The Thief of Hearts

In 1668 King Charles II and his Council launched an unprecedented campaign to destroy a notorious robber band that was threatening the peace of London, its outlying areas, and other parts of the realm. The most celebrated leader of the highwaymen was a flamboyant Frenchman, Claude Duval, who earned as great a reputation for his chivalrous manner and sexual magnetism as for his audacious robberies. An epitaph coined at the time of his eventual execution in 1670 proclaimed:

> *Here lies Du Vall:*
> *Reader, if male thou art,*
> *Look to thy purse;*
> *If female, to thy heart!*

Above all others Duval kindled and defined the image of the romantic highwayman. He inspired such noted writers and artists as Samuel Butler, John Gay, William Harrison Ainsworth and W. P. Frith, and the Victorians and Edwardians turned him into one of Britain's first modern 'superheroes' – storied in numerous novels, penny serials, plays and comics. The myth travelled to North America, where devotees of his fictional adventures included the notorious Missouri outlaws, Frank and Jesse James. The real man, however, was buried beneath centuries of myth and mystification, and has escaped serious research until now.

Sifting the surviving sources, including hitherto unused seventeenth-century manuscripts and pamphlets, John and Philip Sugden have produced an original work of social and cultural history. It not only uncovers a remarkable criminal who became a legend in his own lifetime, and one of the seamier sides of Restoration England, but also the impact that Duval made upon the imagination of the British people in the centuries that followed. "Duval's story, like that of Robin Hood, redefined the mythical history of English outlawry, both here and abroad. He fascinated our ancestors, who made him a household name," say the authors. "We wanted to find out why."

The

THIEF OF HEARTS

Claude Duval

And the Gentleman Highwayman in Fact and Fiction

by
John and Philip Sugden

FORTY STEPS

First published in Great Britain in 2015 by Forty Steps

(40Steps14@pobroadband.co.uk; 13 Inglemere Close, Arnside, LA5 0AP)

A CIP catalogue record for this book is available from the British Library.

ISBN 978-0-9934183-0-3

Book layout and jacket design by Clare Brayshaw

Prepared and printed by:

York Publishing Services Ltd
64 Hallfield Road
Layerthorpe
York YO31 7ZQ

Tel: 01904 431213

Website: www.yps-publishing.co.uk

This book is dedicated to our great friend,
Derek Barlow,
Who showed us the way.

Contents

Illustrations

Preface

Highwaymen have inspired innumerable works of fiction, but relatively little serious investigation, and this contribution could not have been written without the assistance of valuable institutions and individuals. I am grateful to the staffs of the London Metropolitan Archives and the British Library in London; the British Newspaper Library, Colindale; the National Archives in Kew, Surrey; the John Rylands Library in Manchester; and the Central Reference Library, Brymnor Jones University Library and Museum of Transport in Kingston-upon-Hull. I am also indebted to Jackie Pugh and other staff in the Manchester Public Library; Louise Tripp, Assistant Librarian at the University of Lancaster; Jenny Liddle, Images Co-ordinator with the National Trust; Tatiana Yvon of Yvon Genealogie; Victoria Voice, University of East London; and Darren Rawcliffe, Senior Development Officer with Manchester County Council for their kind assistance. April Place offered discerning judgements and youthful enthusiasm, and Duncan Beal of York Publishing Services carefully guided me through what I hope will be the first of several volumes under an imprint of my own. Patrick Pringle, the author of *Stand and Deliver*, one of the most readable of the twentieth-century texts upon highwaymen, was good enough to answer some early enquiries back in the sixties. And, as always, my partner, Terri Egginton, has been a constant support.

My twin-brother, Philip, and I owe much to Derek Barlow, author of the pioneering study of the life and times Richard Turpin, the famous eighteenth-century road agent. A long-standing and true friend, as well as a man of great erudition and knowledge, Derek has ever dispensed encouragement and top-drawer advice, and generously shared material.

Philip and I developed our interests in historical crime in childhood, but while I diverged along other forks in the road he eventually put more than forty years into a definitive study of the London underworld of the early Georgian period. In the course of these studies he became acquainted with much that was relevant to earlier desperadoes, and occasionally suggested to me that there might be unknown records relating to the gentleman highwayman, Claude Duval, an individual who had particularly intrigued me in earlier days. He picked up some items of Duval memorabilia for his library, and alerted me to references that he occasionally stumbled across in his research.

My return to the story occurred fortuitously in the winter of 2012-13. I was writing an account of our pinched but idyllic childhood in a northern town in post-war Britain, and found myself musing once again about the many questions that had excited me as an adolescent. I voraciously devoured literature on almost everything that I construed as old-time romance in those days, but remember being constantly perplexed about where the fiction ended and the fact, if any was to be had, began. Who, for example, was the real Claude Duval, the hero of many boys' adventure stories I encountered in the 1950s? With Philip's encouragement I decided to revisit that particular puzzle and see what I could do with it in the little time I could squeeze out of what was still too busy a life.

Philip's opinions and suggestions were always rich and studied, and he helped run down several important pieces of information. Most crucially of all, he had a command of Latin scripts and ancient judicial processes that few, if any, could rival. He never lived to see the final shape of this little manuscript. He died suddenly in April 2014, but it was only his guidance and skill with the records that enabled me to complete it, and it is just that I should include his name on my title page. The lot of transcribing the last Latin records that I retrieved fell to Kristina Bedford of London, and she performed the task admirably.

The usual caveats are necessary. The project, with any faults it contains, is mine. As this is not, or at least did not start out to be, an academic work, I felt under no obligation to retain the antique spellings of words found in original quotations, or to preserve what was sometimes eccentric seventeenth-century punctuation, but the passages taken from the sources are otherwise rendered as faithfully as possible. With regard to dates, I have kept to the Old Style of seventeenth-century England, rather than converted them to the Gregorian calendar introduced in 1752, but I have dispensed with the obsolete practise of dating the beginning of each year from Lady Day on 25 March. Footnotes were also omitted. They seemed a little out of place in a work of this kind, especially when the contemporary pamphlets about Duval are given as appendices, and the bibliography and text contain the essential sources of information.

John Sugden,
Spring 2015

1

The Prince of Padders

The 'Restoration' is a term widely used to describe a brief period of British history that embraces the return of the Stuarts from exile after the fall of Cromwell's protectorate in 1660, and the troubled reign of Charles II, ending in 1685. It is not a particularly fashionable period among modern historians. Sandwiched uncomfortably between the exciting drama of the English Civil War and its aftermath on the one flank, and the Glorious Revolution of 1688 and much storied eighteenth century on the other, it has not always received the attention it deserved.

Whatever its perceived shortcomings, the Restoration was not a period without a surfeit of colourful and contrasting personalities. Beyond the 'Merry Monarch' himself there stretched a rich *dramatis personae* that included the Lord Chancellor and historian, the Earl of Clarendon, and the rakish Duke of Buckingham; the pioneering scientists, Boyle and Hooke; the diarists Pepys and Evelyn; such literary lions as John Dryden; "pretty, witty" Nell Gwynne, and that salacious courtesan, Barbara Villiers, Duchess of Cleveland, 'the king's whore'; the dashing cavalier, Prince Rupert of the Rhine; the remarkable general and admiral, George Monck; the swashbuckling Henry Morgan who led ragged hordes of privateers and buccaneers to victory over the Spaniards in the West Indies; the rebel Duke of Monmouth; Judge George Jeffreys of the 'Bloody Assizes'; Thomas Blood, who almost ran off with the Crown jewels; and the agitator and pedagogue Titus Oates, who unleashed mob hysteria about a 'Popish Plot'.

It was unquestionably an age of much promiscuity, individuality and extravagance, for good or ill. But among all the men and women who marched into the pages of romance and history at this time, none, perhaps, was more flamboyant, nor impressed themselves more powerfully upon the minds of the common people of Britain in the centuries that followed, than the famous outlaw, Claude Duval. A swaggering Frenchman, his name remained a household property until recent times, and more than any other shaped one of England's most beguiling and enduring myths, the romantic myth of the highwayman, the much publicised 'knight of the road'.

Even today most of us have some sense of that myth, although it found its true home in the Victorian and Edwardian imagination. "Give me a highwayman and I was full to the brim," confessed Robert Louis Stevenson. "A Jacobite would do, but the highwayman was my favourite dish." For this Scottish novelist, who gave the world some of its finest adventure stories, "the merry clatter of the hoofs along the moonlit lane...and the words 'post-chaise,' the 'great North road,' 'ostler,' and 'nag' ...sound[ed] in my ears like poetry."

Stevenson was not alone. In the nineteenth and the early twentieth century the chivalrous image of an English highwayman on a horse thrilled generations of boys and not a few girls and adults. That, of course, was a time when these supposedly exotic figures had become an extinct species, and the threats that they had posed had long since evaporated. As Jerry White has aptly put it in his magisterial study of the English capital, in their heyday highwaymen "haunted the imagination of everyone travelling to and from London," infiltrating their daily peregrinations with fears of robbery and violent attack. The later popularity of the highwayman was to a large extent a literary construct, dispensed through hundreds of novels, plays, bloods and 'penny dreadfuls' at a time when that common fear had subsided.

No one captured the idea of the knight of the road better than the poet Alfred Noyes, a stalwart defender of traditional verse who published "The Highwayman" in *Blackwood's Magazine* in 1906. The poem became a favourite of published anthologies of verse and was recited in scores of drawing-room soirees. Who could fail to stir to the mystery and pace of the story of Noyes's unnamed master of derring-do, smacking of flamboyance and old-fashioned chivalry?

"The wind was a torrent of darkness among the gusty trees.
The moon was a ghostly galleon tossed upon cloudy seas.
The road was a ribbon of moonlight over the purple moor,
And the highwayman came riding –
      Riding – riding –
The highwayman came riding, up to the old inn-door.
He'd a French cocked hat on his forehead, a bunch of lace at his chin,

A coat of the claret velvet, and breeches of brown doe-skin.
They fitted with never a wrinkle; his boots were up to the thigh,
And he rode with a jewelled twinkle,
    His pistol butts a-twinkle,
His rapier hilt a-twinkle, under the jewelled sky.

Over the cobbles he clattered and clashed in the dark inn-yard,
And he tapped with his whip on the shutters, but all was locked and
    barred;
He whistled a tune to the window, and who should be waiting there
But the landlord's black-eyed daughter,
    Bess, the landlord's daughter,
Plaiting a dark red love-knot into her long black hair."

This embellished portrait, while a nineteenth-cum-twentieth-century composition, was not entirely devoid of historical licence. The 'gentleman highwayman', if we may call him such, had, indeed, occasionally appeared, and one man in particular had defined, and to some extent created, the breed: Claude Duval, "a Frenchman born" with "gaudy plumes," who entranced many ladies and danced with one of them on the heath in "his great riding boots." He, it was said, encouraged his ruder English fellows to adopt "the most gentle methods of following the high-pack, taking a purse *a la mode*, mustering his savage Arabians [highwaymen], and exercising them to perform their parts on all occasions with the most obliging dexterity."

Even if Noyes's hero pursued his romantic trysts with an inn-keeper's daughter, a girl of a decidedly more proletarian stamp than the propertied lady who reputedly danced with Duval, we can still see the dandified seventeenth-century French template in the poet's portrait of the "highwayman." The name of Claude Duval was common currency throughout the English speaking world of Noyes's time. It oozed high adventure, flashing blades and fast riding, charged with Gallic charm and sexual chemistry. He had had many imitators, but none surpassed Duval in intrinsic glamour.

This has long been recognized by historians. In 1908 Alfred Marks, writing the first study of *Tyburn Tree*, owned that although "there had been highwaymen before...the great merit of Duval is that he gave a tone and dignity to the profession which it never wholly lost." More recently, Derek Barlow, who single-handedly dragged highway robbery into a new world of serious modern scholarship, agreed that Duval "was flamboyant, and this alone justifies his being regarded as the man who equated romance

3

with highway robbery...In that respect I don't think he can be compared with anyone else." And James Sharpe's study of the highwayman myth contended that "this most remarkable of highwaymen" broke a mould. "With Duval the idea of what a highwayman might be like took on a whole new dimension. Clearly he might now demonstrate the polite gentlemanly standards that were [then]...regarded as desirable." It was exactly that view of the Frenchman that influenced some of Duval's successors as late as 1750, and powered the torrent of popular stories that began in the early decades of the nineteenth century.

In several senses, therefore, Claude Duval may be compared to two earlier much storied desperados, Hereward 'the Wake' and Robin Hood, for all three are as elusive in historical documents as they were in real life, but marched forward into legend as epitomes of the nobler type of English outlaw.

Hereward the eleventh-century Saxon lived on in literature as the classic political rebel and rural guerilla, the champion of a defeated regime, fighting the invading Normans of William the Conqueror. He was a prototype of numerous rebels, displaced by usurpers or factions of one kind or another, who earned notoriety as 'hold-outs' or fugitives from the victorious forces. If we include Scotland, the last of these political outcasts in mainland Britain were probably those associated with the Jacobite rising of 1745-46, adherents of the overthrown dynasty of the Stuarts.

The myths of Robin Hood and Claude Duval were also eventually coloured with political credentials, not unlike Hereward's stand against the Normans in the East Anglian fens. The story-tellers turned Hood into a partisan of King Richard I, whose absence crusading in the Holy Land had allowed the tyrannical Prince John and his partisans to flourish at home. And as Duval metamorphosed in legend, he became a cavalier, seeking to uphold the monarchy against Cromwell's parliamentarians at the time of the English Civil War. Neither the legend of Hood nor that of Duval actually originated in these political causes, but they gathered momentum by acquiring the creed of the patriotic rebel. However, their legends also had original and legitimizing ingredients of their own.

There are those who doubt the existence of a real Robin Hood, although in my view the totality of the evidence very much suggests otherwise. The best guess is that Robin was an early thirteenth-century robber who haunted the north road as it traversed the wild reaches of heath and forest in Barnsdale, Yorkshire. In the late-medieval stories that have come down to us he was neither a peasant nor a noble, but a yeoman of intermediate status. More important, he was also "a good outlaw" who "did poor men much good." He granted amnesty to the yeomen and lowly husbandmen he encountered, and befriended "good" or indigent knights and esquires. His preferred targets were members of the high clergy, and the county sheriff and his cronies. From these thin insinuations grew the post-medieval myth of what has been termed "the social bandit," who flagellated the rich and assisted the poor in a primitive form of class warfare, or who at least was perceived to be so doing by the peasant community that acclaimed him. There was nothing of the social leveller in Hereward. His quarrel was purely with a new regime. The mythical Robin Hood, by comparison, came to express the rebellion of oppressed commoners and the elements of class struggle.

Claude Duval, on the other hand, was neither a political rebel nor a primitive social leveller, at least as he existed in the seventeenth century. The evidence admits of but one interpretation: that he was a predatory rascal through and through. And yet he, too, fathered a popular vision of the English outlaw hero, a third and historically final type that captured public imagination for some three hundred years. Whereas Hereward and Robin were largely foot soldiers, Duval represented the man on a horse. He nurtured the image of the dashing and chivalrous masked rider, skilled with sword and pistol, the precedent for the highwaymen heroes of Edward Bulwer-Lytton, William Harrison Ainsworth, William Powell Frith and Alfred Noyes.

1. Claude Duval: Used to illustrate a printed ballad, *Devol's Last Farewell* (1670), this woodcut or engraving likens the highwayman to a general exhorting his troops in a seventeenth-century military campaign.

And, despite his undoubted criminality, the historical Claude Duval was to a degree as engaging as he was remarkable. In terms of the scale of his misdeeds, he was heralded "the prince of padders" (highwaymen and footpads) in his own time, and one literary source credited him with being even more. He was, it alleged, the master-spirit of an extensive underworld of rogues and vagabonds of every kind that infested London and its environs. On their part, formal historical records depict him as the most celebrated figure in the premier gang of highwaymen in the kingdom, a band that consisted of fifty to a hundred riders, and supported a dependent community that must have numbered several hundred family members, mistresses, receivers, intelligence-gatherers, keepers of safe or 'flash' houses, stable owners and suppliers. The gang threatened all classes, from common travellers and tradesmen to those who served the highest in the land, including the king. It became so notorious that Charles II named and proscribed its members in proclamations reminiscent of the long obsolete medieval statutes of outlawry. But even if all of these suppositions had been true, and Duval had been a master criminal of that ilk, he would still probably have been forgotten if he had been nothing else. He distanced himself from the common footpad, burglar or highwayman in more than the inconvenience of his many robberies. Above all, he was remembered for his style.

He followed a trade that commonly led to a grisly fate on the gallows, and perhaps the roadside gibbet, where the corpses of executed malefactors hung in silent witness to the follies of crime. For that reason its practitioners paid great attention to masking their identities. Apart from using scarves and makeshift visors to shield their faces during robberies on the highway, they adopted multiple aliases and resorted to such devices as placing pebbles in their mouths to distort their voices. Survival, then, depended much upon preserving secrecy. There was, moreover, little about the seventeenth-century highwaymen that was romantic or sophisticated. It is true that the death penalty, and any prospects of obtaining the king's pardon, curbed some instincts to maim and murder, but on the whole these were men moulded by brutal times. They might be compared to the ruthless robber gangs unleashed by the American Civil War in the nineteenth century, when ex-Confederate guerrillas such as Arch Clement, Jesse and Frank James and Cole Younger terrorized the Midwest, pillaging banks and trains and murdering at will. Likewise the English Civil War and its aftermath, laced with religious and political extremism, disrupted, dispossessed and embittered many of its survivors, some of whom took to the highway schooled in and brutalized by violence. It was this mix into which Claude Duval was alleged to have injected his rather different recipe for success on the road.

He had his own formula. Although not immune to the need for secrecy, he also cultivated a personality and celebrity that stamped him as different. His French accent alone was a prominent trademark, and according to the little evidence that survives he often went into action wearing garish and fashionable eye-catching finery that must have required frequent changes of clothes and the services of shrouding riding cloaks at inconvenient times.

Furthermore, he had what might have then been a unique manner. He earned the reputation of a chivalrous gallant, capable of depriving people of their belongings with an apologetic flourish, and treating victims with a measure of sympathy and respect, and he had a legendary predilection for ladies, to whom he was particularly mindful. This brand of audacity, horsemanship, skill with arms, non-violence, exceptional good looks, address and seductive charm made him more than the thief of female hearts found in the seventeenth-century literature and the quintessential story-book highwayman of later days. He stimulated enough imitations to induce modern historians to speak of a breed of gentleman highwaymen found as late as the middle of the eighteenth-century. The phrase is, of course, an oxymoron. But Duval, described by one contemporary as a "famous artist,"

2. A New Kind of Highway Gentility: Howard Pyle, the noted American illustrator, conveyed the blend of terror and courtesy that characterized Duval's 'act' in this drawing of 1890. Here Duval exchanges salutes with his principal victim in the coach.

brought what fashion and style the tawdry and menacing trade of highway robbery under arms could realistically command.

Of course, the historical Duval was a more complex figure. Much of his career was unremittingly squalid, and none who plied his trade could be without a ruthless selfishness, and a readiness, if necessary, to exercise fatal force. Yet unlike the myths of Robin Hood, the essential core of those about Duval sprang from his own lifetime, when much more was known about him than we know now, and when many of his friends, acquaintances and enemies were alive and well. It was the sanitized elements of Duval in those myths that seemed to stick. At their most memorable his thefts resembled pieces of live theatre, in which the robber, conscious of his reputation, played the gallant to the hilt. They make it possible to imagine the conversation of travellers at that time. No one wanted to be stopped by highwaymen, but if the ordeal had to be endured, most would have wished their assailant to have been Duval. A rogue he may have been, but at least he bore himself as a gentleman, and an *avant garde* French one at that.

The myths of Robin Hood and Claude Duval constantly evolved over time, until the real events locked inside them had all but disappeared. Both symbolized eras in the history of English outlawry. If Robin was the medieval rebel in the greenwood, Duval was the daring highwayman on a speedy steed, one of the most iconic figures of the seventeenth, eighteenth and (as far as drama and literature were concerned) the nineteenth centuries. Indeed, the two defining stories of the highwayman as hero – reflecting the myth's twin facets of chivalry and horsemanship – belonged to Duval and his associates. It was Duval who reportedly danced with the lady traveller on the sward, and exemplified the romance; and it was one of his accomplices, Samuel Swiftnicks, who gave birth to the other famous highwayman story, that of the ride from London to York, equally beloved by chroniclers, and later erroneously attributed to John Nevison and Dick Turpin. And if Hood and his henchman Little John were originally associated with Barnsdale in Yorkshire, it was Duval and his comrades who probably cemented the popular connection between highwaymen and Hounslow Heath, that wild four thousand acres of moorland and pasture in southwest Middlesex through which the Bath and Exeter roads coursed towards London at their risk.

As a highwayman, Duval's reputation long remained high. Hanged at Tyburn in London in 1670, he was quickly entrenched in the common mind as the most memorable of his kind. In 1713 Alexander Smith's *Complete History of the Most Notorious Highwaymen* implied that he was more famous than any highwayman "ever...executed within the limits of Great Britain," and that he long sustained this status is suggested by the way in which reprints and plagiarisms of Smith's book hurried the name of the French outlaw into a pre-eminent position, sometimes even on their title-pages. In 1750, for example, was published *Lives of Noted Highwaymen, Viz., Du Vall, Atkinson, Rowland, &c.* Early in the next century the poet Leigh Hunt could still characterize Duval as "an eternal feather in the cap of highway gentility" with the assurance that he yet enjoyed considerable celebrity among readers. Even after the Manchester novelist, William Harrison Ainsworth, revived the reputation of an eighteenth-century highwayman, Dick Turpin, in a best-selling novel of 1834, and ultimately turned him into the most famous of all his tribe, most writers continued to regard Duval as the alternative and in some respects more authentic figure. Taking his cue from seventeenth-century literature, Charles G. Harper, whose two-volumed *Half Hours with Highwaymen* was published in 1908, characterized the Frenchman as an "artist," who had been to highway robbery what Raphael had been to painting. Arthur L. Hayward, the editor of the most popular twentieth century edition of Smith's *Highwayman*, regarded "gay and sprightly" Duval "as picturesque a rogue as ever found his way to the gallows," far removed from those of a "more vulgar cast." And recent historians have endorsed Duval's significant role in the development of highway robbery and the highwayman myth.

By 1962, when I was a secondary school boy with a love of historical adventure stories, Claude Duval had at last all but slipped out of the public memory. Yet it was still relatively easy to find adults who vaguely knew his name, and there remained the stubborn vestiges of what had once been a much greater notoriety. I watched a rerun of an Independent Television series of 1957, *The Gay Cavalier*, which was loosely based upon the story of Duval. I should add here that the word 'gay' at this time had none of the connotations it evokes today; rather, it was a synonym of 'blithe' or 'merry' and accorded Duval the same rollicking devil-may-care persona as Robin Hood and his 'merry men.'

Most obviously at the turn of the sixties I found that the French highwayman was commonly accorded brief if standard entries in English speaking encyclopaedias and biographical dictionaries, even many of the small 'desk' variety, which were comparatively diminutive in size and scope. This struck me as a little strange. The editors of these reference books are constantly reviewing their entries, dropping subjects of little interest to current readers, and replacing them with more topical names and subjects. In 1962 Duval, and the most famous of others like him, were heading for eventual deletion from such august works, as they increasingly failed to enchant those Stevenson once described as "the wiser youngsters of today," but at that particular moment the Frenchman was still usually holding his place. In the 1981 edition of the well-known little almanac, *Pears Cyclopaedia*, for instance, you could still encounter Duval among the fifty-seven pages of "prominent people" that formed one section of that much-thumbed reference work.

An inquisitive schoolboy reading such entries, I asked myself one obvious question. Just who was Claude Duval, and what did he actually do? In 1964, some now forgotten whimsy suddenly deepened my curiosity, and I began raiding newly-encountered tomes of reference and books about highwaymen in an attempt to compile a biographical narrative of the famous outlaw. I stuck with the project for seven or eight months, long enough to hammer out three small manuscripts on an overworked portable Imperial typewriter during my spare time. But I soon realised that most of what I was reading about Duval was sheer nonsense. For example, I traced many of the stories in such fanciful re-workings of the myth as Rex Dixon's *A Book of Highwaymen*, published in 1963, to Alexander Smith's near contemporary *History* of the same subject. The Hull Reference Library eventually came up with a copy of Smith's book, which had first been published in 1713, but the story of Duval I found in it was no more credible for that. At that point I shook my head and gave up. It seemed that the facts about this particular historical figure were irretrievably buried in the most ridiculous fantasies.

When I began the present little volume some three years ago, that first quest of mine, the recovery of the historical Claude Duval, remained almost as unfulfilled as it had been more than half a century earlier. Indeed, opined one of the few modern historians to have considered the subject, so little was known of the real Duval that he could be considered more of a literary creation than a historical figure. Readers of *The Thief of Hearts* will, I hope, get a much sharper picture of Duval than has ever been presented before. But his historical dimensions as a whole still only emerge furtively from the shadows, and we must not expect too much. I have uncovered a good deal of fresh material, including the surviving trial and prison records and hitherto unused contemporary printed sources, and have set the story within its wider context. Armed with this new evidence I hope that I have lifted a once celebrated figure back into history, as it were. Nevertheless, the scant nature of the historical sources will, I fear, ever place the true nature of this unusual man beyond our reach.

However, more recently another question has seemed to me of equal pertinence: why had a highwayman executed three centuries before retained the residual fame I had seen in the 1960s? Why had there been small screen versions of his exploits, and why did he continue to find places in encyclopaedias that had already thrown out entries on far more memorable men and women of the past? True, Duval had attained fame in Stuart England, but other highwayman, before and since, had made transitory names for themselves only to have their memories crushed underfoot in the steady march of Time. Why not this one?

Only one other comparable name had survived: that of Dick Turpin, an eighteenth-century successor. But he, I knew, owed his rehabilitation and revival to a Victorian novelist, William Harrison Ainsworth. Surely, then, Duval must also have enjoyed a similar resuscitation to have remained in the national memory in the mid-twentieth century. The thought suggested the existence of a colourful afterlife of which I knew almost nothing. As the present book reveals, I would discover that if Duval spent much of his professional life impoverishing his fellows for selfish ends, his afterlife enthralled and presumably enriched whole generations of Victorians and Edwardians, who hungrily devoured extravagant interpretations of his adventures in popular literature, drama and art. In short, the encyclopaedias I saw as a boy included Duval because their editors had grown up in a world that knew his name and was interested in him. Indeed, as I would discover, for a century or more Duval was as famous in Britain as Drake, Nelson and Wellington, and in some quarters, even more so. My sortie into cultural history has, therefore, recovered what was a vibrant part of the imagination of our ancestors.

Fifty years ago highwaymen were still largely the stuff of stories, whether purveyed in straight fiction or gullible popular histories. Many of the earliest accounts of these outlaws had been riddled with gross embellishments and outright fabrications, but they were innocently recycled with little regard to historical authenticity. It was not until the 1970s that serious research was published. Derek Barlow led the charge with his formidable study of *Dick Turpin and the Gregory Gang*, still the most thorough biography of a conventional English criminal in print. Although we still await a comprehensive scholarly history of highwaymen in general, some aspects have come under scrutiny and in the present century James Sharpe, Robert Shoemaker and Erin Mackie, among others, have made valuable original contributions, particularly in their reconstruction of the evolution of the cultural myth of these bandits.

Claude Duval's significance has grown rather than been diminished by such scholarship, but he continues to slip through our fingers, as he did so often in his own day. The many who have written about him have drawn their material almost exclusively from the contemporary and unreliable pamphlet by Walter Pope or, what is worse, Smith's partly derivative *History* of the highwaymen. Even modern historians have made little headway with the historical facts of his case. The only serious attempt to unearth the real man was made by Barbara White, who supplied a creditable if brief sketch for *The Oxford Dictionary of National Biography*, published in 2004. The main failing of that admirable entry was the omission of any consideration of Duval's posthumous legend. This pointed to what is still a glaring gap in our knowledge of the subject, for even those scholars who have patiently traced the literary influences of such similar characters as Jack Sheppard and Dick Turpin have been largely unaware of the concurrent stream of memorabilia that focussed upon Duval. No one, therefore, has convincingly explained why this particular seventeenth-century figure had been remembered for centuries after his death. For that I got the most help from a forgotten paper that 'W. Roberts' published as long ago as 1925.

These two pieces, neither more than a few pages in length, were small foundations, mere hit and run raids into largely unknown territory, but if White and Roberts had not journeyed far they had sign-posted the right roads. Here, in this present treatise, I have ventured considerably further; indeed the story, I think it will be conceded, has been radically transformed. But this should not be seen as an exhaustive study. It attempts to salvage information on what had almost become a vanished entity, and to explain how mythology used and transformed Duval into the household property of generations unborn. The subject of this essay, therefore, is both a man and a myth. It visits the history of English outlawry and the literature, culture and folklore of the working people of these islands.

There is more work to do, even though it is difficult to say that the labour would be profitable. It would certainly require a stout heart. The press was still in a primitive state in Duval's time. Despite *The London Gazette*, a skimpy government news-sheet of limited use for students of crime, there were no newspapers as we know them today, and consequently no regular reporting of crimes, even in the capital itself, or discursive comment. Very few of the pamphlets that were published have come down to us.

What survives about London crime in the first decade of the Restoration is largely unpublished, paltry and for the most part undisturbed. Both sets of the handwritten Old Bailey court sessions books – some preserving rough notes of the proceedings and others the more elegant formal summaries – are couched in an archaic Latin legalese that few people know today, as, indeed, are the surviving gaol delivery rolls for Newgate Prison, which in some instances give rather more details of the crimes themselves. Working through the packets of disfigured, damaged, filthy and age-blackened gaol delivery rolls in the London Metropolitan Archives, and those merely the ones the document conservers deemed fit for presentation, was a particularly frustrating process. Most of these papers were so fragile, discoloured and difficult to decipher that it was easy to see why no historian has subjected them to sustained scrutiny. Even J. M. Beattie's magisterial *Crime and the Courts in England, 1660-1800* is relatively thin on the seventeenth century. Yet there were some interesting stories in these ancient and challenging documents, glimpses into a disappeared, difficult and dangerous world meet for a major study of crime, poverty and misdemeanour in the reign of Charles II. They provided me with my tentative reconstruction of the government's hunt for Duval and his associates in the years 1668 to 1670, but if these documents are not properly conserved, and ideally mounted in volumes, they may soon be lost forever.

I see no immediate prospect of the more general work on Restoration crime that is needed being written, for apart from unusual heroism and ability on the part of the historian it would demand considerable resources, particularly in time. The National Archives in Kew contain more than two hundred relevant files of domestic state papers for the period from 1665 to 1672, but crime competes with a raft of other issues in these materials and is often plucked from them in mere fragments. These manuscripts have been copied onto microfilms, which are themselves sometimes difficult to read, but we owe an immense and seldom acknowledged debt to that astonishing Victorian historian, Mary Anne Everett Green (formerly Wood), who calendared and edited many volumes of the domestic state papers for publication, setting new standards in scholarship as she did so. Her volumes, which contain extensive transcriptions, have been another of the great mainstays of the present work.

My focus has been Claude Duval, but even that narrow compass could be explored in yet greater depth. The historical narrative is capable of improvement. Duval's baptism in France has not been found, but there is a slight possibility that the record does survive in some parochial church archive, and that it might reveal itself once such records are coordinated and digitalised for genealogists, as they surely will be in this computer age. Such a discovery would enable us to say much more about the man's family and ancestry.

Then, too, an investigator with more time could widen the focus to trace the complete rise and fall of the particular gang of highwaymen of which Duval was merely the brightest ornament, making a more detailed search of the relevant records between 1660 and 1675. The king's campaign to root the outlaws out, spearheaded by the remarkable William Morton, is a worthy topic in itself, and much could be said of the troubled times that followed the Civil War, and their repercussions on the peace of the realm. A more esoteric inquirer might also consider the Duval affair within the context of the supposed influence of France and Catholicism upon the court and the body politic of Restoration England, as well as upon popular culture, taste, manners and xenophobia. And additionally, the implications of gender, which contributed to the "uproar in this imperial city" that marked the trial and execution of Duval, suggest interesting questions far beyond the scope and competence of this narrative.

The development of the highwayman myth in subsequent centuries throws light upon the nature and springs of the literature and everyday life of what were sometimes termed "the common people." It has, as I have said, already received some scholarly attention. I have principally reconstructed Duval's afterlife from literary sources, including reviews in newspapers and magazines, and surviving copies of the ephemeral literature that appeared. Some of the latter I acquired through the collectors' market, but the finest repository of nineteenth-century bloods and penny dreadfuls is the British Library, which has shown commendable vision in its commitment to this much abused and fragile heritage, and was fortunate in acquiring the huge private collection of Barry Ono.

It is possible that more might be found on Claude Duval, but for all that no one should approach these records expecting to mine a single rich vein. This will always be a topic won by liberating small nuggets from hard ground, and accounting for gaps in the pictures that tentatively emerge. While we can undoubtedly learn more about the times of Duval, and the communities in which he lived, for the most part the unique individuals who peopled this forgotten corner of Restoration England have gone, most with the expiry of their own lives and a few with records that were made and lost. The present volume, therefore, cannot be definitive; it is provisional, a weak flashlight shone into an unrelenting gloom.

But enough has been said to set our scene. It is high time that we began to search for our man on that ribbon of moonlight across the purple moor.

2

Beginnings

Our starting point must be the historical Claude Duval. Just who was he, and what did he do? Almost every step taken to answer these questions is beset with conjecture and uncertainty, and even the most basic of details are difficult to establish. A stubborn obstacle awaits us at the very beginning. I am simply unable to give an exact birthplace, birth date or parentage.

Claude Duval the highwayman operated under many names. He sometimes represented himself to be Lewis (or, in other usages, Lodowick or Ludovic) Duval or Peter Duval, and upon other occasions John or George Brown. It is possible that one of these aliases was a whimsical snub to authority, since a man named John Browne was bailiff of the Sheriff of Middlesex and one of Duval's adversaries. Whatever, partly because he was a French national, and difficult for seventeenth-century Englishmen to trace, the highwayman certainly created confusion about his real identity, and it was only at the end of his life that the designation 'Claude Duval' got the better of the alternatives and became the commonly accepted form. Nevertheless, it is fair to state that at the moment a question remains about whether the subject of this memoir was baptised Claude, Louis or Pierre Duval. The first is only by far the most probable.

The mysterious origin of Claude Duval puts him in the same situation as another notorious French charmer, Jean Laffite, the charismatic pirate, smuggler and privateer who became such a legendary figure throughout the Gulf of Mexico in the early nineteenth century. As one of his biographers has speculated, many of the contradictory stories relating to Laffite's birth and early life may have originated in the different accounts the mysterious outlaw gave to contemporaries. We might say the same about Duval, who was a prime dissembler in what has been described as an age of masquerade.

In his own day rumours abounded that Duval was born of French parents in London or Westminster. People variously placed his origins in Chancery Lane, Drury Lane, Covent Garden, Whitechapel and "many other places." Some said that his father had been a cook in Smock Alley. But no one who considered the matter seriously credited such stories. Duval spent much of his life in the London area and naturally formed associations with various places in the town. He was eventually captured in the Covent Garden area, where he presumably had one of his hideouts. However, as far as we know, no one familiar with Duval took him to be any other than a Frenchman, and I have found no one resembling Duval in the baptismal records of the London area of that time.

That Duval was a Frenchman born and raised was repeatedly attested. Indeed, the vital thrust of attacks made upon him by such writers as Walter Pope and Titus Oates was his Gallic identity. He epitomised what was often seen as the unwholesome political and cultural influence of France upon Restoration England.

Duval, it seems, lived up to the contemporary view of France as a leader of fashion. The ballad, *Devol's Last Farewell*, published in 1670, carols:

"Because I was a Frenchman born,
Some persons treated me with scorn;
But, being of a daring soul,
Although my deeds was something foul,
My gaudy plumes I did display."

Samuel Butler, whose position as secretary of the king's most influential adviser put him in the way of relevant information, saw Duval's flair for chivalry and courtesy as a product of his French nativity:

"In France, the staple of new modes,
Where garbs and miens are current goods,
That serves the ruder northern nations
With methods of address and treat;
Prescribes new garnitures and fashions,
And how to drink and how to eat,
No out-of-fashion wine or meat;
To understand cravats and plumes,
And the most modish from the old perfumes...
In this great academy of mankind
He had his birth and education."

In short, these and other passages in the contemporary literature, pronounce Claude Duval a Frenchman in birth and upbringing, and credit him with importing *avant-garde* Gallic manners and dress into the ruder tradition of English outlawry. Attempts to be more specific about the birth and ancestry of Duval struggle in a quicksand of hearsay and fiction in which little firm footing is to be found. Only Walter Pope, the author of a contemporary memoir of the famous brigand, attempted a connected narrative of his subject's early years.

According to his story, Duval was born in 1643 in Domfront, Normandy, the oldest child of Pierre Duval, a miller, and his wife, Marguerite de la Roche, a tailor's daughter. The parents were described as of good character, and the boy was raised in the Catholic religion, and spoke a provincial form of French. But at thirteen or fourteen years of age he was sent to seek his fortune with a suit, hose, stockings and a modest purse of twenty "sous." Reaching Rouen, he was paid to return some post-horses to Paris, and travelled there in company with "several young English gentleman," who subsequently found him employment as an errand boy or attendant in the 'St. Esprit' tavern, an eating and bawdy house in the Rue de Boucherie, part of the English quarter of Faubourg St. Germain. By some means or other he eventually entered service with a wealthy English family.

Today visitors to Normandy will find that some of old Domfront still gamely resists the ravages of Time. A small hilltop settlement above the River Varenne in north-western France, on the road from Mont St. Michel to Paris, the town's ancient strategic location can still be gathered from the ruins of the extensive medieval fortifications that were for the most part demolished at the beginning of the seventeenth century. And something of the character of the town from which Duval might have begun Life's journey survives in the narrow streets and stone courtyards that were once enclosed by the city walls, and in what is left of the Romanesque church, Notre Dame on the Water.

The Domfront story and its aftermath have been repeated without much reservation ever since, although an obvious question arises: if true, how did such detailed and intensely personal information reach Pope in London in 1670, when his pamphlet was published? The author may have seen Duval at his trial or execution, or, for all we know, have even visited the felon in prison, although he does not say that he did. At least he appears to have spoken to some who had known him. We can, therefore, accept that the age he ascribed to the highwayman at the time of his death, twenty-seven years, might have been a reasonable guess; and even, at a stretch, that he could have picked up a few broad statements about Duval's past. Yet the precise biography related by Pope, with the sort of detail that only the highwayman himself, a relative or very close friend might have furnished, is scarcely credible.

Moreover, the parish registers for Domfront and Saint-Front (an outlying village later incorporated into Domfront) survive in the archives of the Department of Orne in France, and were searched for this project. They are often badly written and difficult to decipher, but no such baptism as Pope describes, under the names Claude, Pierre or Louis Duval, is to be found between the years 1638 and 1647. Not only that, but this search revealed no reference to a Pierre or Marguerite Duval, the supposed parents of the outlaw. We must conclude that Pope's story was either invented or at best markedly inaccurate.

It is, of course, possible that Duval claimed some connection with Domfront, or gave out that his people hailed from those parts, and that perhaps thereby he started a story that merely got confused as it passed from mouth to mouth. It seems pretty clear that Pope for one felt certain that Duval's origins were in Normandy. Apart from his detailed recounting of the Domfront yarn, he quoted the alleged inscription for the outlaw's tombstone, describing him as "the second conqueror of the Norman race."

There is a strut for such suppositions. In 1638 a married man by the very name of Claude Du Val appeared in the baptism register of Saint-Front. On 3 February 1638 one Jean Boysgontier and Julienne Berson presented an illegitimate infant for baptism. They declared the child the produce of Jeanne Boysgontier and a married man named Claude Du Val, and named him Matthias. Jean Boysgontier and Marie Guerin, the infant's godparents, "pledged to take care of him." The following year an Artur (Arthur) was baptized at the same church on 3 March, a legitimate son of Claude Du Val and Jeanne Panart, his wife. His godparents were named as Artur Le Provost and Judith Monestault. Perhaps the existence of a Claude Du Val in the small Domfront settlements at this time is nothing but an odd coincidence, but it is certainly possible that the famous highwayman was named for this Claude Du Val, who was perhaps a relative, an uncle or even his father. Several members of a Duval family also appear in local registers during the last half of the seventeenth century.

Whether Duval was closely related to his namesakes in Domfront will likely never be known, but the better evidence, meagre as it is, places his birth and education not in Normandy but in Paris. An obscure pamphlet, published a few days after Duval's execution, was authored by someone whose claim to have been an "eye-witness" at the highwayman's trial is supported by the close relationship of his account to the official court sessions records. This scribe, whom we will therefore designate Eye-Witness, also maintained that he interviewed Duval in prison, and that the highwayman declared himself to be a native of Paris. Born of parents "he did not boast of," he was also educated in that town.

Whether the phrase Duval applied to his parents suggested that they had been of dubious moral fibre, or merely poor folk of no social significance is unclear. Efforts to verify this Paris birth have so far been thwarted by the sheer lack of documentation, since most of the city records of that period have been destroyed, many during the revolution of the 'Commune' in 1871. But the statement as a whole is the most authentic that we have, coming as it apparently does from Duval himself and a recorder of some integrity. Their unvarnished story eventually dovetails with Pope's account, for according to it the young Duval was fortunate enough to fall in with "a gentleman of quality," who, "liking his person, in which Nature was bountiful, brought him over to England in the nature of a page."

This not only echoes the acknowledged personal attractiveness of Duval, which was throughout life one of his greatest assets, but also a general contemporary belief that he had entered service with an elevated English household while young and through it found his way across the Channel. The supposition of some historians that he came to England at the time of the restoration of the English monarchy in 1660 is highly plausible. In the 1650s many high-born English families, supporters of the Stuart kings overthrown in the Civil War, fled to Paris and other places, where they waited to return if and when political circumstances changed. The fall of Cromwell's Protectorate in 1659 and restoration of Charles II the following year signalled the end of that exile. It was with such a family that Duval probably began his life in domestic service. Though unable to read or write English, as an adult the highwayman was versed in the spoken language, and had clearly enjoyed considerable contact with both the English and the so-called "gentle" society he would have met serving the high-born.

Other sources support Eye-Witness. In the contemporary narrative ballad *Devol's Last Farewell* the hero assures us that

"Unto a duke I was a page
And succour'd in my tender age."

And both *The Life of Deval* and Walter Pope's *Memoirs*, our other surviving contemporary biographies, also say that young Duval became a "servant" to "a person of quality." Pope goes a little further, and tells us that his post was that of a footman, which is extremely likely.

Where has all of this got us? It indicates either that the boy was born and raised in Paris, the principal place frequented by exiled English royalists of the wealthier kind, or, perhaps less likely, that he came from one of the northern regions of France – Brittany, Normandy, Picardy, Artois or the Ile-de-France – and made his way to Paris in childhood or adolescence. Whatever the status of his parents, Duval informed Eye-Witness that he had had a modicum of schooling in Paris, then a city of half a million people. Millions of French men and women were illiterate at that time, and signed marriage and any other relevant legal documents with crosses, but the Roman Catholic Church was making commendable efforts to introduce the poor to basic skills, if for nothing more than to provide a foundation for religious instruction. Duval's close contemporary, Robert Cavelier de La Salle, a Norman from Rouen, destined to carve an empire for his country out of North America, was the product of a Jesuit education, and spent three years teaching school for the order in Alencon, Tours and Blois. Most probably Duval found the rudiments of his education in some such church venture in Paris.

Paris, like London, was a city of contrasts. As a boy Duval probably knew its narrow dirty streets and such places as the Pont-Neuf bridge over the Seine, with its compact houses, market stalls and colourful street entertainers, rather more than any of the grand cathedrals. Few career choices were open to such indigent youths as he. France was at war throughout most of Duval's childhood, seeking with moderate success to break the encirclement of the Hapsburg powers of Spain and central Europe, and it took twenty-four years to restore peace in 1659. But there was little alluring about army life as a member of the rank and file. On the home front, Paris bristled with the signs of tradesmen or artisans, most of whom lived in their workplaces, and some boys were apprenticed. But even if they had the resources to meet the premiums and conditions that masters demanded of novices, and the necessary persistence to become journeymen, such apprentices began a road of uncommon difficulty. So many obstacles, including exorbitant fees, were thrown in the way of aspirants that the guilds that controlled the trades were almost the exclusive domains of the families of existing members. The city contained a numerous class of qualified journeymen unable to enter the hallowed portals of the guilds and doomed to sad and disgruntled hand-to-mouth lives of low wages, threadbare accommodation and long hard hours. Domestic service, perhaps as a page, valet, coachman, ostler or footman in the homes of the nobility or the mercantile *bourgeoise*, was an obvious alternative, and that was the path that Duval followed.

We can only speculate about what Duval gained from his Parisian upbringing. The city was forever on the edge of violence, and it was then the focus of what have been called the Fronde risings, when first the city parliament, defending its supposed ancient rights, and then the nobles challenged the authority of the crown. At that time the French monarchy was represented by Anne of Austria, mother of and regent for the infant Louis XIV, and she ruled from the Palais-Royal with the aid of her astute but controversial and unpopular Italian minister, Cardinal Jules Mazarin. In 1648 the city rose in protest against new tax impositions and the arrest of two of its councillors, and barricades were thrown across the streets while angry crowds massed in the Grand'Salle. The following January all heads of households were called to arms, and a citizen army patrolled the streets and city ramparts, and searched homes for perceived enemies whilst a royalist army under the celebrated Louis de Bourbon, Prince de Condé, blockaded the capital in an attempt to reduce it to subservience. The matter was eventually settled by negotiation in March.

It is difficult to see how the Duvals could have remained unaffected by this turmoil, or, indeed, how Claude could have been unaware of the even more dramatic events of July 1652, when Condé, now trying his strength against the monarchy in a fresh round of conflict, was driven with his followers against the city walls near the Porte Saint-Antoine by a king's army led by that other great warrior Henri, Vicomte de Turenne. A furious six-hour battle between the forces of the two famous military commanders brought Condé's party to the brink of defeat, whilst the Parisian militia stood beside their artillery pieces with lighted matches ready to intervene or defend their town. Duval, like most, probably saw Condé's fugitives flood into the city when the gates were opened to afford them refuge, and heard the guns of the Bastille barking in defiance at the royalist victors. Perhaps, like others, he even strutted about the streets with straw in his hat to proclaim the common solidarity with Condé's rebels, chanting anti-Mazarin ditties. Both the Fronde episodes succeeded in temporarily expelling the Court and Mazarin from the capital, but when order was restored in 1653 it was the country's drift towards royal absolutism, rather than any radical inclinations, that had gained momentum.

A novelist might infer that some of Claude Duval's distant disregard of authority lay in these Parisian protests, but in truth we know nothing about how they affected him. More relevant context may be found in the cultural history of the first city of France. For despite all its travail, the Paris of Henry IV, Louis XIII and Louis XIV was becoming the artistic capital of Europe. The extension of the Louvre; the building of the Pont Neuf and Place Dauphine; the thriving theatres at the Palais Cardinal, Theatre du Marais and Hôtel de Bourgogne; and the Académie Royale de Peinture et de Sculpture and the Académie des Inscriptions et Belles-Lettres, which encouraged the arts and historical enquiry, to name but a few, all went into the meld that attracted the dramatists Corneille, Racine and Moliere, the philosopher and mathematician, Rene Descartes, and the painters Philippe de Champaigne and Claude Lorrain.

This process of gentrification was well underway during the years of Duval's childhood, and one particular significantly touched his career: the reshaping of relationships between the sexes and the notion of what constituted a gentleman. The male offspring of the nobility and well-to-do remained charged with martial ardour, understandable at a time when France was emerging from long and trying wars with Spain and Austria flaunting tangible triumphs. As one foreign observer remarked, Frenchmen were so imbued with a devil-may-care attitude that they went "to their deaths as if they were to rise again the next morning." Duelling was a common feature of public and political life of Paris. But while Duval was yet a child the expectations held of respectable men were also softening and widening, influenced to some extent by the greater profile that women were cutting in Parisian affairs.

When Louis XIII died in 1643, about the time of Duval's birth, it was the capable Anne of Austria who assumed the reins of government as regent for her four year old son, Louis XIV. She ruled until 1661 in an interregnum dominated by the wily Mazarin. However, the noticeable if somewhat transitory increase in female influence was rooted more in literature and society than in politics. Catherine de Vivonne, Marquise de Rambouillet, who hosted readings, lectures, debates and discussions in the famous Blue Room of her *salon* in the Place du Palais-Royal, created a rendezvous for literary and philosophical intelligentsia of both sexes and a forum for challenging new ideas. The 'Hôtel de Rambouillet', as it was called, has been accused of pointing society towards verbosity and ostentation in speech, writing and dress, but at its best in the 1630s it was a seeding ground for intellectual fashions, in which men learned that words, wit and attentions were as important in their moulding as the traditional manly deeds of war.

Some influential literature trended in the same direction by enshrining stylish men. Honoré d' Urfé's *L'Astrée*, a rambling romance about the eponymous heroine and her lover, Celadon, published in five volumes between 1607 and 1627, not only enchanted French readers for decades but offered a blueprint for behaviour. It was, said historian Jacques Boulenger, almost a

> "manual of good manners. The budding man of fashion found in its pages the pattern after which he [the reader] must model his speech, his epistolary style [and] his manner of thought. It taught him how to treat ladies with the respect and admiration that was their due, to discourse to them in language at once respectful, flowery and ingenious; to write them pompous and literary letters; in short all his lessons in politeness and deportment were drawn from...*Astrée*...Add to all this the fact that Honoré d'Urfé's book was entirely devoted to the glorification of the fair sex at a time when the triumph of that sex in French society was greater than it has [had] ever been..."

This, with much that was similar, is credibly alleged to have developed a new type of gentleman, or '*honnete home.*' As Boulenger continued,

> "before long it did not suffice a cultivated man to be well informed. He had also to possess style. He had to express himself clearly and gracefully, both in speech and with his pen. To sum up, in fact he had to be able to please, to fascinate, to amuse, to charm. And it was this art that the men of the world of that day carried to perfection, for they learned it in their childhood and practised it till they died – a very useful art indeed, and even indispensable at a period when nothing was to be had as a right, but everything by favour or by the skill with which the applicant presented his request."

A more recent scholar, John Lough, agreed that a new model of masculinity emerged in Paris during these years: "the rough-mannered warrior was replaced by the gentleman, distinguished for his refinement, good taste, and politeness towards the ladies." The extent to which such ideals prevailed must, of course, be questioned. It was essentially an aristocratic ideal, foreign no doubt to many horny-handed labourers, struggling artisans or poor folk whose lives were necessarily governed by the greater issue of simple subsistence. But it was an image that young Claude Duval encountered while in service in Paris and imbibed.

There is no doubt that French fashions were also beginning to influence the wealthier ranks across the Channel, but Duval was a most unlikely agent. Yet ultimately and paradoxically, it was exactly this genteel model associated with fashionable Parisians that Claude Duval imported into – of all things – the discordant history of English banditry!

No seventeenth-century source that I have seen ventures to name the "person of quality" with whom Duval found employment in Paris, but in 1848 the historian Thomas Babington, Lord Macaulay, appropriated the Duke of Richmond for the role on unknown grounds. Charles Stuart, the 3rd Duke of Richmond, was certainly among the English nobles exiled in France during the closing years of the Cromwellian Protectorate. He usually resided in Paris, married one Lady Elizabeth Rogers, and in 1660 inherited his peerage from a cousin before returning to England with his train towards the end of the year. He was then a handsome young man of but twenty-one years.

It is possible that Duval served him and accompanied him to England, as Macaulay suggested. It is also possible that it was a memory of Richmond's uncle, Ludovic Stuart, Seigneur d'Aubigy, in whose house the duke lived while in Paris, that prompted the alias of Ludovic or Louis that Duval would use in more desperate times. But nothing more than such coincidences as these argue a connection. The source of Macaulay's information has not been found, in lieu of which there seems to be no reason to present Richmond as a more likely candidate for Duval's "person of quality" than any other English nobleman in his situation. Indeed, in the closest account of Duval's origins that we have – that by Eye-Witness – there is no direct statement that the youth's benefactor was so eminent a person of quality as a duke. A dukedom, it should be noted, was the highest rung of the English peerage, rating above those occupied by lowly barons, viscounts and earls.

We have not quite done with Richmond, but at this stage we own that the identity of Duval's patron remains a mystery. There is agreement, however, that once in England it did not take Claude long to tire of the straight and narrow, for him defined as the life of a lackey, and to seek a more exciting career within his own command.

3

Frequent and Great Robberies

We may infer from the statement that Duval reputedly made to Eye-Witness that he prospered for a few years after he came to England. His good looks, address or efficiency ensured that he was passed from one admiring gentleman or nobleman to another as a valued domestic servant. People seemed to have liked him.

It was doubtless during some elite fraternization that the youth was spotted by "a noble and eminent" peer of the realm, who begged that Duval be transferred to his household. Like most peers, the new master had his principal residence outside of London, but an aside in Eye-Witness's narrative indicates that it might have not been situated too far from the capital. Anyway, young Duval lived up to expectations, and was promoted from the post of page to "a more honourable service," presumably that of a footman or valet, and in this state he "continued some years." Conceivably, he might have been a footman to the lady of the house, because it was when she died that Duval's employment ended, and His Lordship placed the young Frenchman with a relative. The narrative refers to this fresh master as "a person of honour," which perhaps suggests that he was a son of the aforementioned peer, or some other relative traditionally addressed as "the honourable" as a matter of courtesy. Whoever he was, he employed Duval for a considerable time with some satisfaction.

Again, there is almost no point in labouring the identity of Duval's employers. It seems evident that the "noble and eminent peer" was a principal bigwig of his time, and that he both liked Claude and treated him well, raising him from page to footman. At the end of his life, while awaiting execution, the highwayman was said to have lamented that he had sunk so low, for "never man had more or better friends." Again, Macaulay's attempt to link Duval with the Duke of Richmond offers one possibility. In some respects Richmond fits the picture of the "noble and eminent peer" who employed Claude in England more than he does the "person of quality" who brought him from France.

Richmond, a Parisian exile returning to Britain after the Restoration of the Stuarts, would likely have known and mixed with any "person of quality" who had shared his circumstances, and could thus have easily seen Duval in service and been drawn to him, as the Eye-Witness narrative implies. Richmond himself was only a few years older than Duval, and was perhaps capable of identifying with some of the qualities if not the circumstances of a lively if liveried attendant. Richmond was also unquestionably near the top of the food chain. Becoming also 6th Duke of Lennox, he was quickly rewarded for his fidelity to the royal house by Charles II, becoming Great Chamberlain and Great Admiral of Scotland, Lord Lieutenant of Dorset, a Member of the Order of the Garter and Gentleman of the Bedchamber. As a member of the Convention Parliament in 1660 and 1661 he may have spent much of his time in London. Richmond, therefore, might well have been Duval's "noble and eminent peer," and his wife, formerly Elizabeth Rogers, "his lady." Our information states that after some "years" Duval's patron relinquished his footman after the death of the lady of the house. Elizabeth, Duchess of Richmond, died in childbirth in 1661, and in the spring of 1662 the Duke took Margaret Banaster as his second wife.

Again, though, this is mere speculation; if Richmond fits the profile it is only a rough fit, which presumes imprecision in the reported facts. It is time to flounder to firmer ground. Whoever he was with, the experience of service probably contributed significantly to the making of the famous outlaw, for it extended his command of the manners and affectations of the wealthy, and enabled him to disport in their company. But, as other sources confirm, although "capable of any employment" and blessed with a fine appearance, intelligence, charm and vigour, he fell into "lewd" company and became "wild and extravagant," frittering his money away on girls, drink and gambling. Living perhaps close to London, a city scourged by pestilence and sudden and early death, as well as innumerable opportunities for youthful improvidence and adolescent high spirits, Duval may have forged a short and merry philosophy of life. Certain it is that driven by the lure of ready money, he quickly became part of "a knot of highwaymen."

According to Eye-Witness, Duval's last master grew concerned with the life of dissipation into which his employee was sinking, and severed his employment, advising him to break with his unsavoury companions and return to France. The parting does not seem to have been made without regret, for the master not only paid Duval all wages due but made him a present of twenty pieces of "broad gold" and an expensive gelding to help him along his way. On his part, Duval later lamented his descent into crime, when no man had been blessed with "more and better friends." Albeit, he left for France, passing through London, either to directly take ship or proceed by coach to the south coast, but he did not complete his journey. Instead he fell "into the acquaintance of some of the Old Gang of Highwaymen, who by debauchery [had] corrupted his nature."

When did Duval commence his lawless career, and what induced him to make such a life-changing step? In his statement to Eye-Witness he reported that he "fell into those lewd and wicked ways" about two and a half years prior to his ultimate imprisonment, which is to say about the summer of 1667. But other evidence indicates that he was an active offender as early as 1665, and possibly even before that. If Duval really made the assertion recorded by Eye-Witness, he may have been trying to minimize his waywardness, and to draw a convenient veil over his earlier exploits. Here, anyway, I have taken 1665 as an approximate date for his embarkation upon a life on the road.

We have alluded to some of the temptations that led Duval astray, but perhaps it is time to look at the prospects that he might have seen in highway robbery. Duval, it must be remembered, lived in highly dangerous times. The ripples from the English Civil War had not yet been spent. The political and religious divisions of that conflict, the economic and social disruption it had caused, the families and fortunes that had been divided and broken in violence, the resentments sown, and the large numbers of men, trained in arms only to be thrown upon their own resources when the war ended had fed disorder and crime. Party strife continued to fuel it for several decades. It was not until 1685, when the Duke of Monmouth's rebels were defeated at Sedgemoor, that the last major battle was fought on English soil. Then, too, large mobilizations to meet the threats of foreign enemies, such as those mustered to resist the Dutch in 1667, added to the numbers of common men drilled with weapons. In a nation familiar with horses and arms, it was almost inevitable that armed crime, at least, would thrive.

Francis Jackson, himself a highwayman, recalled that many in that profession had been soldiers. "Highwaymen, for the most part, are such who never were acquainted with an honest trade, whom either want of money or employment prompted them to undertake these dangerous designs. To make their persons appear more formidable, and to gain respect, they dub one another Colonel, Major, or at least a Captain, who never [actually] arrived to a greater height than a trooper disbanded, or at the utmost a lifeguardsman cashiered for misdemeanour." His point is stretched, but it has some validity. It was partly for this that the latter half of the seventeenth century was probably the great age of highway robbery. Unlike the eighteenth century, in which roads, communications and law enforcement all steadily improved, and highwaymen usually operated alone or in small parties of perhaps two or three, the seventeenth century occasionally suffered large robber bands to make boot of the countryside.

The highwayman's trade, if such it was, had attractions in Duval's day. The primary motive was pecuniary gain, and the money to be had from small valuables such as watches and jewellery, occasional mail packets and bulk goods, could yield high dividends. But on the negative side, it was deemed an extremely serious offence. Victims were placed in fear of their lives and every robbery was pregnant with potential violence. Furthermore, some contemporaries were alert to the economic consequences of the principal arteries of inland trade and business being threatened by thieves, and clamoured for tough action. For these reasons the penalties meted out to highwaymen were ferocious, and many offenders ended their lives kicking and struggling for breath under a gallows.

But for all that, the chances of highwaymen evading capture at this time were reasonable, and many, among them Claude Duval, operated brazenly by day as well as by night. A well-mounted robber could normally outpace victims as well as the feeble enforcers of the law, even if a general hue and cry, inviting all good citizens to join in the pursuit, was raised. In the London area, where urban as well as rural crime was a problem, patrols were still effectively in the hands of parish or ward watchmen, who were merely untrained civilians serving obligatory and transitory terms of public duty. Supported by the ratepayers, the local watch was supervised by a beadle, who might call upon the services of a constable, armed with a staff of office and wooden truncheon. In the city of Westminster these officials were appointed by a High Steward responsible to the Court of Burgesses. They were capable of handling a modest level of crime and disorder, but ill-equipped, on foot and often undermanned, they were inadequate to tackling heavily armed and ruthless gangs. Moreover, they generally confined their patrols to the hours of darkness.

If routine enforcement was not a great deterrent, neither was the legal system itself. Although prosecutions were made in the name of the crown, they remained driven by the victims of crime. It was the victims who registered their complaints with magistrates and bore the onus of identifying offenders and supplying witnesses, and only a particularly angry or affluent victim persevered with what was a potentially protracted and expensive procedure. Court administration fees and the costs of having witnesses subpoenaed, warrants issued to constables, and recognizances prepared to bind essential participants to appear in court, all fell principally upon the victim as prosecutor. Not surprisingly, many and perhaps most victims declined to expend additional time and treasure, and decided to take their losses on the road philosophically. Others found it cheaper to advertise rewards for the return of their property, or to approach 'thief-takers' able to broker private deals between victims and offenders. Both parties stood to gain through the agency of such dubious intermediaries. The victim might retrieve his property more surely and for less money than a public prosecution promised, and the thief secured part of the value of his haul and immunity from further legal proceedings.

Although the law was undeniably severe in the seventeenth and eighteenth centuries, it was by no means as heavy handed as conventional wisdom declares. Juries often strove to mitigate offences in cases that aroused their sympathies, and not all courts were entirely indifferent to those showing apparent remorse, or the play of unfortunate circumstances that might drive a defendant to crime. Even if the case was vigorously pursued to a successful conviction, even a capital conviction, there were several ways in which a felon might escape the direst consequences. He might hope for a pardon, and if all else failed, there was one card he might successfully play several times. In return for a reprieve, or reduction of sentence, he could inform upon his mates, and, if necessary, appear as witnesses against them in court. As this study will show, some rogues repeatedly used this practice, selling their associates for reprieves, and happily returning to their trades ready to play the card again if need ever arose. At least one of the highwaymen who rode with Duval, George Woodrington, used the system so efficiently that one suspects that he was leading a double life, as both a thief and a government spy and informer. When he could he lived off the proceeds of armed robbery; but he probably kept the authorities at arm's length by feeding them intelligence at appropriate times, and squealed when captured.

Finally, time was often on the side of the highwaymen. Witnesses, where and when available, frequently soon disappeared as they resumed their daily business, and most cases that went to trial concerned recent offences. The older and staler the crime, the more difficult it was to gather the supporting evidence needed for a satisfactory conclusion.

In short, the highwayman certainly followed a dangerous profession, but he had distinct hopes of lasting for several years and even of ultimate escape with or without the benefits of his ill-gotten gains. Some lived down their shady pasts, with the result that one occasionally meets individuals in the records following one legitimate career or another, who were described as former highwaymen.

Idleness, easy money, a spirit of adventure and revulsion at the long arduous hours and skimpy rewards demanded by honest toil all contributed towards the attractions of highway robbery. Duval's London was also the London of the Great Plague and the Fire, tragedies over which he had no control, but which may have fostered notions that life was short and had to be taken at a run. In 1665 the plague cost a reported 70,000 Londoners their lives, some fifteen per cent of the city's population, and the dread march of funeral carts and isolation of infected houses became chilling but familiar sights. By comparison, the fire that raged for five days in September of 1666 cost relatively few lives, but destroyed some two thirds of the city, including more than 13,000 houses. We can only imagine the psychological impact of such calamities, and how they might have moulded attitudes to life. The likes of Duval, for instance, may have weighed the costs of the gallows against a future over which disease and misadventure hung like black clouds.

We cannot positively identify the highwaymen with whom young Claude Duval set himself upon the uncertain path to Tyburn, but he would shortly be running with a desperate set of characters headed by Edward Maddox, John Ashenhurst and Richard Dudley. Of these, Maddox may have been the original leader, although we know little about him. He may have been the "Edmund Madocks" who pleaded for a pardon after being convicted of a serious offence about 1664. If guilty of bloodshed, this Maddox claimed, he would submit to the decision of the law, but he had served his country at Dunkirk, and remained a soldier until the disbanding of the troop under a Major Bridges. He had returned to civilian life only to suffer unemployment, and had fallen in with ill company. If this was our man, he escaped the noose to continue his criminal career.

Four years later Maddox appears to have been the recognized leader of the gang, and was ambitious enough to consider graduating from highway robbery to piracy. In September 1668 a Richard Bulstrode travelled to Bruges in Flanders on behalf of the crown, pursuing reports that some of the gang had been apprehended in the town. From his destination he wrote Sir Joseph Williamson, the head of the king's intelligence and security systems, on 21 September, informing him that according to his information "there is not above five or six principal highwaymen of the gang now about London, of which Edw. Madocks is chief, and one Brixhist, whose brother waits upon the Speaker of the Commons, is another. This crew will be found very busy [robbing] towards Newmarket during His Majesty's progress. They had a design on foot, if Oxenden had not been taken, to have gone to sea upon a desperate attempt. The [sea] captain who was taken with Oxenden was to have been their [sailing] master, and they say that he has not his fellow in England, and that he was lately a prisoner in Dover Castle in a dungeon...and broke through the walls where the sea came in and made a miraculous escape upon the rocks...They had a ship ready at Flushing, had they not been prevented. [Thomas] Granger [an associated thief] betrayed them because he was cheated of the £1000 amongst them, Oxenden having got £500. Granger, besides, laid out the money to [corrupt] the postmaster [in the execution of a swindle in Newcastle], and was at £100 more charge [expense] in preparing the business. In France they employed Mr. Roch, that went over [the Channel] as [a] major to Col. Stanniers, but he being dead, they sent another to Paris to lay their design."

By Bulstrode's evidence the gang that inducted Duval were no local hoodlums, but national and perhaps international criminals, with members close to government. They were also opportunists, gathering where pickings were rich and many, as the reference to the king's fashionable horse races on Newmarket Heath in Suffolk testified. Nevertheless, Duval rapidly increased in notoriety among these brigands. His lawless exploits, we are told, were many, but most have been lost. The fullest pamphlet of the time merely states that they were too well known to bear repetition, and were of the same character as those of James Hind, the most famous highwayman of the mid century. Duval certainly became a serious as well as a frequent offender, eventually leading a powerfully armed "company" of malefactors capable of halting large cavalcades of travellers and intimidating the small forces of law and order.

The major roads serving London were favourite hunting grounds for highwaymen, and all of them had their black spots. The Great North Road included notorious stretches through Enfield Chase and Finchley Common, while travellers taking the Dover road risked Shooter's Hill and Blackheath. Duval seems to have favoured the western approaches to London, and such untamed regions as Hounslow and Bagshot Heaths on the Exeter road and

Maidenhead Thicket on the Bath Road. Hounslow Heath in particular entered the lore of highway robbery. No other place in the country so loudly evokes the images of masked riders and flourishing pistols. It had long been known as a dangerous place. In 1552 four thieves were executed at Tyburn in London for robberies of one kind or another on the heath, and in 1650 a trio of highwaymen, John Selllinger, John Carrowe and William Halton, were indicted for a similar offence. But it was arguably the prolific spate of robberies committed by Duval and his followers in the late seventeenth century that indelibly stamped Hounslow Heath with its forbidding reputation.

Through his operations Duval attained a greater infamy than any other outlaw of his time. If the contemporary ballads, poems and pamphlets did not describe many of his depredations in detail, they reflected their general nature. Thus the ballad *Devol's Last Farewell* has the bandit claiming that

"If I my crimes to mind shou'd call,
And lay them down before you all,
They would amount to such a sum,
That there is few in Christendom,
So many wanton pranks did play."

While in a mock heroic style, the secretary of the Duke of Buckingham, Samuel Butler, claimed in his "pindarick ode" *To the Happy Memory of the Most Renowned Du Vall* that the outlaw often targeted the cavalcades of traders going to the markets, as well as coaches and other travellers. Indeed, so prolific were these robberies that

"No convoy e'er so strong with food,
Durst venture on the desp'rate road."

Butler compared Duval's gang of highwaymen, infesting the roads feeding into London, to enemy soldiers blockading the city.

"And if he had but kept the field,
In time had made the city yield."

According to the same piece Duval and his associates grew increasingly bold as time passed:

"From these first rudiments he grew
to nobler feats, and try'd his force
Upon whole troops of foot and horse
whom he as bravely did subdue
Declar'd all caravans [convoys] that go
Upon the king's highway the foe;
Made many desperate attacks
Upon itinerant brigades of all professions, ranks and trades."

Moreover,

"He vanquished the most fierce and fell
Of all his foes, the Constable;
And oft had beat his quarters up,
And routed him and all his troop."

The contemporary *Life of Deval* contents itself with stating that to satisfy his extravagant living and "his girls" Duval made "many rich prizes" and "harass[ed] the country to purpose, taking rent from many tenants." But it confirms Butler's allegations that the outlaws paid special attention to the caravans of traders who passed to and from the London markets and fairs. This particular work, which often involved intimidating or overpowering large companies of wayfarers, some armed with cudgels, swords or even pistols, was largely beyond the smaller gangs of highwaymen, but was capable of paying high dividends. Duval and his associates probably operated loosely, for much of the time breaking into small units to work different roads or pursue independent targets, but also coalescing to tackle such bigger game as the trade caravans.

So dangerous were the robbers that some traders took to remaining in town overnight after busy markets in order to avoid travelling home in the dark with their takings. Even the sheep, oxen and hogs of butchers were confiscated by Duval and his companions. We are given details of one such outrage, when a band of a dozen or fourteen "market folks," men and women both, completed their business in London early and headed "merrily homeward" with their profits, thinking that they were safe from attack. It was yet daylight, but they were ambushed in a narrow lane, and their money taken. The unfortunate merchants were made to sit on the ground, beside the hampers stripped from their horses.

We have some contemporary reports that probably reflect the activities of Duval, or if not he, members of his band. These concern large numbers of highwaymen who occasionally commanded the main road from London to Portsmouth. It was an artery of major national importance, linking the capital with its principal naval base on the south coast, and was in regular use, not least for the movement of the massive amounts of provisions and stores that were needed for His Majesty's ships. On 1 November 1666 one Hugh Salesbury informed security chief Williamson that "on Monday the Portsmouth wagons were robbed at Redhill, near Ripley, twenty miles from London, by nine horsemen, who staved [stoved] all trunks and chests in search of money, but met with none. They carried away a great deal of goods on their horses." This attack upon a provision convoy is exactly the sort of adventure of which Duval's contemporaries, the author of the *Life of Deval* and Samuel Butler, complained. Butler specifically referred to attacks on "ammunition carts." The following year a similar episode occurred. From the same informant, in a document of 23 November 1667, Williamson learned that "the wagons coming from London [to Portsmouth] this week with shop goods were plundered near Cobham by sixteen or seventeen robbers, who carried the plunder towards London." This report also implicates the nest of highwaymen associated with Duval, especially as the thieves retreated towards London, which was, of course, their base of operations.

Alexander Smith, an early eighteenth-century chronicler whose fictional account of Duval credits him with absurd acts of confidence trickery as well as other thefts, concurred that "his robberies were many." In that he was probably right. Large scale attacks, like those on the convoys, were probably based upon considerable planning, but the bandits also often rode out with a no more complicated design than merely to hold a road and see who came along. Active by day and night, Duval would have regularly perpetrated several robberies on each such outing. As his career lasted for five or so years, he probably committed several hundred robberies. Many were petty beyond belief, but others involved considerable risk and plunder. The accounts of Duval published at or shortly after his death need not be taken literally, but printed when much about him was still within common knowledge, they portray no small time villain, operating with one or two comrades, but a leading light of a formidable robber band, a "knot of highwaymen," that posed a serious threat to public order.

Historical records furnish the names of some fifty active robbers in the accord, and these were admittedly less than the whole, for others had already been captured, or escaped being named because the authorities were preparing to arrest them and were wary of causing premature alarm. When the number of the gang's collaborators – the receivers and fencers of stolen property; the 'thief-takers' and other brokers willing, for a consideration, to negotiate between robbers and victims to the mutual advantage of both; the informers and suppliers; the innkeepers, ostlers and stable-owners; the tenants or landlords of safe houses willing to turn blind eyes for profit; the mistresses, whores, and game-house hosts; and the colluding or dependant friends and relatives – are added, the total network of economically interdependent persons probably summed several hundred.

Soon after the Frenchman's death, the playwright Thomas Duffett went further still, characterizing Duval as the lynchpin of a "New Utopia" or underworld, in which he operated as the "chief commander of all the padders [highwaymen], jugglers [tricksters], priggers [thieves], ditchers, bulkers [street thieves and prostitutes] and pickpockets..." By either reckoning, Duval's place was among the great bands of brigands spawned in the unsettled period of the mid and late seventeenth century. There were other such leaders, sung or unsung. Both Hind, who preceded Duval, and Whitney, who followed him, are said to have worked with similar large bodies of men. If true, they stand in contrast to their eighteenth century successors, who operated in less disorderly times and against increasingly sophisticated forces of enforcement, and who typically moved in small units.

However, as Butler pointed out, Duval's contemporary reputation stood on two legs rather than one:

"Both fully satisfy'd; the one
With those fresh laurels he had won,
And all the brave renowned feats
He had performed in arms;
The other with his person and his charms."

And it was actually the latter, those "charms," that particularly secured Duval a lasting and prominent station in the ranks of highway robbers. His attentions to women, if highly unlikely to have been honourable, nevertheless accorded him a surprising female following. As the author of the *Life of Deval* put it, "They [Duval and his associates] will truck with them [women] for their maidenhoods if they have a convenient opportunity, for which kindness the maids resolve to gratify them with their prayers when they go to be hanged, and cry them up for the *handsomest* men they ever saw."

As far as this particular facet – chivalry with an attendant sexual chemistry – was concerned, Duval was doubly advantaged over most of his predecessors and contemporaries on the highway. His extensive experience in the service of the aristocracy in England would alone have educated him in the manners and customs of the elites. But over and above that was his nationality and Parisian heritage. The French were setting the pace in the worlds of fashion, manners and courtship. Many, especially, it was said, women, fiercely admired France as the home of civilization and taste. Indeed, so many did so that in some quarters there was a jealous reaction. Thus, a news report of 25 September 1668 acidly maintained that "several Frenchman having attempted to 'debauch' our Englishmen to instruct them in France in the mystery of weaving silk stockings were brought before the [privy] council and committed to the Tower." Duval, with his first-hand knowledge of the new men espoused in Paris and his life of service, was fully equipped to exploit his country's reputation in clothes, speech, gestures and gallantry.

More than any other highwayman, Duval stayed in the national memory less for what he *did* than for the type of man he *was*. Little in the way of violence was ever charged against him, but, extravagant in appearance and address, he robbed with a singular gentility, flirting with the ladies and engaging both sexes in a disarmingly amiable banter. In the process he carved a niche for himself that no one else quite filled. In Butler's words he

"Taught the wild Arabs [robbers] on the Road
To act in a more genteel mode;
Took prizes more obligingly than those;
Who never had been bred *fi lous*;
And how to hang in a more graceful fashion
Than e'er was known before to the dull English nation."

A rogue indeed, but Duval exuded glamour. He was handsome, virile, intelligent, well-spoken and, when occasion served, courteous and sympathetic, and if a dandy of sorts he was assuredly no milk sop, and excelled on a horse or with a sword and pistol. Hiding his dishonest purposes beneath a sweeping and disarming civility, he refrained from violence whenever he could, and was known to be a compulsive lady's man. We have no portrait to show us Duval's face, nor even a half decent description; only a thin inference to be drawn from a contemporary sneer that "a dapper fellow with fine black eyes and a white peruke" had gulled the English ladies. In short, he was a veritable story-book knight of the road.

This is really why Duval stood out. Among the dozens of highwaymen with whom he consorted there were other prolific thieves, and some of them masters of the same manly arts of riding and fighting. In those respects they were equally deserving of notoriety. This was no ordinary band. Upon his death one member, Richard Dudley, was described as "the great robber," who, according to another account, was "known and dreaded all over the country," though the considerable wealth he pilfered "was as soon dissipated in riot and extravagance." John and Humble Ashenhurst, Edward Maddox, John Blanchard and Samuel Swiftnicks, among others, likewise gained unenviable reputations for their wrong-doings. But it was Claude Duval alone who had the style and aplomb to become a lasting celebrity of the road.

The first intimation of Duval's new career that has so far been found in the official records is an indictment of 5 April 1665, referred to after the highwayman's eventual capture in 1669. At his trial in 1670 he was charged under the earlier indictment with murdering one James Tirrell near the 'Golden Lion' alehouse in the Strand in the spring of 1665. It is possible that the allegation against Duval was lodged at the time of the offence, and that a jury found sufficient grounds for a formal indictment, but had to leave it in abeyance as the supposed culprit remained at large. The records of the sessions of 1665 show that John Fitzgerrard, Titus Gold and Denby Stoland then appeared before the court to answer for the crime, and in 1670 it was said that a Dutchman had actually been convicted of it.

It is, however, also possible that Duval was only connected with the murder retrospectively in 1669 and 1670. The indictment against him in 1670 rested largely upon the statement of George Woodrington (or Withrington), a London butcher turned thief, who almost made informing a third profession. He testified that Duval had once boasted of killing a man in Durham-yard in the Strand. On that occasion the jury may have known something of Woodrington's status as a regular informer. As early as 1667 he had found himself incarcerated in Dorchester gaol with another robber named Richard Laurence. Woodrington told the authorities that Laurence had admitted to him that he was involved in a papist plot to assassinate the king as he walked in St. James's Park and raise a regiment of malcontents, including highwaymen, with which to march through England. He had a scheme to liberate all the Catholics in Dorchester gaol. What favour Woodrington bought with such a yarn is not clear, but his career as a highwayman continued, as did his propensity to gain advantage by timely if unreliable intelligences to the authorities.

In 1670, however, the jury chose to doubt Woodrington's interpretation of Duval's supposed confession with respect to the murder of Tirrell. If such a claim was made, they speculated, it might well have been merely the idle boast of a young man, "the better to fit himself for so wicked a company, of which he was then to be a member." The jury acquitted him of the murder charge outright. Whether Duval's name had come up in 1665, or simply arose in 1669 as a result of a fresh allegation of Woodrington, the episode suggests a rough date for the beginning of the Frenchman's career as a professional criminal. By one interpretation he was charged with a capital offence in April 1665, and lived thereafter under its shadow, a wanted man. By the other, he was held to have boasted of murdering Tirrell as a means of ingratiating himself with a criminal band which he aspired to join. In other words, he had not been fully integrated into the highwayman knot before the date of Tirrell's murder.

If Duval became a highwayman in 1665, he made speedy progress, for one of the few surviving 'on the spot' reports of a robbery alleged against him comes from a printed newsletter dated 1666. In the absence of a regular press, government newsletters were an important means of disseminating information in Restoration England. This one, discovered by Charles G. Harper, intimates that four years before his death the Frenchman was considered a leading actor in a notorious gang of robbers. Although the identity of the highwayman referred to in the newsletter was not confirmed, the affair had all the hallmarks of a Duval exploit. The opportunism, in this case fed by the number of wealthy gamblers being drawn to celebrated races; the courtesy and amiability of the malefactor; the apologetic tone of his approach, with its explanation of an urgent need of money; and the worthless promise to return the loan were all features that would reappear in the spare records of the French highwayman. In fact, when we consider that in 1666 Claude Duval was only one of several notable highwaymen acting in loose association, it is plausible that it was the *manner* in which this robbery was conducted that led to him being specifically named as the probable perpetrator. If this construction bears any weight, Duval's fame as the gentleman highwayman had developed extremely quickly. The passage is worth quoting in full:

"Last Monday week in Holborn Fields, while several gentlemen were travelling to Newmarket, to the races there, a highway man very politely begged their purses, for, he said, he was advised that he should win a great sum if he adventured some guineas with the competers

[sic] at Newmarket on a certain horse called Bopeep, which my Lord Exeter was to run [in] a match [race]. He was so pressing that they resigned their money to his keeping (not without sight of his pistols), he telling them that, if they would give him their names and the names of the places where they might be found, he would return to them that had lent, at usury [with interest]. It is thought that his venture was not favourable, for the gentlemen have not received neither principal nor interest. It is thought that it was Monsieur Claud[e] Du Vall, or one of his knot, that ventured the gentlemen's money for them."

Apart from the untested allegation respecting the Tirrell murder, which does not seem to have become a matter of public knowledge, it does not appear that any act of serious violence was ever credibly levied against Claude Duval, and Walter Pope, the hostile author of the contemporary *Memoirs*, seeking to counter his subject's popular reputation as the ultimate gallant, could only discover one occasion to tarnish it. Duval's party stopped a coach on Blackheath, and the Frenchman robbed the ladies of a child's sucking bottle, apart from their watches, rings and money. In this story an associate insisted that Duval return the bottle to the tearful child. It has often been told as the chronicler intended it to be, as evidence of a hidden brutality in Duval's nature, and yet it arguably points towards the opposite conclusion. For at a time when robberies were regularly accompanied by physical and verbal violence of every kind, including murder, this relatively insignificant anecdote was all that could be unearthed from a long and active career on the road that worked to Duval's disadvantage in this respect.

Duval seems to have liked cultivating his victims, using his acquaintance with the manners of the gentry, as if in amelioration of his acts. The contemporary *Life of Deval* describes how he and an accomplice stopped two gentlemen on their way to the city, and presented pistols at the breasts of their servants without taking anything from the masters save a sword and belt, which they almost as soon returned. The highwaymen freely gave their names, and "called the gentlemen by theirs" as if to establish familiarity, and they explained that they would not have stopped the travellers had they not been down to four shillings which had to support a dozen of them. Moreover, they disingenuously agreed to repay what they had taken "at any place on the road they would appoint." Evidently proud of his armoury, Duval showed the gentlemen his pistols, and remarked, as if they were worthy confidants, that he was resolved never to be taken alive.

By far the most famous incident in Duval's career became one of the two iconic and endlessly retold highwayman stories. He and four other horsemen overtook a coach one night in which there travelled a knight and his lady, with her serving maid. In the words of the *Memoirs*,

"He, with his squadron, overtakes a coach which they had set [waited for] over night, having intelligence of a booty of £400 in it. In the coach was a knight, his lady, and only one serving maid, who perceiving five horsemen making up to them presently imagined that they were beset, and they were confirmed in this apprehension by seeing them whisper to one another, and ride backwards and forwards. The lady, to show she was not afraid, takes a flageolet out of her pocket and plays. Du Vall takes the hint, plays also and excellently well upon a flageolet of his own, and in this posture he rides up to the coach side. 'Sir,' says he to the person in the coach, 'your lady plays excellently, and I doubt not but that she dances as well. Will you please to walk out of the coach, and let me have the honour to dance one currant [coranto] with her upon the heath?' 'Sir,' said the person in the coach, 'I dare not deny anything to one of your quality and good mind. You seem a gentleman, and your request is very reasonable.' Which said, the lackey [footman] opens the boot [door], out comes the knight, Du Vall leaps lightly off his horse, and hands the lady out of the coach. They danced and here it was that Du Vall performed marvels, the best master in London, except those that are French, not being able to show such footing as he did in his great riding French boots. The dancing being over, he waits on the lady to her coach. As the knight was going in says Du Vall to him, 'Sir you have forgot to pay the music.' 'No, I have not,' replies the knight, and putting his hand under the seat of the coach, he pulls out £100 in a bag and delivers it to him, which Du Vall took with a very good grace, and courteously answered, 'Sir, you are liberal, and shall have no cause to repent your being so, this liberality of yours shall excuse you the other £300,' and giving him the [pass]word that if he met with any more of the crew he might pass undisturbed, he civilly takes leave of him."

Some recent historians have questioned, and even ridiculed this story, and scepticism is certainly not out of place. Pope was at best a blundering historian and perhaps worse. But we must not rush into simple denigration. Duval's reputation with women was not a fiction. As this book shows it was attested at the time in poems, pamphlets, legal documents, reminiscences and contemporary creative literature. It was current within Duval's lifetime and the lifetimes of those who had known him. And if it was not the whole picture, we have to accept that it had roots somewhere.

3. Duval's Dance: William Powell Frith's classic interpretation of the defining moment in the evolution of the myth of the gentleman highwayman, painted in 1859.

Pope's version of the dance need not be taken as a faithful record in all or even many of its particulars. That would simply be setting up a straw man for cynics to knock him down. In its broader respects the story is not, it has to be said, as improbable as it appears. The use of the flageolet, for example, was one with the time. A French flute, usually with six tone holes, it was an easy to play and accessible musical instrument then increasingly popular in England, partly as a ready recourse. Indeed, it was the subject of Thomas Greeting's *The Pleasant Companion*, published in 1675, which praised its everyday use and portability.

But apart from the equivocation about the details of the Pope account, a dance similar to that described could certainly have contributed or even created the wider contemporary reputation that Duval clearly acquired. Pope, ever eager to debunk the highwayman, described it with a degree of grudging acceptance, as if it was an inconvenient but well-known episode that he was obliged to acknowledge. And that something of the sort actually occurred, or was believed to have occurred, is indicated by its prominence in an entirely independent contemporary source, the narrative ballad, *Devol's Last Farewell*, in which Duval claims

"Upon the road, I do declare,
I caused some lords and ladies faire,
To quit their coach, and dance with us;
This being done, the case was thus,
They for their Musick needs must pay."

This was the only specific robbery to find a place in *Devol's Last Farewell*, so we may be sure that the anecdote was fairly well known at the time. It is possible to imagine that such a reputation made Duval the subject of considerable speculation among the fashionable women of the day, and incited more than a little curiosity. That, at least, would explain the appearance of so many of them during his subsequent imprisonment, trial and execution. Moreover, the incident almost begs for romantic embellishment in fiction, film and art. Innumerable stories have sprung from it, picturing gentlewomen as participants in illicit liaisons with highwaymen that were as exciting and romantic as they were dangerous.

Duval operated at a time when there was little of a popular press, and no daily newspapers; worse, few of the official documents then made have been routinely preserved. As a result, hardly any documentable robberies are known. Alexander Smith, who produced an account of Duval early the next century, filled it with transparently fictitious episodes set in Oxford, Beaconsfield and Paris. Only one of his stories smacks of authenticity. It stands out on account of its brevity, its prosaic and unvarnished character, and because it alone actually named the victim. Smith told how Duval stopped "Squire Roper," master of the king's buckhounds, who he found hunting in a "private thicket" of Windsor Forest. Since Norman times the forest, which lay south of Windsor and the Thames in Berkshire, and west of Hounslow Heath, had been a royal hunting preserve, and it had been enclosed in the thirteenth century. Ignoring such pretensions, Duval invaded the forest and ran upon Roper. He, Smith said,

"commanded him to deliver his money, or else he would shoot him. The squire...gave a purse of fifty guineas to Du Vall, who then tying him neck and heels, with his horse fastened by him, he rode away.

All the pastime of hunting was over before the squire was found out by the forester, who...unloosed the bound person, who then making what haste he could into Windsor was met in the town by Sir Stephen Fox, who asking him whether he had met with any sport, he replied in a great passion, 'Yes, Sir, I have had sport enough shown me by the son of a whore, but he made me pay damned dear for it; for tying me neck and heels, he then took fifty guineas to pay him for the trouble of taking such pains about me.'"

4. Duval's robbery of Squire Roper, as depicted in this recognisably eighteenth-century engraving from Alexander Smith's *Complete History of ... Highwaymen*, first published in 1713.

It is possible to identify this "Squire Roper." Edward Roper, sometime known as Squire Roper of Eltham in Kent, would have been thirtyish at the time of the robbery. Subsequently, he became master-of-hounds for the Duke of Monmouth and Lord Grey in Charlton, Sussex, and had the dubious distinction of founding the Charlton hunt. He was important enough to have his portrait painted, and two likenesses reputedly exist today; one is owned by the Goodwood Social and Sporting Club, in Sussex, and another can be seen in a National Trust property, Hardwick Hall. The Duval story was first published in 1713, within Roper's lifetime; he died at the age of 84 in February 1723 without ever having contradicted the account, as far as is known. That despite the book's continuing popularity (a fifth and expanded edition appeared in 1719) and the fact that the episode was one of the few to be graced with an imaginary full-page engraving.

As for Roper's acquaintance, Sir Stephen Fox, he, too, was a follower of the king. An important government financier, he was at this time also paymaster of the king's guards, and would ultimately become the grandfather of the famous eighteenth-century Whig politician, Charles James Fox.

5. Edward Roper (c. 1738-1723), master-of-hounds, said to have been robbed by Duval in Windsor Forest, from an oil painting in Hardwick Hall, possibly painted by Jonathan Richardson the Elder. The picture is reproduced by the kind permission of The National Trust.

Stephen Fox died in 1716, and was therefore also still alive when Smith's story of Duval and Roper appeared in print. Again, there is no evidence that he objected to it.

So this anecdote of Duval may have preserved a true incident. If so, it demonstrated that no part of the realm, not even royal domains such as Windsor Forest, were immune to Duval's incursions. It could not have endeared him to the political establishment.

4

Manhunt

On 19 June 1668 Richard Bulstrode took up his diary and recorded that "a considerable knot of highwaymen and robbers were yesterday and ye day before apprehended here in town [London] by ye diligence of Justice [William] Morton principally." The entry is significant since it represented the starting gun of an extraordinary campaign on the part of Charles II and his government.

As far as we know, the state had not troubled itself with the doings of a particular highwayman, or gang of highwaymen, before. But for some time the activities of Duval, Dudley, Ashenhurst, Maddox and their followers had been growing in intensity. A series of measures had been introduced to check the outrages, but none of them seem to have been very successful.

On 7 March 1667 Henry Muddiman, the journalist and publisher who had founded *The London Gazette* and remained a government confidant, wrote that "there have been so many robberies lately that a new office of Marshal of England is created, with a fee of £50 a month and power to seize all suspected persons and keep the road[s] clear of highwaymen." This fresh post, which should not be confused with a ceremonial function of a similar name that had been evolving since the Middle Ages, apparently produced no significant results.

In a separate initiative that same year a certain Thomas Martin, claiming an extensive knowledge of the offending highwaymen, with "most" of whom he was intimate, was empowered by the Lord Chief Justice to bring them before the courts. It was the old story that to be a thief-taker one first needed to be a thief. Unfortunately, according to Martin's story, some of his former associates learned of his perfidy, and arranged for him to be accused of stealing £30. Witnesses to that effect were produced, and the would-be thief-taker was hauled before the Surrey Assizes and thrown into the

Marshalsea Prison. In September Martin was reprieved, but his mission had been discredited.

On 23 November 1667 a warrant was issued to Thomas Walkedene and John Hope authorizing them to commandeer the services of one or more constables and search "all places where highwaymen are suspected to keep their horses, to seize all that can be proved to belong to highwaymen, and to give account of their proceedings to the Secretaries of State." There is no evidence that this was any more successful than the earlier strategies.

Such, then, was the background to the entry in Bulstrode's diary: a history of failed attempts to arrest or alleviate increasing public and government concern about the highwaymen plaguing the capital and neighbouring counties. It was time for a serious fight-back, and in the spring of 1668 the government counter-offensive took shape, with a distinct chain of command. Beneath the king and his privy council authority rested with his two secretaries of state, especially Sir Henry Bennet, Baron Arlington, who was not only the Secretary of State for the Southern Department but also the holder of such relevant offices as postmaster-general and commissioner for trade. From his base in Whitehall, close to the Treasury, Arlington was a member of most of the committees appointed by the crown and acted as the principal conduit between government and the country's local authorities, such as justices and deputy lords lieutenant. To him came the correspondence from all quarters, letters and reports that furnished detailed information about the state of the nation, and upon which Arlington was required to arbitrate. He was, then, a maker as well as an implementer of state policy.

Acting as his under-secretary was a formidable protégé, Sir Joseph Williamson. In his mid-thirties, Williamson was a brisk-for-business self-made man then emerging as one of the crown's most effective bureaucrats. It was in the hands of this pair – Arlington and Williamson – that the safety of the king and his realm in these uncertain and turbulent times substantially rested. As part of their brief, they were developing an efficient intelligence and espionage system to penetrate potential enemies of the state, be they external foreigners or domestic republicans, religious nonconformists or dissidents. Several weapons were to hand.

As postmaster-general Arlington had control of the postal service, which had become a monopoly of the state by acts of 1657 and 1660. During this period hand-written letters were the staple of communication, and Arlington and Williamson quickly turned their privileges to account, intercepting, rifling and copying mail as they thought necessary. No less crucial to the intelligence service was the widespread use and reward of spies and informers, a practise authorized in the interests of state-security by the penal laws against dissidents and recusants. The power to hire under-cover agents was extended to local officials, such as justices, enabling Williamson to create local networks of intelligence. Spies fraternized with suspect organizations or individuals, shovelling up a farrago of information, from confidential meetings to tavern talk, and feeding it through local authorities to Whitehall. Sometimes prisoners were also used. Incarcerated enemies of the state, facing the ultimate penalty, were often willing to betray their friends for a reprieve. And some went further, agreeing to become underground government agents themselves. Arlington and Williamson became adept at protecting the most useful of these informers. The government might arrest and interrogate them, furnishing a means by which they could impart their secrets without arousing the suspicion of their comrades. And at an opportune time an apparent escape could be staged to allow the spy to return to his work with his cover intact.

As historian John Alan Marshall has shown, under the patronage of Arlington, Williamson created an efficient intelligence service that would today justify the terms security-chief and spymaster. His methods were just as applicable to nests of criminals as to religious and political rebels. But the workhorse of the new campaign, which would turn the crushing powers of the state upon Claude Duval and his highwaymen, was the third, and in some respects, the most crucial member of the triumvirate: Sir William Morton, a man of almost demonic determination and judge of the King's Bench under its Chief Justice, Sir John Kelyng. It was he, according to Bulstrode, who made the first significant break-through in June of that year.

Sir William was by all accounts an indefatigable officer of the crown. A lawyer and soldier by profession, he was a staunch Anglican and royalist, and had served his king in the Civil War, reaching the rank of lieutenant-colonel in the army. He was compelled to surrender Sudeley Castle in Gloucestershire after a siege in 1644, and suffered imprisonment in the Tower of London and loss of land for his fidelity to the losing side, but was compensated by a knighthood in 1643, and after the restoration returned to grace and favour. Morton became the king's sergeant in 1663 and a justice of the King's Bench two years later. A learned, grave, iron-willed and grim-faced zealot, he was in some respects the ideal man to confront such an intractable problem as highway robbery. About sixty-three years of age in 1668, he turned the job into an obsession. If he was justly accused of undue severity, he also brought much-needed energy and purpose to the hunt. Four years in pursuit did not quench his fire. In 1672 Richard Hals, a highwayman in Newgate Prison, attempting to obtain a pardon, described Morton's passionate hostility as a "fury" and considered him "implacable."

Morton's methods were already well oiled. Williamson's battle against rebels and nonconformists and Morton's campaign to rid the country of highwaymen were different faces of the same coin. Gilbert Thomas, for example, was appointed provost-marshal for Westminster, Middlesex, Southwark and Surrey in 1664, charged with confronting both criminals and Quakers suspected of sedition. These were twin missions relying upon a rehearsed cocktail of infiltration, intimidation, informers and rewards.

6. Sir William Morton (1605-1672), who led the hunt for Duval and his gang. This engraving of a portrait at the Inner Temple, attributed to Gerard (Gilbert) Soest, suggests the energy, intelligence and violence he brought to his work.

The arrests in London on 17 and 18 June, alluded to by Bulstrode, may have had something to do with that accomplished highwayman and informer, George Woodrington, who we met in the preceding chapter. He was in custody again, this time in London in the April of that year. He had fallen afoul of a thief-taker named William Miller. Miller, a self-styled soldier and servant of the court, had offered his services as a thief-taker to John Browne, bailiff of the Sheriff of Middlesex, and a gentleman named William Hastings. Ordered to "discover" highwaymen, Miller succeeded in finding three of their horses, which were identified as belonging to Woodrington and another notorious road-agent, John Blanchard. Both were members of the robber band that also included Duval, Maddox and the Ashenhurst and Dudley brothers. However, apprehending the bandits was another matter. Woodrington initially escaped, but then brazenly approached one of the justices engaged in the hunt with an offer to sell his companions for a pardon. By his statement, both he and Miller had participated in a robbery in Essex and quarrelled, and the latter had impugned him in a spirit of revenge. In addition to playing the informer, therefore, Woodrington bargained upon securing freedom from prosecution by discrediting Miller, who was the only witness against him in the present instance.

Woodrington's allegations against Miller were dismissed after Hastings and Browne issued an affidavit on 26 June, verifying that they had authorized Miller to act as a thief-taker, as he had claimed. But once in the hands of the authorities, Woodrington was a useful instrument in the state's hands. Pressed by Morton or his officers to identify notorious associates and their haunts in return for his liberty, the highwayman had no qualms about squealing. In May and September a John and an Anna Woodrington were likewise rounded up by the authorities. It is likely that one or both were relatives of George, and that all belonged to a family that would produce a dynasty of thieves.

As Morton pieced together his information he perhaps realised for the first time that he was not confronting a proliferation of single or small groups of offenders. He was up against an extensive criminal network. It became clear that one large gang or "knot" of robbers was behind the most threatening disturbances of the peace. But at last the names of the main culprits were known, and law enforcement officers could raid known hideouts and supposed safe houses to arrest offenders or their accomplices. Every associate taken into custody was capable of being threatened or bribed to reveal more. The hunt gathered a fearful momentum.

In the autumn two very big fish indeed fell into the net, John Ashenhurst and Richard Dudley. Ashenhurst, an exceptionally active highwayman, housebreaker and burglar, was evidently taken in September, and a formidable list of indictments was thrown at him in a Middlesex court session of November. The most serious offence charged was his participation in a damaging raid that a gang of thieves had made upon the home of Lancelot Johnson, a propertied and influential gentleman of the Inner Temple. At a time when banking was in its infancy people generally kept their valuables in their own homes, and house-breaking and burglary could yield much higher returns than robbery on the highway. The Johnson robbery was deemed a major heist of the day, and it appeared in one indictment after another for over a year as various members of the gang were brought to justice.

The date and place of the robbery are uncertain, although these details could well survive in gaol delivery rolls that are now considered too dilapidated for presentation. Johnson's "domo mancionali" mentioned in some of the indictments literally suggests a manor house, and in 1669 this particular Esquire was indeed in possession of Cowley Hall, a manor house in Hillingdon in the western environs of London, north-north-west of the notorious Hounslow Heath. It was, therefore, close to the main roads between London and the west which Duval and his friends frequented. It is likely that Cowley Hall (not to be confused with the later construction that occupied the site) was the scene of the robbery, but as the Latin phrase was also simply used to describe a dwelling place or residence, we cannot be sure. As for the date of the Johnson raid, that too has not been found, although the indictments indicate that it occurred in 1668.

The attack was daring and well-planned. A substantial gang, including a quartet of famous highwaymen, John Ashenhurst, Claude Duval, John Blanchard and Edward Maddox, gathered outside Johnson's house in broad daylight when he was known to be away from home. Some of thieves, no doubt respectably attired, knocked upon the door, and told a servant that they had business with the missing owner. Affecting disappointment at his absence, they begged to be admitted so that they could leave him a written note. Once inside, the robbers quickly gathered and neutralised the staff, opened the doors and allowed their other comrades inside. No one was hurt in the robbery, but the place was systematically ransacked, and a very large amount of valuable property removed. It had gone strictly to plan.

Two of Ashenhurst's confederates in the raid, Francis Eaton and Hannah Cledon, were indicted and convicted with him, but others still at large included Duval (who may have been mentioned in an indictment drawn up on 9 December) and George Woodrington, who would happily inform upon the others if he was caught. The case of Hannah Cledon was an interesting one. Although she confessed that she had participated in the robbery of Johnson's house, she was able to "read books," and therefore claimed 'benefit of clergy'. Originally a device to protect men of the cloth from prosecution in criminal courts, benefit of clergy had come to rest upon success in a literary test, and in the seventeenth century was consequently available to a much wider public than churchmen. A defendant who could read, whether an ecclesiast or lay, and who was charged only with any of the stipulated "clergyable" offences, could escape serious punishment by claiming benefit of clergy. In 1623 a statute had in some degree extended the privilege to women. Providing that she could read, and had not been convicted of the theft of property worth more than ten shillings, Hannah could theoretically evade the grosser penalties of the law. Serious offences such as burglary, murder, rape, violence to the person and highway robbery were considered to be beyond the reach of benefit of clergy, but in this case the prisoner was allowed the privilege so it must be assumed that the court regarded her part in the Johnson robbery as a trivial one. Hannah may have been one of those on hand to carry away the large amount of booty secured; anyway, she was spared the noose, but condemned to be branded on the hand so that all might know of her misdemeanour.

Ashenhurst himself had no such luck. Condemned to death for the raid on the Johnson home, he also faced capital indictments for six additional offences. He had robbed John Andrews, James Worsfold, James Neck, Roger Living and Thomas Collett on "the king's highway," and also taken money from a widow named Anne Long. For the first of these hold-ups, that of Andrews, Ashenhurst was jointly indicted with a fellow highwayman who styled himself 'Captain Dudley.' Captured about the same time as Ashenhurst, Richard Dudley was an old offender who needed no new capital offences to mark him as gallows bait; in fact, he had already been sentenced to death on a previous indictment. Crime ran through the Dudley family, as it did among the Woodringtons and Ashenhursts, and both Richard and his younger brother William had rode with Claude Duval.

According to a brief but apparently reliable contemporary account of his career, Richard Dudley hailed from Swepston, Leicestershire, but his father had lost his once considerable estate through extravagant living and been driven to London, where he was subsisting upon a frugal stipend. Nevertheless, Richard did well enough for a while, benefiting, no doubt, from the influential connections that his family had made in their better days. He married "a gentlewoman of a good fortune" that netted her some £140 a year. But rather like Duval, Dudley revealed a feckless streak, and soon became a leading luminary in the same gang of highwaymen. His biographer, whose title-page proclaimed his subject "the great robber," averred that "there was scarce any notable robbery committed in which Dudly [sic] had not a hand." Before long, he had also inveigled his brother William into the same capricious trade.

In November 1668, when Dudley appeared in the Old Bailey with John Ashenhurst, he was judged to have already forfeited his life by a previous indictment, but somehow neither that nor any fresh villainies succeeded in nailing the fugitive. Probably he bought his freedom with information. Whatever, he "escaped that bout" and in 1669 was again robbing upon the roads with his brother and other companions-in-arms.

If Dudley slipped away, Ashenhurst and probably Eaton paid for their misdeeds by swinging from the gallows at Tyburn while the government simultaneously embarked upon another and remarkable step to bring their surviving accomplices to justice. Informers, spies and thief-takers were yielding important dividends, both in arrests and in information that Morton needed to build a picture of the gang. But now something more was required. On 20 November Bullstrode recorded that "the frequent and great robberies" that had lately been committed had forced the king and his council to address the "enormities."

In medieval times fugitives could be declared outlaws, placing them beyond the protection of the law, so that they could be taken dead or alive by anyone without retribution, and their goods and chattels confiscated by the authorities. It was from this practise that the term 'outlaw' originated. It had long fallen into disuse, although it was effectively and remarkably re-enacted in the Australian colonies in 1865 and 1878 when Felons Apprehension Acts were passed against the Hall and Kelly gangs of bushrangers operating in New South Wales and Victoria. Confronted with the robber band associated with Duval, Charles II and his council came close to reviving the declaration of outlawry in England. On 23 December 1668 a Royal Proclamation proscribed the entire remaining nest of malefactors, and published the names of twenty-three of them, undoubtedly distilled from interviews with those already apprehended. It was the severest and most comprehensive assault upon highwaymen within living memory.

Most of the outlaws were using aliases, partly to allow them to address each other during robberies without revealing their true identities to the victims. Consequently, the authorities were sometimes in doubt as to their real names. In the order of listing, the offenders named in the proclamation were Edward Mad[d]ox, alias Morgan; John Blanchard, alias Major; Lewis [or] Lodowick [Ludovic], alias Peter Deval [Claude Duval]; John Mawer, alias Marr; William Wood[r]ington, alias Widrington, a brother of George; Humble Ashenhurst, alias Needham, a brother of the late John; Swift Nix [Samuel Swiftnicks], alias Clarke; John, alias William Philips, commonly called Captain Philips; William Dudl[e]y, the brother of Richard; Howard Coney; John Cassel[l]s or Castles; Laurence Clarke; John Martin; Thomas Lambert; John Hawkin, alias Jekins; William Moore; William Stavely; a man known only as Tripp; David Lloyd; William Stanesby; Thomas Bradshaw; George Poynter; and Henry Lassells, "all...notoriously known to...daily commit such offences" as highway robberies, burglaries or murders. Importantly, the proscribed men were "all...well known to be of one party and knot, and commonly keep company the one with the other, and with others who already are convicted of those offences." The absence of Richard Dudley from the list indicates that at the time it was drawn up he was still in custody.

To break the gang a raft of new measures was enacted: Justices of the Peace were told to "use all diligence and endeavour" to apprehend the criminals, and to ensure that "watches and wards" were properly patrolled by both horse and foot officers; all vintners, and the keepers of inns, gaming, lodging and other houses were threatened with "punishment" if they failed to watch for and attempt to apprehend such of the robbers as came within their cognizance; and the owners of horses at livery or for hire in London, Westminster, Southwark, Middlesex and Surrey were commanded to register their animals with the Justices of the Peace, and informed that they would be prosecuted if any of their stock was discovered to have facilitated crimes. Moreover, if any offence was committed a hue and cry was "immediately" to be "raised and [the perpetrators] pursued with diligence by horse and foot." To encourage the public to inform upon or assist in apprehending the named offenders, a reward of £10 per head was payable within fifteen days of conviction, the cost to be borne by the Exchequer. A speedy result was anticipated, since the reward was only offered until 24 June 1669. A week after the proclamation, on 30 December, the king was induced to extend the campaign to all highwaymen and robbers, and offered £10 per conviction on that account. But to preserve the original focus of the operation – the Duval gang – the reward for each of its members was increased to £20. Given that twenty-three gang members had been named in the proclamation, on this score the Crown stood to pay out £460 or more for the whole knot, no mean sum at that time.

These proclamations had some effect, owing not a little to the energetic co-ordinator of the hunt, Sir William Morton. According to a twentieth-century scribe whose authorities, if any, are unknown, serious efforts were made to deal with the outrages on Hounslow Heath. Decoys were sent to draw the highwaymen out, where they might be pursued by armed patrols following close behind. Nevertheless, as late as 10 May 1669 Sir Joseph Williamson, the king's security chief, was still being reminded by Daniel Fleming of "the late boldness of the highwaymen in divers places."

The situation remained more fluid than Morton would have wished, for some of the highwaymen who had been apprehended simply struck bargains to provide information in return for their freedom. If they had all reformed upon release the peace of the realm would have benefited, but recidivism was common. A notable recidivist was the more formidable of the Dudley brothers, 'Captain' Richard Dudley, who had been convicted with John Ashenhurst in 1668 before escaping in one way or another and returning to the road. Another figure who slipped in and out of the hands of the establishment was John Cassells. Two warrants of February 1669 granted him temporary protection provided he abided by the law, and the government omitted him from a new list of the most wanted on 21 March. It is not clear how Cassells came to an understanding with the authorities, or what services he offered, but it had no lasting effect, for within weeks he had also rejoined the ranks of the outlaws.

Another probable consequence of the manhunt was dispersal. As established haunts became unsafe, some of the robbers seem to have fanned out to fresh grounds. Humble Ashenhurst turned some of his attention to the Midlands. Humble was almost certainly a brother of the late John, and appears to have been a fairly young man. In 1666 and 1667 he and his wife baptised two sons, Robert and Humble, in the church of St. Giles Cripplegate in London. In addition to his boys, Humble would seem to have felt a responsibility for the daughters of one Edward Ashenhurst of Dudley in Staffordshire. He may also have been a man of means, perhaps garnered from the proceeds of highway robbery, for in June and September of 1668 a "gentleman" with that unusual name was attempting to purchase nine and a half acres of land near Kings Norton, Worcestershire, from Edward Parkeshouse of Sedgley in Staffordshire. This as Morton's manhunt was getting underway. Given these and no doubt other connections in the Midlands, it is perhaps not surprising that Ashenhurst was one of the gang members who extended their activities into that area.

We have several documents adverting to forays in the Midlands. According to a letter Ralph Hope of Coventry wrote to Sir Joseph Williamson on 4 January 1669 Humble Ashenhurst and two or three other members of the gang had been active around Curdworth Bridge in Warwickshire. A man in one group of victims managed to escape, although wounded in a shoulder, but the others were divested of their valuables, including their horses. Ashenhurst then seems to have retreated back towards London. The following month, on 24 February, Hope reported that a band of men had stopped five carriers upon the road between St. Albans and London the previous Saturday, cutting away their packs and taking much of value, including a horse. Humble Ashenhurst, William Dudley and others, said Hope, "have been seen near, but none dare seize them. They are so vigilant and well armed that they have openly ridden through several towns." In the summer Humble would again be reported in the Midlands.

In March 1669, however, Morton achieved another major success. The Dudley brothers had remained active around London, and now paid the terrible price. About eight o'clock in the evening of 20 March 1669 five men arrived at the horse ferry at Millbank, Westminster, upon suspiciously "hard ridden horses." The upshot, as reported in *The London Gazette* and developed in Richard Dudley's contemporary biography, was that the ferryman, fearing a misdemeanour, barred entry to his craft and left the suspects to shift for themselves. Lodging their horses in a couple of nearby stables, the thieves split. Some found a boat and rowed themselves across the river to Lambeth, while Richard Dudley and probably his brother put up at a convenient house. Unfortunately, a hue and cry was already afoot, and a posse led by a constable recovered the stabled mounts, and tracked Dudley to his hideout, which was immediately stormed. Richard attempted to barricade himself in a cellar, where he stood ready to receive attackers with sword and pistol in hand, but he eventually thought the better of it when the cellar door was breached, and surrendered. Moreover, pursuers also apprehended the highwaymen who had fled to Lambeth. Morton committed all five to Newgate – Richard Dudley, alias Armstrong; William Dudley, alias Hall; William Jeffreys, alias Lovell; George Cox, alias Waters; and William Warwick.

In April 1669 the Dudley brothers and William Jefferys were tried at the Old Bailey for the highway robbery of Katherine Weedon and the theft of goods and geldings belonging to William Baker; all three were convicted and sentenced to hang. One, and probably both, of the Dudleys informed against those mates who were still at large but this time it availed them little. The contemporary life of Richard Dudley recorded the inevitable end. In Newgate "gentlemen...came in great companies" to see the famous thief, who protested that if he had robbed many he had never spilled the blood of a victim. "On Wednesday [four days after receiving his death sentence] he was carried from Newgate [to the gallows] with the rest of the prisoners. His brother was very sick and lay all along in the [death] cart, but he and Blancher [John Blanchard] rode in a cart together, looking very cheerfully all the way they went." Another, more embellished report of uncertain authority, claimed that the bodies of the Dudley brothers were placed in separate coffins and conveyed to their disconsolate father, who was so distraught at the sight that he "sunk upon the dead bodies and expired. Thus, the father and the two sons were buried in one grave."

It was probably stirred by this coup that Morton struck again at the remaining holdouts of the outlaw band, especially Claude Duval. On

21 March, the day after the capture of the Dudleys, Morton supplied Williamson with a revised list of his main targets. Claude Duval headed this fresh list, followed by Humble Ashenhurst, Philips, Blanchard, Lloyd, Maddox, Stanesby, Martin Bromshurst, John Conyses [?], Swiftnicks, Matthew Bromfield and Christopher Mansfield, alias Mansell, all "notorious highwaymen" guilty of "several offences." Morton suggested that "Claude Devall" and sixteen other criminals should be noticed in the next *London Gazette*, although he had "emissaries" out after others and did not wish to see them prematurely alerted. This was the same as saying that Duval and the sixteen to be papered by the *Gazette* were not yet even in the government's gun-sights, although Blanchard would, in fact, soon be taken. The wanted list had certainly been reduced since December, but four of the names on Sir William's new list had not even featured on the original proclamation, indicating that Morton's knowledge of the "knot" was still expanding.

Informers were crucial to Morton's campaign, providing the names and descriptions of robbers and their connections and hiding places, which could then be investigated or raided by posses. Some were also prepared to bear witness against their former friends in court. In short, it was they, more than any others, who spelled disaster to Duval and the surviving outlaws. The remnants of the gang lived with constant suspicions, forever looking over their shoulders for fear of betrayal. The authorities had bled the Dudleys for what information they could get, and were also making good use of George Woodrington.

A brother, William Woodrington, had been omitted from the wanted list of March, perhaps because his arrest seemed imminent. He was eventually arrested in July 1669, but presented a harder nut to crack. That month he was arraigned with three other characters, Arthur Evans, John Carpenter and Edward Russell, and thereafter found himself bound over from one court sessions to another until October. Perhaps, like George, he finally agreed to provide information, but the delays might rather have related to Morton's difficulty in making a case stick against him.

Anyone remotely connected with the outlaws was liable to be hauled in for interrogation. In April 1669, for example, Richard Bassett, Lewis Billingsley and John Holmes found themselves before the Middlesex sessions "for being in the company of Swiftnix and Castles, being...nominated in His Majesty's proclamation for highwaymen." Perhaps there was nothing to substantiate anything criminal, because they were bound to appear before the next session in order to have the charges dismissed, but it is possible that their speedy release was also an acknowledgement that they had told all they knew. Descriptions of Duval and other principal outlaws, garnered from witnesses and informers, were apparently published, but sadly it seems in a government news-sheet now missing.

Under Morton's onslaught the number of offenders and offences declined, although acts of defiance continued. In the summer of 1669 John Cassells and Humble Ashenhurst made another foray into the Midlands. On 6 August 1669 Bullstrode confided to his diary that "an attempt of a robbery it seems was designed upon Dunsmore Heath [southwest of Coventry in Warwickshire], which appears to have been laid by Cassells and Ashenhurst, but ye traitor that should have continued it, having not carried it so warily, was discovered and upon suspicion was apprehended and carried to Coventry gaol." More appears from letters of Ralph Hope and Captain Robert Manley, the Lieutenant-Governor of Jersey, written in July and August respectively. The two highwaymen had planned to ambush Manley, his lady and servants as they journeyed by coach to London, but the plot was leaked to the authorities by one Richard Bourke, who had been arrested on suspicion of being in league with the bandits. Manley reckoned his escape an extremely fortunate one.

But one by one the gang was being hunted down, most of them in London and the surrounding district. Thomas Lambert was taken about February 1669, John Blanchard in April, and Edward Maddox and John Philips in July. All were committed to Newgate and brought before the Middlesex sessions. These were senior members of the outlaw fraternity, and their loss a serious blow. Blanchard and Maddox had even preceded Duval on the first proclamation. The two capital convictions that destroyed Blanchard in April both concerned robberies that had also involved the Frenchman: the raid on Johnson's house and the robbery of Thomas Hastings upon the highway.

In February 1669 Maddox had also been indicted for the raid on Lancelot Johnson's house in absentia, but when he was brought to trial in July he admitted that he had committed the offence. He also confessed to a second indictment concerning the robbery of William Davies upon the king's highway. These offences had not involved violence to the person, and Maddox attempted to reinforce his claims for a reduction of sentence by cooperation. Condemned to hang, he begged to be transported.

The rest was almost predictable. On 12 July 1669 a warrant was issued to Sir John Howell, the Recorder of London, and the Sheriff of London to reprieve Maddox "on account of his services in discovering several notorious malefactors who have thus been brought to condign punishment."

A document of the following month also referred to "his former loyalty" as a reason for the pardon, by which was no doubt meant past services to the king as a soldier. Maddox had got a remarkably good deal. He was to be transported, presumably to the West Indies or the American colonies, but providing he supplied sureties for his good behaviour, he would be released from prison and allowed up to two months to prepare for his journey. Understandably, Morton and his fellow justices were reluctant to release such a noted malefactor; the pardon was withheld and the case referred back to the king and his advisers for reconsideration. It was not until 24 June 1670 that the pardon was upheld and Maddox was ordered to be released.

While the case against Maddox floundered, Morton and his colleagues pressed their attack upon the other highwaymen. On 5 July 1669 the magistrates on the Middlesex bench, determined to convict offenders already in custody, bound half a dozen individuals (Peter Williams, Marmaduke Holland, Anna Adlington, Jonathan Pridoux, Randolph Cobbett and John Gynoway, if the names are deciphered correctly) to appear at the next sessions, when charges against them would be dismissed providing they gave evidence against some or all of Maddox, Philips and William Woodrington. In other words the prisoners were told to give evidence for the prosecution or they would themselves be prosecuted.

By one means or another nineteen of the twenty-seven men 'papered' in December 1668 or March 1669 were gathered in towards the close of the latter year. True, some of them had thrown in with the crown to secure their liberty, and were therefore free to offend again. But despite this occasional recycling, Morton's campaign had undeniable effect.

Little is actually known of the careers of Duval's associates, although all of them were infamous in their day. The Woodringtons (or Widdringtons or Withringtons), were probably older members of a family of criminals, of whom the youngest, Jack, is *said* to have perished at Tyburn in 1691. A John Martin, perhaps the same as another of the old Duval gang mentioned in the royal proclamation of 1668, was sentenced to death at the Old Bailey on 15 October 1679 for burglary and house-breaking.

These men were all enterprising thieves, but apart from Duval himself the only member of this desperate association to achieve lasting fame of a kind was Samuel Swiftnicks. Of him more will be said presently, but by November 1669 it was Duval and Swiftnicks who headed the list of those still at large. The original deadline for claiming rewards under the proclamations of 1668 had been passed in June. Consequently a new proclamation of 19

November 1669 was needed to reinvigorate the attack upon the holdouts. Of those now mentioned, eight had been papered before: "Lewis, alias Lodowick, alias Claude Deval, alias [John] Browne"; "Swift Nix," alias Clerk; Humble Ashenhurst; Martin Brom[s?]hurst; John Castells [Cassells]; Bromfield, alias Spencer; William Stanley [Stavely?] and William Stanesby. The new names revealed by the continuing hunt (Thomas Stanley, Nicholas Greenbury, William Talbot, Richard Wilde, William Connel, Nicholas James and Herman Atkins) raised the total number of gang-members proscribed in 1668 and 1669 to thirty-four. The £20 reward for each was restored, and made payable up to 20 June 1670. The thirty-four men thus outlawed raised the crown's total liability to some £680 in reward money. Today the purchasing power of that sum would be worth about £100,000, and considerably more measured against average earnings.

Throughout this legal storm, Claude Duval continued to pursue his profession of robbery under arms, but he knew that the net was closing around him, and every confederate who fell into the hands of the law increased his danger, threatening to bring fresh evidence upon him or expose his associates or refuges. He and those close to him lived in a climate of acute suspicion. Moreover, with so many of his former associates seized or fled, Duval had to find new confederates. He took up with a thief named Patrick Mackee or Magee. Mackee had featured in none of the king's proclamations, at least under that name, and he was probably a newer hand. One wonders if he had the experience of the older brigade, but at least he seems to have been reliable.

Feeling the heat, Duval told "a gentleman he met on the road" that he intended returning to France, and it appears that he did so, but only for a brief period. Despite the proclamations he had remained active, working the western roads that led into London from Exeter, Bristol, Bath and Windsor. On 10 February 1669 Duval and his party, "with force and arms," robbed Thomas Harris on the highway in the parish of Hanwell, Middlesex, taking £14 15s. Few fry were too small, and Harris was a poor man who protested that as the thieves had stolen all he had, they might as well take his life too. Some members of the gang jested, and asked whether he preferred to be shot, ran through with a sword or have his throat cut, but "God restrained them that they did him no other hurt, leaving him to lament his loss." The same month the band stopped a man named William Hopkins and deprived him of a bridle worth twelve pence and cash to the value of eleven shillings. Although Duval remained free, he was indicted for the Hopkins robbery on 17 February.

Before the spring of 1669 had grown old Duval, with a band that included John Blanchard and George Woodrington, stopped a coach on the highway and robbed its passengers, Thomas Hastings and his wife, of goods worth £14.10s. as well as £3 in cash. The presence of Woodrington was ominous. He had been netted by the man-hunters the previous year, and secured his freedom by supplying much of the detail that went into the ensuing royal proclamation of 1668. Likely he also promised further information, and in time he would appear as a witness for the crown against Duval in the Old Bailey. Woodrington must have squared himself with his colleagues somehow, or they would perhaps have put a pistol ball into him. Perhaps the government had engineered an "escape" so that he could return to the streets a criminal hero rather than a mere poltroon. Whatever, here he was, a viper in the outlaw nest.

Duval's sojourn in France must have occurred shortly after the robbery of Hastings. Probably he slipped back to Paris, and for the last time visited members of his family, but the interlude cannot have lasted long. Running out of money, no longer familiar with his native land, or simply missing some of his friends or mistresses, Duval was soon back in his usual places in England attempting to resume his wayward career. On 30 November 1669 he held up Thomas Browning in the parish of Heston, Middlesex, a little north of Hounslow Heath, taking ninety yards of woollen cloth valued at £30. Browning seems to have been a carrier, because the goods actually belonged to a widow named Mary Trotman. It is conceivable that Duval had actually stopped a small trade convoy on this occasion, and that Trotman and Browning were the only victims willing to fund a prosecution.

The decision to return to the London area was a fatal one, however, for "before he had done anything of great glory or advantage to himself" Duval was taken. He chose to spend Christmas Eve, a Saturday, at the small 'Hole-in-the-Wall' tavern in Chandos Street near Covent Garden. This tap-house was probably one of his regular resorts, and it is possible that the authorities had learned of it and put their spies in the place, or that some opportunist saw the chance of a reward. However, a message flew to the authorities, and a posse led by John Bennett, the Head Bailiff of Westminster, arrived to find the notorious highwayman drunk and incapable, although he had three pistols, one double-barrelled, and a good sword with him. *The London Gazette* and Anthony Wood, a diarist, recorded that Duval was taken "in the night-time," which may indicate that he had actually retired to an upper room at the inn, where he lay in a drunken stupor.

7. 'The Hole-in-the-Wall' tavern in Chandos Street, where Duval was captured in 1669, is believed to have been the foundation of the modern 'Marquis' in Chandos Place, Covent Garden.

Duval was known to be a skilled, courageous and determined fighting man, and his Christmas revel might well have been fortunate for the law enforcement officers. As the highwayman's biographer, Pope, remarked, "As well it was for the bailiff's men that he was drunk, otherwise they had tasted of his prowess...I have heard it attested by those that knew how good a marksman he was, and his excellent way of fencing, that had he been sober it was impossible he could have killed less than ten. They farther add, upon their own knowledge, [that] he would have been cut as small as herbs for the pot before he would have yielded to the bailiff of Westminster." There is no need to doubt that the highwayman would have made a desperate resistance had he been able. The author of the *Life of Deval* reported not only that he had long asserted his determination not to be taken alive, but that in prison he remarked that it was his greatest regret that he had been too drunk at the time of his arrest to make a fight of it.

Now, with the most wanted highwayman in Britain in their grasp, the authorities were determined not to slip up. With almost unseemly haste, they brought Duval to judgement.

5

Old Tyburn's Glory

According to *The London Gazette* it was Sir William Morton himself who immediately tumbled out to deal with the notorious highwayman that cold Christmas night. Duval, probably still under the influence of Bacchus, was likely held for a short time in a local watch house before being thrust before a magistrate on Christmas Day. It was then, on a day betrothed to goodwill towards all men, that he came face to face with his arch and implacable enemy for the first time. Without much ceremony, Morton committed Duval to Newgate Prison, which housed not only the felons of London and Middlesex but also national offenders such as the more wanted pirates, highwaymen, traitors and other state prisoners.

Apart from the debtors, most of the inmates endured relatively short periods in Newgate whilst awaiting trial, acquittal or punishment. This "English Bastille" straggled across a roadway where Holborn and Newgate Street merged. The road passed beneath a formidable gatehouse, which formed the core of the prison. Duval would have been received at a lodge near the entrance to the gatehouse, where he would have been shackled before being conducted to appropriate quarters. His final destination in Newgate was probably the 'condemned hold', a dark stone cell not far from the lodge which communally held all felons convicted of capital offences, but it is possible that he initially found more salubrious and select quarters, either through the generosity of benefactors, or to facilitate the large number of lucrative visitors who arrived to view so celebrated and intriguing a prisoner.

No trembling or resentful felon, Duval generally maintained a cheerful persona in prison, and indeed throughout his remaining trials. Obviously a brave man, he appeared to have accepted his fate with rather more equanimity than one might have expected from one in his parlous situation. Although kept under heavy security, he established reasonable relationships with his custodians. Duval was not a particularly religious man, but would likely have tolerated the ministrations of the 'Ordinary' who preached on Sundays and extolled the benefits of repentance. The office was held by a Londoner, Edmund Cressy or Cresset. Cressy believed in the deterrent value of strict justice, but he also contended that true remorse deserved its reward and thought enough about his vocation to write an advisory tract about spiritual work in prisons and hospitals. "I have walked in a path untrodden by others before me," he wrote in it, "but all along have sincerely aimed at the spiritual good of those that have come under the direction of my pen. It is very meet that in this, as in all other actions, the main end that I propound to myself should be the honour of God and the good of souls." No doubt any advice he gave Duval, with its asides to such figures as the thieves who died beside Jesus at Golgotha, dwelt upon the importance of repentance, remorse and spiritual salvation. How much allowance was made for the minority of prisoners who, like Duval, were ostensibly Catholics rather than Protestants is not clear. Other preachers often supported the ordinaries, and the provision of papists, if for no other purpose than the administration of last rites according to the Roman religion, was accepted. Indeed, the prison had become a holding pen for Catholics during the years of papist persecution, and would have been familiar with the spiritual needs of men and women of that persuasion. A Catholic priest was certainly furnished Duval at the time of his execution.

The Keeper of Newgate, John Woodall, had purchased his office that year, and the absence of complaints made against him during his stewardship suggest that he was better than many who had or would hold the post. Appointed by the Court of Aldermen, he had not only paid for his position but also bore financial responsibilities for the gaolers or 'turnkeys' and part of the maintenance of the prison. He was, however, unsalaried and expected to recover his expenses and turn a profit from fees and perquisites. Likewise, the turnkeys, who bought their offices from the keepers, had an eye to what they could make from the prisoners or their families. Since the early 1630s the aldermen had also reaffirmed a tradition of prisoner self-regulation, in which the keeper worked with a steward and his assistants, elected by and from the inmates to manage their affairs. By the early eighteenth century this system had morphed into another layer of corruption and abuse, in which the appointees, or 'partners' as they were then designated, bullied prisoners and skimmed them of their resources on one ground or another. The situation in Duval's day is less clear, but the highwayman would not only have interacted with officials charged with his imprisonment, but also with elevated inmates affecting to represent the incarcerated community. One wonders how these last reacted. Perhaps they had little to do with the formidable new figure in their midst, who had to be kept in strict security, but what dealings they had with him perhaps aroused unusual feelings of awe or jealousy.

Because the keepers and turnkeys ran the prison as a business, the unfortunates entering the gaol were customarily dunned for entry fees, the rent of chambers and such 'easements' of their condition as light shackles and access to windows, fires, candles, beds and improved victuals. Although the authorities supplied bread, for example, the prisoners themselves had to provide the balance of their food. We know that at this time the excessive fees paid in Newgate were raising public concern, for in 1670 Parliament ordered the city to devise a schedule of fixed fees for which prisoners were liable.

All in all, Newgate was a miserable place. Daniel Defoe, who was held more than once in a renovated and more elaborate Newgate than Duval knew, described it in his novel *Moll Flanders*, published in 1722. "Newgate, that horrid place!" said he. "My very blood chills at the mention of its name...the hellish noise, the roaring, swearing and clamour, the stench and nastiness...an emblem of hell itself, and a kind of an entrance into it...Oh! If I had but been sent to any place in the world, and not to Newgate, I should have thought myself happy." Others said much the same, but it is important to remember that prisoners were not all treated alike. Different sections of the prison held different types of offenders, and those in any section could, if they had access to money, buy themselves more congenial conditions.

Duval seems to have done comparatively well for one of his notoriety. Among the "comforts" he contrived to receive in Newgate was the privilege of having his "wife" with him over Christmas. Her name was Elizabeth Morris but she was sometimes known as Elizabeth Duval. The likelihood is that the two were never formally married, although this was a time when 'private marryings' that avoided the use of churches and public ceremonies were not uncommon in London. As historian Peter Earle has described, 'clandestine marriages' of the cheapest kind involved nothing more than couples meeting in a house or a tavern and using a rudimentary version of a church service and the administrations of a willing clergyman, whether practising or no, or even a layman to bind them together without any other outside interference whatsoever. Elizabeth was probably a comely girl of uncertain morality who had been drawn into bad company, and assumed the role of mistress to a man of legendary magnetism. There is nothing in the records to suggest that she had been involved in serious criminality, or ever been pushed into the courts before.

Duval was a likeable and on the whole cheerful prisoner. One who met him in those final days remarked of his many visitors that "whatever their opinions were before they went up [to see him], they pitied his condition when they came from him, which I impute to his youth. He was very temperate as to drink, his actions very modest and discourse civil." In other words, if this testimony is to be believed, the highwayman melted hostility, and won people to his side.

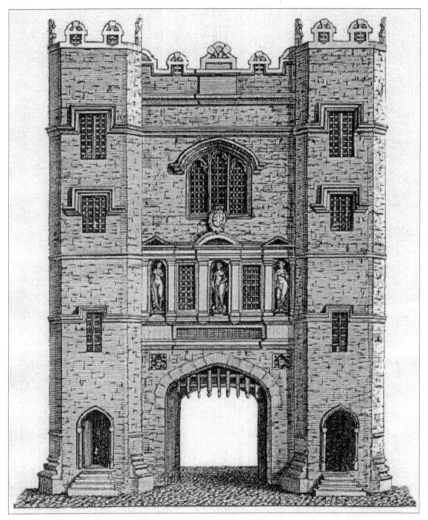

8. An early engraving of the gatehouse, the most famous view of Newgate, the most feared gaol in England.

But that was not the major reason, perhaps, for any favours he received in prison. At this time a new phenomenon manifested itself. The prison found that it had a genuine celebrity, a greater than it had ever held, and one whose vaunted looks and address had hitherto been a mystery to the general populace. Visitors, curiosity seekers and interested parties thronged to see the highwayman, most of them women, among whom many were "not of the meanest degree." Dudley, "the great robber," had drawn large numbers of sight-seers the previous year, but Duval was held to have set a new record. He, claimed Eye-Witness, was "the present subject of all persons' discourse...Never had [a] prisoner such a concourse of people come to see him." In particular, a powerful female lobby was developing, clamouring for the pardon of the country's most famous malefactor. Be that as it may, these visitors, whether men or women, provided an exceptional source of income for Keeper Woodall and his turnkeys. Probably they were charged admission to the exotic exhibit, and almost certainly it was some of their sympathetic purses that secured the 'easement' of the highwayman's conditions of confinement.

Whatever he received must have been welcome. There was little opportunity to stage a break-out from the prison. A few weeks after Duval's execution the justices were warning that unless Newgate was strengthened it would have to close. Perhaps their concerns had been intensified by the fears for the security of such a celebrated prisoner as Duval, but although the prison was obviously in a poor state, the speed with which Duval's case was prosecuted and the attention he attracted in it allowed him little space to plan or execute an escape. He had to stick it out, and needed all the comforts he could command in December and January, the coldest months of the year, when death rates in that perishing fever-ridden place generally rose.

The capture of Duval raises some interesting if unanswerable questions. Despite his French accent and great fame, both of which must have stamped him as an unusual man, he had remained at large for several years, and for eighteen months had even withstood the most relentless manhunt that the state had mounted against a criminal gang that century. This surprised his pursuers, who had initially anticipated obliterating the main culprits within six months. It was no doubt with some annoyance that they had had to extend the period in which the rewards could be paid.

There had always, of course, been individuals who sheltered or succoured highwaymen for a share of their plunder. Thus Thomas Hill, "a great padder during the plague [years] in London," was known to have used Cobbet's inn at Kensington and Maxwell's premises on Upper Chancery Lane and

Holborn. Both innkeepers were believed to have been complicit in Hill's activities. Duval was an active thief, and probably dispensed his ill-gotten gains with a liberality that reflected the ease with which he expected to replace them. If there were palms, he was seldom without the means to oil them. Accomplices won by such means, however, were rarely reliable, and that Duval survived such heat for so long suggests that something more than mercenary gain may have been involved.

It is surprising that in a world of poverty, crime, rewards, spies, informers and dog-eat-dog the government's inducements had not reaped speedier dividends in Duval's case. No doubt his peripatetic lifestyle was one factor in his longevity, allowing him to slip from one place to another as circumstances changed, and confound attempts to predict his movements. But sometimes more personal factors could contribute. Take, for example, the more documented case of Henry McCarty, known to American history and folklore as Billy the Kid, whose career has been most convincingly rescued for us by the historian Robert M. Utley. In 1881 law enforcement officers in New Mexico were temporarily obstructed by the outlaw's ability to endear himself to members of the poor Hispanic population around Fort Sumner, particularly, it seems, the local *senoritas*. However reprehensible the Kid's crimes, he was sheltered, fed and protected.

Duval may have been similarly favoured. Unlike most of his partners in crime, his looks and flamboyance radiated personality, and his relatively good cheer and carefree manner may have earned him popularity. To account for his professional endurance, even when papered by the king, one is encouraged to believe that he inspired a degree of loyalty among those who knew him.

Duval probably relied upon a reasonably extensive support system, harnessed by economic and personal ties, and for long it sustained him even as the man-hunters closed in. Around 'town' (as London was then called), he must have used 'flash' or safe houses, kept by friends, mistresses, or people with whom he shared his successes, but no evidence now tells us their locations. In the early nineteenth century there was a tradition that he used a refuge in the Holloway district, but no earlier testimony to that end has been found. At the time of his capture he was drinking heavily in the Covent Garden area, which indicates that secure lodgings were probably close by. Beyond that we cannot go.

Many prisoners being held for grave offences sustained themselves with the hope, however thin, that remorse might buy them a reprieve or a lighter sentence. Despite his fame, even Duval consoled himself with such prospects. He knew that substantial offences against property could reap the death penalty; but he was probably also aware that juries were not always the creatures of prosecutors, and were sometimes willing to resist capital sentences or seek pardons for those who could show mitigating circumstances. Prominent as he was, Duval was not without cards to play. His youthful appearance, lack of violence and expressions of remorse, as well as the many influential people interested in his plight, encouraged hopes that he might yet cheat the gallows.

There were, for example, those early connections he had had with aristocratic employers, including the "eminent" peer who had once befriended him. Probably Duval wondered if any goodwill towards him remained in those circles. We cannot identify that most prominent of his patrons, and the name of Richmond is the only one to have ever been advanced. In 1670 Richmond's star was still ascendant. Although his third marriage, to the famous court beauty Frances Teresa Stewart, a royal favourite, in 1667 might have temporarily damaged his standing with the king, he was still receiving prestigious marks of affection, and in 1668 became Lord Lieutenant and Vice-Admiral of Kent. Hopes of potent intervention from some such source, or simply influential well-wishers, were also no doubt encouraged by some of his powerful visitors in Newgate, who must have related to him any efforts they had made, or intended to make, to save him.

But all such aspirations were straws in the wind from the start. His own people – those politically small people who had harboured and supported him during his years as a highwayman – had probably been silenced or neutralised by the majesty of the law. Apart from those willing to profit from selling information, they were no doubt happier keeping their own heads down to avoid persecution. No help was to be had there. And true, the authorities were mindful of the more vocal and potentially powerful lobby that was developing for the French gallant, particularly among ladies of gentle birth, but they remained steadfast from the onset that in this case the law would take its full course. As soon as Duval's capture was announced the king declared that no pardon would be granted, whatever intercessions were made.

It seems that His Majesty wanted to quash at birth what may have been embarrassing calls upon his favour, and to allow no room for doubt about his determination to make an example of a man who had continued to defy his authority, even after the issue of two royal proclamations. Those proclamations, as pronouncements of the royal will, should have deterred

Duval from committing further offences, or at least interested him in making his peace with the authorities. But he had simply kept on robbing, setting the law at defiance.

Moreover, Duval had shown on other occasions that he had been willing to tweak the royal proboscis. Indeed, two of the charges currently being prepared against him related to the theft of property belonging to George Villiers, 4th Viscount Grandison. Grandison, a member of the Irish peerage, was no common aristocrat. He was a relative of George Villiers, 2nd Duke of Buckingham, one of the wealthiest and most powerful men in the realm. A royal favourite, Buckingham was the first in a cabinet cabal that advised the king. Not only that, but Grandison was also the uncle of the king's long-standing mistress, the voluptuous Barbara Villiers, Duchess of Cleveland. If Duval's common notoriety damned him most of all, it was not the only argument telling against him. He had insulted people close to the king, his strongest minister and his mistress.

Duval's blatant contempt for the king's writ injected a political dimension, perhaps even a touch of treason, to his case. It is significant that some of the most notorious highwaymen in the land, men such as Richard Dudley, Edward Maddox, Humble Ashenhurst and Samuel Swiftnicks were eventually allowed their liberty in return for evidence against their fellows, but no such deal was contemplated in the case of Claude Duval. Nor, to do the Frenchman full justice, is there the slightest evidence that he ever sought to strengthen his case by betraying colleagues. It is doubtful, anyway, that any such ploy would have worked. As the biggest fish in the pond, Duval would not have been released merely to facilitate the capture or conviction of decidedly smaller fry. No, for the authorities the matter was clear. Duval had to be destroyed to discourage others from challenging the king's peace.

Morton's first job was to put the charges against Duval before a court in order to secure a jury's agreement that they constituted a 'true bill,' that is a credible case for prosecution. This was, in many respects, a different age than the eighteenth century that followed, not least in its lack of newspapers. There were occasional government newsletters, and the official *Gazette*, but these were threadbare substitutes for a regular and discursive press. News of Duval's capture had largely to travel by word of mouth, but although the next gaol-delivery session at the Old Bailey, the first of the eight scheduled for the year, swept swiftly forward the hurried gossip still brought crowds to gape or commiserate at his plight.

On Friday, 14 January Duval was marched with several lesser felons to the Middlesex Sessions House in the Old Bailey. The sessions house had been gutted by the Great Fire, and proceedings were now being held in a substantial wooden structure erected in the shell of the old building until it could be completely renovated. The court was crowded with interested persons, many of them men and women of rank, eager to see the glamorous highwayman and learn his fate. It was clear from the beginning that the authorities were determined to rid themselves of this most embarrassing of miscreants, and to despatch the business quickly and comprehensively before the volume of intercessions from the public could obstruct the path. Combing through an extensive list of offences that had been put down to the highwayman, Morton and his assistants had assembled a heady collection of capital crimes capable of being supported in the relatively short time available. Three of these charges rested on older indictments lodged against Duval while he was still at large. But most were of recent origin, presumably because the prosecuting victims and witnesses were close at hand.

Since only one capital offence had to be proven to secure a conviction, seldom had a criminal been confronted with such a determined judicial assault. The indictments lodged against Duval were capable of yielding no less than eight death sentences, and it was remarked at the time that others charges lay furtively in the wings, ready to advance if that first squad failed. John Ashenhurst had confronted seven such indictments in 1668, but even that was unusual. Edward Maddox, for example, was indicted for two offences in 1669; Jack Sheppard, the famous house-breaker, faced three counts of robbery, two of which failed, in 1724; Jonathan Wild the thief-taker fell afoul of two counts of theft the following year; and in 1739 Dick Turpin, the most notorious highwayman of the eighteenth century, was hanged in 1739 on two indictments for stealing horses. None of these famous deviants inspired the official malignance that faced Claude Duval.

It is probable that on that account alone all of the presiding justices of the court were present at one time or another during the proceedings against Duval. They were a truly unyielding cast of characters, a "knot" of a different kind, from whom little mercy, sympathy or even fair play could be expected. All middle-aged to elderly dignitaries, they comprised Sir Samuel Starling, the Lord Mayor of London, and a member of the Worshipful Company of Drapers; Sir John Kelyng, Chief Justice of the King's Bench, and sometime the Member of Parliament for Bedford and the king's sergeant-at-law; Sir William Morton, of whom enough has been said; Sir Thomas Allen, a former Lord Mayor of London who also served as Deputy Lord-Lieutenant and Member of Parliament for Middlesex; Sir John Lawrence, an alderman and member of the Haberdasher's Company who had also once been the

Lord Mayor of London; and Sir John Howell, the Recorder of London since 1668.

If Morton was the attack-dog who led the proceedings against Duval and his associates, at least three of the other gentlemen, Starling, Howell and Kelyng, developed reputations for severity, the manipulation of juries and coercive, even illegal, practices. Starling, elevated to Lord Mayor in 1669, would taint the history of the jury system by his trenchant pursuit of William Penn, who was tried for unlawful assembly in 1670. He, backed by Howell the recorder, wilfully obstructed the attempts of the accused Quaker to defend himself, and bullied, punished and disregarded jurors in order to ensure a successful prosecution. Kelyng was cast from a similar mould, and in 1667 had barely avoided being tried himself, after the House of Commons censured him for gross malpractices. These were not men to let the niceties of the law get in the way of a pre-determined result. Starling may also have had personal motives for seeing off Duval. After his death in 1674, his widow, Mary Starling, married George Villiers, Viscount Grandison, which suggests that the two families had been close associates. As Grandison was the victim of two of the robberies for which Duval was being held to account, it is possible that Starling had a private axe to grind.

After consideration a jury found the charges against Duval a 'true bill' and formally indicted him on multiple counts. Duval pleaded not guilty to them all, and declared that he would be tried by his "God and country," or, in other words, by a regular jury. Those rounded up as confederates or accessories enjoyed mixed fortunes at the session house. They included Robert Wallis and Alexander Benny (or Benning), who were held as accessories after the fact to robberies by Duval and Patrick Mackee, and Robert Cooke and John Neale, who were similarly suspected. All four were likely to have been part of the network that had supported Duval, but while Wallis and Benny were bound over for trial, Cooke and Neale were released, as no substantial evidence was found against them. Just as lucky was "Elizabeth Morris, alias Duvall," the highwayman's mistress, who had also been held as an accessory to robberies and felonies. An accessory after the fact was deemed to have succoured an offender, but not actually participated in his crimes, and in Elizabeth's case there was also a failure of clear evidence, and she was not held over. In accordance with the usual practice, however, she remained in custody for several days until the end of the sessions before being released without trial.

Patrick Mackee, Duval's partner in arms, who had been transferred to Newgate from his former prison in the Westminster Gatehouse, was presented with two persuasive capital indictments, but one William Mitchell, who appeared before the court with him, was merely accused of being an accessory to a felony. For some reason Mitchell was committed to the City of London for further proceedings. A final figure in these doings was William Piggott, who was indicted twice, as an accessory after the fact to both Duval and Mackee. He, too, was bound over for a full trial. He pleaded not guilty to both offences, and asked to be tried by jury.

Morton had successfully paved the way for a trial that could only go one way. The preliminaries over, Duval was returned to Newgate to await his decisive day in court. Mackee, who shared two of his indictments, made the journey back to prison with him, as apparently did Elizabeth Morris, whose eventual freedom had, however, been secured. Their wait was a short one, for the government was determined to dispose of Duval quickly in order to pre-empt any developing difficulties. There was almost no time for the two highwaymen to prepare their defences, even by simply thinking them out. The very day after the true bill was found, Saturday, 15 January, the indictments were put to the test in summary trials at the Old Bailey, again in a court-room crowded with excited spectators, many said to be members of the aristocracy, including interested ladies.

Those who shared the sessions with Duval that day met mixed fortunes. Some were sentenced to death, including three thieves, Thomas Boyd, William Braine and Thomas Meade, and a John Smallwood who was convicted of murder. Probably they were all destined to share the death cart that would carry Duval to Tyburn. Two women were charged with murdering illegitimate children, but Frances Caswell was held pending a coroner's report and Elizabeth Holder was spared death in favour of a public whipping. Anna Phillips, accused of stealing goods worth eight pence from William Crispe, and George Doggett, facing charges of house-breaking and theft, were bound over for another day, and Jenkin Morgan escaped Tyburn when the charge of murder was dropped in favour of one that would now be called manslaughter and he pleaded benefit of clergy. Instead, he was branded on the hand. These and other cases filled a busy session, but the main business, and the one that had packed the court, concerned Claude Duval.

The jurors all possessed a freehold worth at least £20 per annum, and were composed of persons of the "middling" sort, such as established householders, artisans and shop-keepers. They were not in themselves stooges of the prosecution, and were capable of exercising independent judgement, but they would have little leeway here. During this period there was neither a counsel for the defence, nor often for the prosecution. The judges effectively controlled the proceedings, calling and examining the witnesses in as partial or impartial a fashion as they wished. A glance at these witnesses would have told Duval that his fate was sealed. They included the victims of his atrocities, ready to identify him as the perpetrator of the misdeeds described, and the informer George Woodrington, who likely shifted uneasily as he stood across the room from the man he was about to betray.

First up, Duval was charged with the highway robbery of one Thomas Lawrence, involving the theft of goods worth £1 and a horse valued at £10, the property of George Villiers, Viscount Grandison. This was one of the charges that might have accounted for some of the aristocratic interest in the trial, and the court heard that Lawrence, one of two servants of Grandison present on the occasion of the robbery, had made a heroic stand, and traded severe blows with one of the highwaymen, Humble Ashenhurst, before he was overpowered. Mackee, another Duval accomplice, faced an identical charge. There are disparities between the rough notes made on the day and the fair copy that constituted the official record, but Mackee seems to have eventually confessed his guilt and sought leave to petition to be transported, a relatively lenient alternative to the rope. His sentence was therefore held over. Bracketed with the record of this offence is the name of William Piggott, indicted with being an accessory after the fact. He pleaded not guilty, but when the jury found against him, conceded the charge and also begged to be allowed to petition the king for a sentence of transportation. His plea was ultimately denied and he suffered the severer penalty. But when the jury returned a verdict of guilty on Duval there was no such prevarication. The death penalty was simply and immediately secured. The court recorded that no financial assets or significant property had been found on the prisoner.

Technically, no more than the Lawrence robbery was needed to hang the two highwaymen, but Morton piled fuel on the fire. His second indictment raised an interesting novelty. Duval and Mackee were charged with robbing John Cox on "the king's highway" and taking goods worth £5 belonging to his master, the aforementioned Lord Grandison. The surprising abbreviation "cogn" is applied to both defendants in the rough notes of the sessions, meaning "cognovits." This literally means that the defendants pleaded *guilty* to the charge. On the face of it this was tantamount to inviting another death sentence. It is likely that the robberies of Cox and Lawrence, both relating to property owned by Grandison, occurred at the same time. If so, the finding of the jury could hardly have been in doubt. Mackee was still clutching at the straw of transportation, and Duval may have reasoned that further resistance to a charge already proven against him might have been unnecessarily provocative. Still, with two capital offences proven his chance of escaping the noose was fast disappearing, if it had existed at all.

Benny and Wallis were charged with being accessories after the fact in relation to this robbery, and aping Piggott pleaded not guilty until the jury found otherwise, when they appealed for leave to petition for sentences of transportation. It is possible that both men had supplied some information leading to the case against Duval and his partner, and hoped to curry favour. Whatever, their tactics enjoyed a measure of success, for the court postponed making a decision until another time. Eventually both Benny and Wallis were granted the right to petition the king, and did so on 29 June. The petition went before King Charles and his council, and Benny and Wallis were spared punishment, but ordered to quit the realm for the Americas within two months of the pardon without the right to return to England within seven years.

With two death penalties over his head, Duval was next found guilty of the famous raid upon the home of Lancelot Johnson, when goods of "magni valoris" (great value) had been taken. This rested upon an existing indictment of 9 December 1668, but while the jury now found Duval guilty, there were doubts about the aptness of the charge. In the end the jurors declined to convict Duval of "burglary," that is specifically, breaking into a house at night, but declared him guilty of felonious theft. In theory, the jury might have been exercising clemency on this count. Burglary would have incurred another outright capital sentence, but daytime theft was deemed a less serious offence, partly because it did not always involve actual breaking into a house, and partly because it could occur when no one was at home to be threatened with violence. That being the case, an offender convicted of felonious theft was eligible to escape severe punishment by claiming "benefit of clergy" and satisfying the requisite literacy test. If the jurors had offered a thread of hope to Duval on this head, it was useless to him. According to the later report of Titus Oates, Duval was able neither to read nor write in English. More than that, it is impossible to envisage the court suffering such a notorious figure as Duval claiming ecclesiastical protection whether he passed the test or not; nor would it have protected him from the other capital convictions, which related to offences that were not, in the parlance, "clergyable."

This and the next case, another revival of an old indictment, were couched against Ludovic (rather than Claude) Duval. This reflected the name the victims had used in progressing their complaint, and which had therefore passed into the original indictments of 1668 and 1669. Duval had used the names Claude and Ludovic, and it only seems to have been about the time of his capture that the familiar Claude Duval came to be regarded as the authentic nomenclature. The highway robbery of Thomas Hastings, which now occupied the court, had been levied against Duval as early as 21 April 1669. Hastings recounted his misfortune and established the fact of his loss, but he was unable to identify Duval at the bar. For this Morton had the informer George Woodrington, who had been present at the Johnson robbery, again at hand. He claimed to have been one of those who had robbed Hastings, and confirmed Duval's guilt. The jury brought in their verdict, and a third capital sentence was secured.

Four more indictments were tested. One returned to the old indictment of 5 April 1665, charging Duval with the murder of James Tirrell. This was probably an important indictment for Morton, since a conviction for murder would have greatly retarded public sympathy for Duval, even among the interested ladies gathering to his support, and pulled the feet from under any attempt to wheedle a pardon from the king. However, the Tirrell murder does not seem to have ever been widely credited to Duval, despite the tendentious indictment. Although the highwayman had effectively threatened people with extreme violence every time he brandished a pistol and called for their belongings, and would undoubtedly have defended himself from attack or killed to escape, his career had not suggested an inherently violent nature. Putting aside the Tirrell indictment, there was no evidence that he had ever injured, let alone killed, anyone. Indeed, as late as November 1669, a little more than a month before his capture, the royal proclamation itself had alluded to his "robberies and burglaries" rather than killings, and it is difficult to believe that a more serious offence such as murder would have been omitted if there had been any strong ground for alleging it. None of the contemporary pamphleteers had a whiff of real violence to allege against Duval, not even Walter Pope who was patently hostile to the Frenchman, and in reporting his death *The London Gazette* referred to him as "that notorious highwayman and *robber*, Claude de Val."

If Morton ventured the murder indictment to undermine support for Duval and sabotage any lingering appeals for a pardon, as seems likely, he failed. Duval denied the charge, and extended the routine defence that as he had not fled at the time of the alleged homicide, it could be assumed that he had not been the perpetrator. The jury was unimpressed with the evidence, and returned a verdict of not guilty. Duval would at least hang without blood on his hands. The final three indictments, for the highway robberies of Thomas Browning, Thomas Harris and William Hopkins, all secured successive convictions.

At the end of these proceedings the court had secured at least six capital convictions, covering the robberies of Lawrence, Cox, Hastings, Browning, Harris and Hopkins. This may have been the implication of a reference in *The London Gazette*, which stated that Duval suffered for six counts of robbery. However, the Johnson robbery probably also earned a capital conviction, in which case Duval would have netted seven death penalties. It is possible that the *Gazette* had boxed the Lawrence and Cox robberies into one, since both, preying upon the property of Lord Grandison, had probably occurred at the same time. Mackee, his partner in that attack, who at least appears to have resisted the temptation to save his life by informing upon his companion, also paid on the scaffold.

The trial was notable for the great public interest it aroused, "The concourse of people [on] both these days [14 and 15 January] being such as the like hath seldom been seen on such an occasion," as the contemporary *Life of Deval* averred. According to *Devol's Last Farewell* the proceedings were attended by "many noble Lords...and Ladies." In this, perhaps, lay Duval's only hope of escape, for it was an age when justices could be bribed, and both the king and his government were vulnerable to the intercession of influential persons. Unfortunately, although Duval could not be convicted of murder, he had forfeited his life too many times, and we know that other charges were waiting if those submitted failed to stick. Appeals for clemency were lodged, but the king stood by his original decision to resist "upon what intercession soever." The protests were effectively silenced.

On Monday, 17 January, Duval made his third appearance at the Session House, this time for sentencing, which in his case was merely a confirmation of what he already knew. When the judge or perhaps the recorder reached for the dreaded black cap, donned whenever the death penalty was pronounced, it was no surprise. The 'dead warrant' as it was called, presumably signed by the recorder and the king, was rushed to the prison without delay.

Duval now knew that he had no hope. It was said that back in his quarters in Newgate the highwayman became disconsolate and penitent. "Never man had more or better friends, and worse success," he confessed. Four days after sentencing the fateful day arrived, Friday, 21 January. Across the street from the Old Bailey stood the shell of the church of St. Sepulchre-without-Newgate, now badly damaged by the Great Fire, but still sporting an impressive tower. It was this church that kept the time for the execution of prisoners in Newgate. An officer of the church, by tradition, carried a hand-bell beneath the windows of the condemned at midnight and early in the morning, announcing that the day of death had arrived and calling upon them to repent and beseech the lord for forgiveness while there was still time. In the morning, as the condemned prisoners were prepared for their final day, the doom-laden great bell of the church tolled grimly, signalling to all and sundry that the unfortunates were about to begin their last journey and that it was time to pray for their souls. "I hear my summons for another world," Duval is said to have remarked.

He and his companions received the sacrament in the chapel, and were then led to the press yard, where their shackles were struck off and they were delivered to the officers of the sheriff. A flight of stone steps led to a horse-drawn cart, in which, escorted by mounted lancers ready to control encroaching crowds or frustrate attempts to escape, the prisoners would be transported to the gallows at Tyburn. The slow journey lasted about an hour. Outside the church of St. Sepulchre the procession halted to allow a bellman (perhaps a parson) to call a large and excited crowd to attention with his hand-bell and lead them in a prayer for the condemned. Then the cavalcade passed westwards along Newgate Street, down Snow Hill and along Holborn and High Holborn between the excited and jostling gazes of innumerable excited spectators, many of whom fell in with the march, swelling the throng as they did so. Duval's capture and trial was said to have thrown the city into an "uproar," and needed no newspapers to become the talk of every citizen. Crowds routinely gathered on 'hanging days' but when Claude Duval went to the gallows they must have been tremendous. The capital would have to wait for more than fifty years, and the execution of Jack Sheppard, to witness a scene of comparable excitement at "the triple tree."

Somewhere near the church of St. Giles-in-the-Fields prisoners were traditionally allowed to imbibe spirits to steel themselves for their gruesome fates. Then a brief journey along Tyburn Road, now more sedately styled Oxford Street, brought Duval to the grim spectacle of the triple tree gallows, located in a large open space in the middle of the southern terminus of Edgware Road, just north of the present junction of Oxford Street and Bayswater Road. There the greatest throng of all stood waiting expectantly. In due course the cart passed beneath the gallows, and after some preliminaries a rope was fastened around the highwayman's neck.

There was no measured drop to break the necks of victims in those days. When the horse was whipped forwards, Duval was simply left to strangle in the air.

9. A seventeenth-century engraving of a routine hanging on the "triple tree" at Tyburn. Duval's execution drew huge crowds to the site, which is commemorated today by a plaque at the junction of Edgeware Road and Marble Arch.

According to the diary of Anthony Wood, who appears to have either seen Duval die or spoken to some who had, "he received extreme unction upon the ladder by a popish priest." Elsewhere it is recorded that Duval made a speech acknowledging that he had "taken many men's money" and been "a very lewd liver," but hoped for the forgiveness of God and those he had injured. "After that he was turned off [hanged] and soon dead." Eye-Witness, who was probably also present, reported that Duval "prayed very earnestly that God would forgive him his world of sins, and that the world would forgive him; that he died in charity with all men, and craved the prayers of them all, and that they would take example by him to amend their lives lest they fall into the like ways, for then God's judgements would overtake them, as it had done him. And so committing his soul to God Almighty, and often calling upon Christ for mercy, the executioner discharged his office."

In his pocket, biographer Pope claimed, was found a speech to the "fair English ladies," thanking them for their support. The references towards the close of the supposed speech, adverting to his fear of falling victim to disease, may have inspired remarks to that effect in the contemporary *Life of Deval*. If the copy given by Pope is a faithful one, the highwayman was at least determined to play his chosen role to the end. It is best given as it came:

"I should be very ungrateful (which, amongst persons of honour, is a greater crime than that for which I die) should I not acknowledge my obligation to you, fair English ladies. I could not have hoped that a person of my nation, birth, education and condition could have had so many and powerful charms to captivate you all, and to tie you so firmly to my interest that you have not abandoned me in distress, or in prison, that you have accompanied me to this place of death, of ignominious death. From the experience of your true loves I speak it; nay, I know I speak your hearts. You could be content to be with me now, and even here, could you be assured of enjoying your beloved Du Vall in the other world. How mightily, and how generously, have you rewarded my little services. Shall I ever forget that universal consternation amongst you when I was taken; your frequent, your chargeable [expensive] visits to me at Newgate; your shrieks, your swooning when I was condemned; your zealous intercession and importunity for my pardon? You could not have erected fairer pillars of honour and respect to me had I been a Hercules, and could have got fifty sons in a night. It has been the misfortune of several English gentlemen [royalists], in the times of the late usurpation, to die at this place upon the honourablest occasion that ever presented itself, the endeavouring to restore their exiled sovereign [Charles II], gentlemen, indeed, who had ventured their lives and lost their estates in the service of their prince. But they all died unlamented and uninterceded for, because they were English. How much greater, therefore, is my obligation, whom you love better than your own countrymen, better than your own dear husbands? Nevertheless, ladies, it does not grieve me that your intercession for my life proved ineffectual, for now I shall die with little pain, an healthful body, and I hope a prepared mind. For my confessor has showed me the evil of my way, and wrought in me a true repentance. Witness these tears, these unfeigned tears. Had you prevailed for my life, I must in gratitude have devoted it wholly to you, which yet would have been but short, for, had you been sound, I should soon have died of a consumption; if otherwise, of the Pox."

Duval's body could easily have been purloined by the authorities to decorate some roadside gibbet as a warning to others, or shipped to a surgeon for dissection purposes, but if such intentions existed they were thwarted by the highwayman's friends. According to the *Memoirs* the body was taken down by "well dressed" persons, hired by rich ladies, no doubt, and conveyed by a mourning coach to 'The Tangier Tavern' in St. Giles-in-the-Fields, where it was laid out for the night attended by eight cloaked guards. Numerous visitors were admitted to file by the coffin, some to satisfy their curiosity, others to pay their respects, and all in "great silence...for fear of disturbing this sleeping lion." Morton was scandalised by the display, which accorded the highwayman the treatment that might have been bestowed upon a public figure or hero, and ordered it closed, but the hurried burial the following day was accompanied by "many flambeaus, and a numerous train of mourners, most whereof were of the beautiful sex."

That funeral apparently took place in the nearby parish church of St. Giles-in-the-Fields, where one Robert Boreman was serving as rector. A traditionally poor parish, St. Giles had suffered much during the plague, and many of its victims lay in the churchyard. There, according to the burial register, 'Peter de Val' (another alias) was interred on 22 January, the day after the all-night vigil. This is almost certainly our man, although the acknowledgement is at variance to the well-known account given by Walter Pope. His *Memoirs* of Duval asserted that the highwayman was laid in the middle aisle of a church in Covent Garden, under a stone of white marble, "whereon are curiously engraved the Du Vall arms, and under them, written in black" the following epitaph:

"Here lies Du Vall: Reader, if male thou art,
Look to thy purse; if female, to thy heart.
Much havock has he made of both; for all
Men he made stand, and women he made fall.
The second conqu'ror of the Norman race;
Knights to his arms did yield, and Ladies to his face;
Old Tyburn's Glory, England's illustrious thief;
Du Vall, the ladies' joy, Du Vall the ladies' grief."

The stone with its famous epitaph has never been verified. Pope's "Covent Garden church" has been taken to be St. Paul's, which as the parish church was truly situated in that area, but its burial registers contain no reference to Duval. This dissonance between the 'Peter Deval' of the burial register of St. Giles-in-the-Fields and the Covent Garden location given by the *Memoirs* begs an explanation that is not easily offered. One serious possibility is that Pope simply invented both church and tombstone, but a deeper consideration raises doubts. Pope published anonymously, but can hardly have convinced himself that he would escape being identified, especially if the *Memoirs* sold well, as he patently hoped they would, and as in fact they did. A scholar, he constantly emphasized his wish to be judged an honest chronicler, and would surely have known that thousands of his readers, most of whom were Londoners, were quite capable of visiting the alleged gravesite of such a public sensation. To state so obvious a falsehood was merely soliciting exposure and condemnation.

Another possibility is that Pope erred in identifying the site, and that the stone was erected in St. Giles-in-the-Fields. The two churches are within a short walk of one another, and the pamphleteer's language was loose. Yet another alternative is that Pope, who rushed his pamphlet into print, stated something that he believed was going to happen. Such an elaborate memorial would, after all, have taken a considerable time to create. Pope seems to have been on the fringes of women who admired Duval, some of them very wealthy women, and may have learned that the stone he described, with the quoted epitaph, was in train. The vigil over the body was cut unexpectedly short by the intervention of Morton, and it is possible that a more hurried funeral than was planned then became necessary. It is even possible that Pope picked up talk of an exhumation of the body and reburial in a more suitable location. If so, the church of St. Paul's, which served Covent Garden, may have been the obvious choice. Duval's capture suggests that he sometimes resided in that area; one wonders if he had been drawn to celebrate his final Christmas there because his mistress and any offspring, what family he had in England, were inhabitants of that quarter. Conceivably, the transactions Pope described were meditated, aborted and finally surrendered in the face of dwindling interest, resignation or continued official obstruction.

We do not know, and as both churches, with their middle aisles, were destroyed in the eighteenth century, the existence of the stone at either site, cannot satisfactorily be established. Nevertheless, whether sculptured, proposed or merely the whim of a poet, these lines of 1670 depict more graphically than anything else a popular view of the time, and encapsulate the highwayman's myth.

The role of the women, especially the wealthy women, also raises one of the more interesting aspects of the Duval case: the gender dispute, if we may so call it, which distinguished the highwayman's end. Nothing approaching

10. St. Giles-in-the-Field church, where Duval was apparently buried, as it appeared in 1718, a little more than a decade before it was demolished. This is a lithograph by George Scharf after a work by John Hall.

it seems to have occurred before or since. Whatever else may be said of Duval, he did not die unloved. Of course, some men may have also regretted his end, and there were women who no doubt thought him well rid of, but if the contemporary comment is to be believed, opinion markedly divided on the lines of gender, and numerous women in particular were aggrieved that the state should exercise such lethal force against one who had, for all his faults, never practised violence against those who had fallen into his hands. According to Walter Pope, female sentiment in Duval's favour was so strong that men risked being ostracised or threatened for condemning the French charmer. Pope's mistress threw him out of her house, and in his pamphlet the aggrieved scribe declined to name Morton as the man behind the abrupt closure of the display at the 'Tangier Tavern' lest "he should incur the displeasure of the ladies."

For those few weeks in January 1670 a group of women stood loyally behind Duval. They visited him in prison, interceded for a pardon, attended his trial, followed him to the gallows and buried him. It was presumably they who bore the considerable expense of improving the felon's comforts in prison, hiring a mourning-coach, staging the laying in state at the 'Tangier Tavern' and perhaps trying to arrange a respectable burial and memorial. Duval cannot have been insensible of the efforts of these angels, and if his parting address is to be believed, tried to thank them. These women who tried to rescue Duval from his cruel fate unsuccessfully pitted themselves against a male establishment determined that justified or not the forces of the law must prevail.

It was a small but apparently passionate skirmish of the sexes, and an interesting aside upon Stuart England, and it ultimately led fiction writers to nominate Duval the "the ladies' highwayman."

6

The Knot Undone

With eyes fixed firmly on ridding the country of the outlaws, the government was unmoved by the entreaties of ladies, and busied itself with winding up the hunt. With the death of Duval one senses a tipping point had been reached in the law's war against the "knot" of highwaymen that had bedevilled London for so long. Most of the leading lights of the criminal community had been put out. But there was a messianic zeal in Morton, and perhaps in Williamson, and it did not brook half measures. In April 1672 Sir William was claiming indemnification for large expenses he had incurred in the pursuit, including £100 paid for spies. The significant sums he had advanced were evidence of his energy.

As the crushing power of the state destroyed the leaders of the gang, the rest either informed to save their necks, scuttled underground or scattered. One of the fugitives was Thomas Hill (or Hull), whom Morton described as "the great and notorious cheat, and Granger's right hand." Hill's story, as far as we can salvage it, is worth giving as an illustration of the numerous ways in which these criminals attempted to enrich themselves. As we saw in the last chapter, Hill had come to the attention of the authorities as a persistent highwayman of the mid 1660s, but his career diversified into fraud and confidence trickery. In this he was associated with Laurence (or Walter) Clarke, another "great padder," whose name had found a place in the royal proclamation of 1668. Both men had been active participants in the Duval-Maddox outlaw band.

Hill and Clarke also ran with two other villains, one referred to in the records only as Oxenden, and the other "a notorious cheat" named Thomas Granger. Granger specialised in disguise, deception and fraud. Posing as Sir Thomas Morton, a fine gentleman (the ironic choice of the surname was probably deliberate), Granger approached a London mercer named

Nicholson in 1668. Nicholson was paid £200 to issue a bill of exchange for the same amount, which could be presented to and cashed in Newcastle by another man of business, Mark Milbanke. It was a seventeenth-century credit transfer, allowing one man to pay money in London so that another could claim the amount in Newcastle.

But Granger was crooked. Using Nicolson's bill of exchange as a model, he forged a second for the sum of £1000, also to be presented to the unwitting Milbanke. To consummate his subterfuge he had also corrupted a postmaster on the mail road north, and through him intercepted a letter of advice Nicholson had sent to Milbanke. Again deploying his counterfeiting skills, Granger provided an authorization for both payments and returned it to the mail carrier. Although the £200 was covered by the deposit left with Nicholson, Milbanke was thus swindled out of £1000, an enormous amount of money in that day. Naturally, the fraud was eventually flushed out, and Milbanke fiercely pressed for the capture of the fraudsters.

Unfortunately for them, thieves often fall out. Granger accused Oxenden of purloining an unfair share of the takings and betrayed him, with the result that the latter was arrested, along, coincidentally, with the daring sea captain that Maddox and perhaps Duval had hoped would take them pirating. On his part, Oxenden, incarcerated in the King's Bench prison, ratted to the authorities about Granger's fraud. In a separate initiative, Hill and Clarke, the accomplices of Granger, were apprehended in Bruges, Flanders.

In September 1668 the crown sent Richard Bulstrode to Bruges with a warrant from George Monck, Lord Albemarle, to bring Hill and Clarke to England for trial. But Bulstrode discovered that Hill was held in Bruges for some civil matter, and could not be surrendered against his will. However, Hill was ready to bargain for his freedom, and revealed that Granger, the instigator of the fraud, and one who still had "great designs in foot," was then in London, and that he and no other could bring him to justice.

Whatever happened to Granger, Hill, highwayman turned fraudster, contrived to continue his career. Almost two years later, on 3 February 1670, Morton told Williamson that Baron Arlington, the Secretary of State for the Southern Department, had authorised him to bring Hill from Exeter for trial. The fellow had been committed to Newgate, but was afterwards transferred to the King's Bench prison to face charges of having swindled the Bishop of Winchester of £600, Milbanke of £1000, and "divers others" of £10,000. However, Hill escaped from the King's Bench, it was thought with the connivance of the deputy marshal, and had "since been cheating in Norfolk."

There Hill's story may have begun its epilogue. By 28 January 1670 an individual named Thomas Gill, who claimed to live in Faversham in Kent, had been imprisoned in Norwich on suspicion of being a member of Claude Duval's gang. His appearance matched a description of the wanted highwayman published by *The London Gazette*, and he was held by the Norfolk authorities pending intelligence as to whether he was among "those accused by Dudley and Widdrington [Woodrington]." Notified by the East Anglian magistrates, Morton immediately suspected that Gill was in fact the fugitive Thomas Hill. "I know Gill, confined at Norwich, to be a great cheat, having had him on my list," his letter to Williamson ran. "He has been confined in Salisbury, Reading, Newbury and other gaols, and it is, therefore, fit he should not be admitted to bail until he has been viewed by one who knows him." So keenly did Morton view his mission that he determined to go to Norwich himself to satisfy himself that he had his man.

The principal witness ready to identify Hill, if such was Gill's true identity, was none other than Humble Ashenhurst, now cooperating obediently with Morton as a new informer. Ashenhurst, readers will remember, had featured in all three lists of the Duval gang, and had been free as late as December 1669, robbing under the alias of 'Captain Cary'. At the end of the year, however, *The London Gazette* reported that the authorities were hot on his trail, and cautioned surgeons as well as law enforcement officers to watch out for him. "He is a tall man, thin-faced with black eyes, and bow-legged," said the paper, "and was in a late robbery wounded on the left side of his head and in his neck, which wounds are not yet cured." Within weeks 'Captain Cary' was sitting in prison, and like Woodrington and Dudley before him, offering to turn king's evidence. Apart from the obvious desire for self preservation, Ashenhurst had a family to support, and it is not difficult to imagine his dilemma. But such a prominent member of the Duval "knot" was clearly a valuable acquisition, and his readiness and ability to identify Hill further testifies to the connections between the fraudsters and highwaymen.

Whether Ashenhurst did play a part in Hill's destruction is unclear, but he did not benefit greatly from his collaboration with the authorities. Playing the system for all it was worth, he sold enough information to remain free, but instead of leaving it there he merely embarked upon fresh rogueries. It did not last long, and his end is fortuitously recounted in two sets of letters. A couple of letters of Henry Muddiman, the government journalist, survive in the National Archives, and they are supplemented by personal letters of William Lilly, a notable astrologer, who was then enjoying a peaceful retirement in the village of Hersham, Surrey, southwest of London.

Early in July 1670 Ashenhurst reconnoitred Lilly's house with three accomplices, one a well-known thief named Berkenhead. Lilly and one of his neighbours chanced upon them as they slept while resting their horses in an orchard. Deciding that they were suspicious, Lilly wasted no time in reporting to a magistrate named Andrews, who immediately got up a party of seven to apprehend the gang. In a brief skirmish two of the thieves fled; another, Berkenhead, was arrested; and Ashenhurst himself fell fatally wounded as he attempted to escape. Lilly graciously tended the dying Ashenhurst, who was carried to a public house in nearby Walton-upon-Thames and placed in the care of a doctor. Assisting, Lilly gave Humble a cordial and an enema, and chided him by saying that he knew the highwayman by sight, having watched him suspiciously passing his house several times. The rogue owned that he had been casing the place, but maintained that all ideas of raiding it had been abandoned. Lilly the thieves knew to be elderly, but he had been described to them as "a lusty old man," capable of giving trouble.

Ashenhurst's wound was a severe one, a pistol ball having lodged "one finger deep" in his back, and although he was speedily committed to prison he died within three days of receiving his injury. Lilly retained one of the highwayman's pistols as a keepsake. Humble was described at this time as a resident of St. George's parish in Southwark, but what gains he had made in life may have already evaporated. As required by law, his widow was charged with detailing his estate to the registry of the Prerogative Court of Canterbury. She asserted that she had no knowledge of an estate, but promised to account for anything that came subsequently into her hands. However, since these "inventories" normally included leases, stock and assets but not actual real estate, her declaration may not have been a comprehensive reflection of her late husband's holdings. As for Berkenhead, Ashenhurst's last lieutenant, he fared a little better in the short run. He was imprisoned but escaped to steal another day.

Apart from Ashenhurst, the principal remaining member of the outlaw band was the alliteratively named Samuel Swiftnicks. Swiftnicks, no less than Ashenhurst, had already once fallen in with the authorities only to return to crime. He had been convicted and pardoned. After the death of Duval he tried to regenerate the broken "knot" of robbers, but in May 1670 four of his new recruits, John Hickes, alias Lloyd, a victualler, Alexander Nowell, a soldier, John Richardson, a servant, and one William Norris were arrested on the orders of Justice Morton and thrown into Newgate. "They are all of a new gang, and drawn in to commit robberies by Swift Nix and Ashenhurst," Morton told Williamson, "and had [been] appointed to meet in a house in St. Giles, where they were arrested. But Nix and Ashenhurst kept away for fear of discovery. I hope to have them shortly." This close call, and Ashenhurst's death soon after, may have told Swiftnicks that the net was inexorably closing around him. At any rate, he again made his peace, and on 15 October 1670 was granted a full pardon for all the crimes he had committed. This time he turned his back on highway robbery and reclaimed a place among the ranks of the law-abiding.

Another old lag, George Woodrington, who had shamelessly used the system to sustain a dual career as highwayman and informer, also ended his rebellion about this time. On 6 May 1670 he was granted a pardon, although whether this enabled him to reform we are unable to say.

Nevertheless, the great manhunt was coming to its end. The credit was due to Morton, more than anyone else. His had been a frustrating task, for his principal weapon in destroying the outlaw band had been the use of informers, and they had often been major offenders themselves, who used what privileges they received to return to the ranks of active highwaymen. Morton believed it a worthwhile strategy, nonetheless. True, he captured and released robbers, but always to land bigger fish. George Woodrington lived on, but the man he had impeached in January 1670, Claude Duval, died on the gallows. Thus for Morton, the step backwards was always worth two or more forwards, and slowly he broke the spine of what had possibly been the most formidable combination of highwaymen in English history.

Reflecting upon it in a letter to Williamson on 9 April 1672, Morton remarked that it had been four years since he had undertaken to prosecute "the highwaymen who so infested the roads that scarce any that travelled... that were worth robbing could escape their clutches. But now they are almost totally reduced, only six or seven that I can remember being left at liberty, but either hanged, transported or imprisoned there being no less than a hundred of them, notorious rogues, when I first undertook them." Nor, he added, was his four-year war at its end, because he was committed to suppressing any new gangs that attempted to replace the old; indeed, said he, only the day before he had apprehended and imprisoned seven such neophytes. It was, undoubtedly, a major achievement, if one that few historians have recognised.

Nevertheless, not all the ripples set running by the manhunt worked towards the peace of the realm. As the outlaws were struck down in and about London, some dispersed, looking for safer regions in which to ply their trade. It was, perhaps, such a dispersal that contributed to one of the bloodiest affrays in the history of highway robbery, an event that took place in the north of England and ultimately cost the lives of twenty-seven people.

Ironically, the episode occurred upon the fourth anniversary of Duval's execution at Tyburn, on Wednesday, 21 January 1674. It demonstrated more graphically than any other incident how a profession that Duval had invested with a veneer of glamour could rapidly descend into mayhem. Two of the highwaymen involved later confessed to having been members of the late Frenchman's gang, a fact that was considered so significant that it was placed upon the title page of a pamphlet describing the events, *Bloody News From York-shire*. Inside, this interesting information was left to form the final paragraph of the account, and for emphasis it was printed in italics thus: "*Two of them* [the surviving highwaymen, held at York Castle] *upon examination have since acknowledged that they were first initiated in the discipline of the road by that famous artist Du Vall, who brought out of his own country into England the gentle methods of following the high-pack, taking a Purse Alamode, mustering his savage Arabians* [fellow thieves], *and exercising them to perform their parts on all occasions with the most obliging dexterity. For which and other excellent accomplishments he was about five years since deservedly preferred at Tyburn.*"

It is, of course, possible that the offenders were simply claiming an idle association with the great man of their profession, although it is difficult to see what clemency they could have gained by admitting such antecedents. Furthermore, the attack north of York did in some respects bear the stamp of a Duval coup, and perhaps throws light upon his *modus operandi* as well as that of the perpetrators. It was a large scale heist, involving twenty robbers, and targeted a convoy of fifteen York butchers making its way to a famous fair and market at Northallerton. This recalls Duval's penchant for scourging the "market folks" and "itinerant brigades" of the southern counties, as described by the author of *The Life of Deval* and Samuel Butler. Indeed, the latter actually referred to Duval's raids upon "savage butcher[s]."

If butchers had a reputation for ferocity, they lived up to it on this occasion. They were "marching in such a body [that they] had not the least apprehension or fear of being set upon by thieves." Yet twenty desperadoes staged a well-planned attack, perhaps following the tactics that had been practised successfully by Duval's outfit. One robber innocently fell in with the butchers on the road, travelling with "a melancholy" air that encouraged enquiry. After exchanging greetings the solitary traveller expressed his gratitude for being allowed to continue his journey with the security of such a large and powerful convoy, and fell to its rear in better spirits. Presently, some three miles further, the company approached "a place where the way was very narrow, having a high hill on the right-hand and a large thick wood on the left," and it was here that the new recruit suddenly "fell a-singing, which he performed so well that the butchers...began to tune their pipes" (probably flageolets) and added to the merriment.

The song, however, was merely a signal to the other highwaymen secreted in the wood, who quickly deployed in two parties, cutting the road ahead and behind the convoy, and calling upon it so surrender. With naked blades they demanded, "Damn ye, ye dogs, deliver!" These tactics might have worked in the past, but on this occasion the stroke foundered upon the unexpected recalcitrance of the victims, who fell to what weapons they had to hand (five swords and innumerable bludgeons, as well as the knives and cleavers that were their tools of trade) and lustily set about their attackers. At the outset one highwayman, unsuccessfully thrusting his sword at an uncooperative butcher, found himself unhorsed by a stunning return blow from a cudgel. "A most terrible conflict there was with much fury above an hour," recorded the contemporary pamphlet, "both parties showing extraordinary courage and resolution." The highwaymen appeared to have been reluctant to use lethal force, but after three of their number had been killed and others wounded and some of the butchers injured, they resorted to their pistols and shot seven of the tradesmen dead. Two other butchers had their horses killed beneath them. This broke the deadlock. The remaining eight victims sued for mercy, and the surviving robbers bound their bloodied assailants, sequestrated their purses and rifled the dead. That done, they fled into the woods carrying their own dead with them to prevent identification. It was estimated that they had made off with £936, which was at that time a huge amount of money, illustrating what spoils were to be had in such high risk games.

It was not long before other travellers came upon the surviving butchers, and gazed in horror at a "place all dyed with blood." A hue and cry was raised, and alarm sped throughout the countryside. About ten o'clock the same night a villager noticed a number of worn horsemen gathering at "a small tippling house" in some remote country spot, and hurried to the nearest magistrate. A makeshift posse of watchmen and other enforcement officers soon enfiladed the robbers' refuge and tried to force the door with halberds, but "the thieves with naked rapiers stood on their own defence," and ultimately drove the assailants back. Reinforcements then arrived to swing the balance against the robbers, and a murderous fire was poured into the house. Four outlaws were slain and the remaining thirteen captured, all "desperately wounded in several parts of their bodies." They were soon languishing in fetters in York Castle. Interrogations revealed that two members of the captives had been members of Duval's gang, probably driven north by the ferocity of Morton's manhunt.

If so, it was a bloody end to the activities of one of the most active outlaw gangs of the century.

By then the man who more than any other had masterminded its destruction was himself dead. Sir William Morton died on 23 September 1672, and his remains were laid to rest in the Temple Church in London. He had been fighting to the finish, mopping up the old gang, and suffocating any successors at birth. In February of that year, for example, the government allowed an imprisoned highwayman named Henry Hitchins to escape so that he could renew his connections on the road and betray them to the justices. If the demolition of the Duval knot had been the crown in Morton's career, it must be seen as only the epicentre of what became a more sustained onslaught on the criminal gangs. Morton's career had been a salutary lesson to law-breakers, and deserved to be remembered in the history of law enforcement in London.

In breaking the outlaws Morton had pioneered methods that were tried again and again. By 1690, for example, a new large-scale "knot" of highwaymen had developed, and it provoked another royal proclamation, papering the fifteen known members still at large. Three years later rewards for the successful prosecution of highwaymen were offered at £40 per head. Other proclamations would follow.

Morton did not bring an end to the large robber bands, but their sun was setting. One of the last, led by James Whitney, operated principally in the London area until his execution at Smithfield in 1693. He was alleged to have mustered numerous followers in his day, and in 1692 offered to bring eighty "stout" men into the king's service in return for a pardon. Although a humble butcher by trade, he also assumed the appearance and manners of a gentleman. Perhaps he was remembering Duval.

For something remarkable had already begun to happen. The gang of Duval, Maddox and Swiftnicks was gone, and the eighteenth century, rushed impatiently forward. The day of small armies of raiders was all but done. Sir William Morton was dead, and quickly forgotten. But the man he had sent to the gallows in January 1670 was finding a new stage. Dead in life, he would live on in legend and literature.

7

From Life to Legend

The process of encrusting Claude Duval in legend began quickly. As it snowballed over the centuries the need to retain the history diminished, and a fictional Duval emerged from the chrysalis, able to serve every popular whim, and even to slip from one century to another, rather like a primitive 'Timelord' in the well-known television series of our own day. Only three essential ingredients were needed to identify this developing Claude Duval to his public: he had to be French, a daring highwayman, and a gallant, fond of rescuing damsels in distress.

The real Duval had operated at an inopportune time for those who would reconstruct his real career. The extensive Old Bailey sessions records, with their full statements of witnesses and defendants, are not available until 1674 – four years after his execution – and it was not until 1695 that the lapse of the Licensing Act, which had restricted the growth of the press, allowed daily and weekly newspapers to flourish and record a wealth of detail on matters great and small. Scholars of the eighteenth century have thus been bequeathed an enormous body of information about crime in London. The eighteenth-century lives of Jack Sheppard, Jonathan Wild and Dick Turpin have been recovered richly accoutred. Indeed, their very fame, especially that of the burglar and escapist Jack Sheppard, who was executed amidst much excitement in 1724, was in part a creation of the explosion of the popular press that occurred in the first years of the century.

By comparison, even the brief notice of the execution of "that notorious highwayman and robber Claude de Val" in *The London Gazette*, a two-page broadsheet reserved for subscribers and confined to little more than state affairs, foreign news and occasional asides to the doings of the aristocracy, was probably unprecedented. The documents that do remain about him are few and disappearing. Many of the relevant gaol delivery certificates, which were kept for posterity, have now disintegrated beyond use. As far as historical documentation is concerned, therefore, Duval belonged with the pauperised past, not the future.

For all their fame, neither Duval nor John Nevison, who attained a considerable reputation as a highwayman in Yorkshire a few years later, are much better placed, in terms of the footprint left in historical records, than Gamaliel Ratsey, a noted thief executed in Bedford in 1605, or James Hind the mid-century royalist partisan. The exploits of Ratsey and Hind are known to us through fanciful pamphlets, ballads or poems and a mere handful of brief allusions in the historical records. Indeed, compared to their well-documented successors in the eighteenth-century, the seventeenth-century fugitives are closer to such famous medieval predecessors as Hereward the Wake, Eustace the Monk, Fulk Fitzwarin, Robin Hood, Roger Godberd and Robert Stafford (the fifteenth-century original of Friar Tuck). One and all, they were fodder for entertaining embellishment rather than serious history. Their stories were circulated in romances, verses and fictional biographies, and they lived before the routine preservation of large quantities of relevant records, or the development of a regular press. They are, and will forever remain, outlaws on the edge of history, known to us only as shadowy indeterminate creatures of an impenetrable past. Like Professor Challenger, the ebullient creation of Arthur Conan Doyle, anyone hunting them today journeys *In the Land of Mist*.

We do not know how many contemporary pamphlets or broadsides testified to Duval's end, but none of those we now have provides an account that is both authentic and comprehensive. The most popular and perhaps the fullest is the anonymously published *Memoirs of Monsieur Du Vall*, printed for one Henry Brome at 'The Gun' tavern in 1670, but it was as much as anything a satire on the ostentatious but beguiling flippancy of French manners, with Duval the glamorous thief playing the part of their exemplar.

The wider context behind this and some of the other polemics against Duval is worth mentioning. England was a Protestant country, and one with a traditional history of conflict with France. The reign of Charles II was marked by considerable religious and political unrest, in which popular xenophobia and anti-Catholicism found a convenient target in everything French. The king was suspected of favouring both France and the Pope, perhaps not unnaturally for one who had found a safe asylum from Cromwell's parliamentarians across the English Channel. Although the 'Merry Monarch' postponed declaring himself a Catholic until he was on his deathbed, he maintained a steady discourse with Louis XIV of France throughout his reign, partly in order to frustrate any potentially threatening alliances the French might make with the Dutch. By secret clauses in the Treaty of Dover in 1670 Charles even promised to convert to Catholicism in return for a French subsidy.

The king was wise to act covertly. In England popular suspicions of the drift towards Catholicism fuelled a determination to block the king's younger brother, the Catholic James, from the royal succession and kindled hysteria and reaction. In 1678 the inflammatory Titus Oates stirred a furore with his tales of a 'damnable and hellish' treason against the state (the 'Popish Plot') and legitimized the hounding of Catholics, some to the death. In Westminster the government's Test Acts of 1673 and 1678 barred Catholics from public office, and during the 'Exclusion Crisis' of 1679 to 1681 the king found it almost impossible to work with his parliaments and resorted to an absolutism dangerously reminiscent of the events that had overthrown his father little more than three decades before. If Claude Duval's Gallic ancestry scored points with fashion-conscious ladies, it also struck others as another unwelcome influence from across the Channel.

This brings us back to the anonymously published *Memoirs* of Duval. According to Anthony Wood (1632-95), an antiquary, they were written by Dr. Walter Pope, something of a libertine himself, whose fiancé ("the Miss of our author Pope") had been one of the women enamoured of Duval. The pamphlet, said Wood, was "written upon offence taken from a gentlewoman who, having a respect for his [Pope's] person, left him upon the sight and company of Du Vall." An element of jealousy was suggested; it seems, indeed, to have been at the heart of Pope's interest, and to have led him, for example, to acquire a "muster roll" of the people who had visited the highwayman in Newgate. One wonders if he expected to find the name of his estranged mistress therein.

Pope's own account of his discomfiture attributes it to the wider tendency of the English ladies to lionise French fashion and company:

"Being once in the company of some ladies, amongst other discourses, we fell upon the comparison betwixt the French and English nations. And here it was that I, very imprudently maintained, even against my mistress, that a French lackey [Duval?] was not so good as an English gentleman. The scene was immediately changed. They all looked upon me with anger and disdain. They said I was unworthy of that little breeding I had acquired, of that small parcel of wit (for they would not have me esteemed a mere fool because I had been so often in their company) which nature had bestowed upon me, since I made so ill use of it as to maintain such paradoxes. My mistress forever forbids me the house, and the next day sends me my letters and demands her own, bidding me pick up a wife at the plough-tail, for it was impossible any woman well bred would ever cast her eyes upon me."

To whatever personal animosity Pope had for Duval was added, therefore, his marked prejudice against the French, those "strangers" to good nature in word or deed. For all its protestations of objectivity the author's treatise was a hostile one, written, he admitted, in "in great indignation."

Pope, a graduate of Wadham College, Oxford, had succeeded Christopher Wren as professor of Astronomy at Gresham College, London, and from 1668 served as registrar of the diocese of Chester. A fellow of the Royal Society, he also left poetry and travelled widely in France, experiencing the Gallic way of life. His modest pamphlet on Duval was certainly a success. According to Wood, it "took so well and sold so much that 'tis thought there were 10,000 of them printed." It certainly outsold all of its rivals.

By comparison the other two surviving biographical pamphlets are briefer, a mere eight pages apiece, but more down-to-earth and reliable. The author of *The Life of Deval* is unknown, but the item was drawn up for a topical sale, and licensed by Roger L'Estrange, who oversaw the national press, on 22 January 1670, the day after the execution. It was printed by 'W.R.' Also in January appeared *A True and Impartial Relation of the Birth and Education of Claudius du Val, Together with the Manner of his Apprehending, Commitment to New-gate, &c.* The printers were by T. Ratcliff and T. Daniel, who sold it from their house in New Street, between Shoe and Fetter Lanes.

We are not able, as yet, to name the anonymous author of the *True and Impartial Relation*, although we have called him Eye-Witness because he was certainly present at Duval's trial and reported it accurately. He said, and there is no reason to doubt it, that he also interviewed the prisoner in Newgate. In later times the Ordinary of Newgate customarily marketed confessions of doomed felons, but this pamphlet does not bear the stamp of Cressy's work, and we should beware of crediting works too hastily. Ignoring the many unsung and unknown scribes, historians have constantly stumbled in attributing works of this period to this or that famous author. With relatively little regard to serious evidence, the eighteenth-century writer and entrepreneur, Daniel Defoe, for example, has been assigned pamphlet 'lives' of Jack Sheppard, Jonathan Wild and Robert McGregor, as well as the famous compendium on pirates published under the sobriquet of 'Captain Charles Johnson'. We had best leave *The Life of Deval* and the *True and Impartial Relation* as the works of unknown hands.

Although the *True and Impartial Relation* was close to the events it describes, it is weak on all that concerns Duval's career as an outlaw. Most likely the reluctant hero could not be drawn upon such matters during his prison conversations. In addition to the three surviving prose narratives of the highwayman, however, we also have two in verse, the ballad *Devol's Last Farewell* (1670), and Samuel Butler's well-known *Pindarick Ode* (1671). They treat the subject in a light vein, but both contain echoes of a life that was then well known, and provide insights into public perceptions of the man.

Butler, a noted satirist and poet famous for the classic *Hudibras*, had just become secretary to George Villiers, 2nd Duke of Buckingham, the king's most powerful advisor and courtier, and was therefore in an excellent position to tap government thinking about Duval, and probably also information known to or suspected by the authorities that is no longer available. Given his interest in Duval it is difficult to believe he did not discuss the subject with the Duke or those close to him. However, the *Pindarick Ode* was something of a two-edged sword. Written in a mock heroic style, it grossly exaggerated the highwayman's achievements, as if to deride those who had lionized and supported him. But Butler's expose of delusion and hypocrisy also extended to those who had damned Duval's misdeeds whilst occupying less than moral high ground themselves. As the poet insinuated, Duval had at least been an open rogue, whereas many of his victims, the ostensibly upright and wealthy,

11. Samuel Butler (1612-80), poet and satirist famous for his burlesque *Hudibras*, penned a mock tribute to Duval. Written while Butler was secretary to the Duke of Buckingham, the "ode" contains undertones of admiration. This portrait was engraved by James Heath from an original painting by Gerard Soest and published in 1810.

came by their gains by furtive sleights of hand. Thus, in a sense, Duval's predation inflicted fitting punishment upon extortionate tax-collectors; forestallers, who accumulated goods through underhand private purchases and sold them in the open market for immoral profits; "enhancers" with their excessive charges; and "dreadful" lawyers, "fierce" hagglers, "savage" butchers and bullying drovers. In his readiness to contrast the obvious crimes of an executed felon with the dubious practises of some of those who professed good citizenship, Butler foreshadowed Henry Fielding's famous satire on *The Life of Jonathan Wild the Great* (1743), with its thinly veiled animus against corrupt political magnates who abused their power.

In 1713 one styling himself 'Captain Alexander Smith' supplied a fanciful account of Duval in his *Complete History of the...Most Notorious Highwaymen*. It drew much on Pope's *Memoirs* but added unbelievable and frankly silly episodes that he had either invented or quarried from some other source that no longer exists. Newspaper advertisements establish that Smith's work was first issued in November 1713, and his subsequent *Comical and Tragical History of the Bailiffs of London and Westminster*, published a decade later, indicates that he had some acquaintance with law enforcement in London if little with the pursuit of truth. The few historians who have considered Smith have noted his plagiarism.

Cumulatively, all of these sources established the historicity of Duval, and broadly his contemporary reputation, but contain relatively little solid information. Nevertheless, the ambiguous cocktail of charm and terror that distinguished Duval, the extraordinary efforts made by the government to break his gang, and the endurance of his name all bespeak an uncommon criminal remembered long after the multitude of hanged rogues were forgotten. England would have to wait more than half a century until the execution of Jack Sheppard in 1724 to see a criminal of comparable celebrity. As far as highway robbery itself is concerned, John Nevison, James Whitney, James Maclaine, Richard Turpin, William Page, Jack Rann and Jerry Abershaw all achieved temporal fame without usurping Duval's standing as the classic example of their business, especially in regard to its romantic pretensions. It was not until the Victorian period, when the novelist Ainsworth recast Turpin's character and reputation in the same vein that a comparable, and in some respects even more potent, fictional knight of the road emerged.

Duval left the memory of one who had brought chivalry of a kind to highway robbery. Perhaps, in a subtle way, he had also demonstrated that gallantry and non-violence might be a worthwhile investment. True, he had been just too infamous to escape the noose, but he had famously won surprising public support, support that might have saved a lesser outlaw. Non-violence and courtesy did not even cost the highwayman much. Whilst the common footpad had an incentive to physically injure his victims lest they rallied to pursue him or impede his flight, the highwayman rode a fast horse that gave him good prospects of escape. For one reason or another, the 'gentleman' highwayman became something of a stock in trade during the eighteenth century, although no successor had the flair to topple Duval's reputation as the premier practitioner.

James Sharpe, in a recent history of the highwayman myth, concluded that Duval "established the highwayman as a romantic swashbuckling daredevil... [He], possibly more than any other of his profession, established the image of the highwayman which was to prove so resilient in later generations." Degrees of civility had, of course, been part of earlier outlaw legends, and not just that of Robin Hood. In reviewing the blend of fiction, legend and fact that passed for stories of highwaymen in the early modern period, some scholars have suggested a few names as possible precursors of Claude Duval, but of most of these candidates there are few, if any, authentic details. Unquestionably, some men who took to the road hailed from the gentrified classes, including a number dispossessed during the troubles of the Civil War, but none left any great reputation as a gentleman highwayman *per se*, and they died forgotten. To have made a contribution towards the creation of the gentleman highwayman as a distinct breed, inspiring copycat practises on any scale; to have generated a *myth*, demanded an unusual degree of celebrity. In that sense, only one serious contender can be advanced as a significant forerunner of Duval.

James Hind, who was brutally executed in Worcester in 1652, stands alongside Duval as one of the two most significant highwaymen of the seventeenth century. His contemporary renown cannot be disputed. His death occurred during a brief free-for-all that occurred between the collapse of the old system of press regulation in 1640 and the imposition of new and relatively illiberal controls, and no less than seventeen pamphlets about Hind survive to attest to his considerable standing. Hind was reputedly the son of a humble Oxfordshire saddler, and took to robbery to escape the drudgery of life as an apprentice butcher. He is unlikely to have commanded the excess of manners and etiquettes that marked Duval, but fictionalised accounts of his life represented him to have been capable of acting the gentleman, and spoke of his reluctance to visit violence upon victims, his courtesy to women and tendency to rob "with grace." Speaking more generally, one pamphlet described Hind as "an absolute artist in his profession," words which would reoccur in the early literature of Claude Duval.

In these respects, there are distinct similarities between Hind, as rendered by the pamphleteers, and Duval, with the differences being rather of degree and emphasis. While Duval's highway manners and relations with women were forefront, the earlier ruffian made the greatest play of his royalist credentials and opposition to the Parliamentarians. Indeed, some of the Hind authors went further, and fancied their hero not merely a political dissident thrown into the wrong by the Civil War, but also an egalitarian who championed the poor and underprivileged against the dishonest, avaricious and tyrannical. As the historian Karsten Piep has explained, he became a clothes-horse upon which all manner of political and social grievances might be hung. How much any of this reflected the real James Hind is beyond our investigation, but it clearly places him nearer to the legends of Hereward and Robin Hood than to the relatively apolitical Claude Duval.

James Hind was the first great highwayman hero, and in that sense brought a new glass through which the subject might be beheld. The possibility that a highway robber might be heroic in some way went forward through literature if not in real history. But it is to be doubted that Hind was the prototype for the image of the gentleman highwaymen seen in the eighteenth century. As we shall see the notable illustrations of that idea, such as the career of James Maclaine and the social comment of Wilhelm von Archenholtz, align with the memory of Duval rather than that of Hind. It is conceivable that Duval had heard of Hind, whose death had occurred within living memory. It is even possible that he used Hind as a template. But it is also clear that Duval had much more obvious mentors in the Paris that had raised him and the elevated families in which he had moved, and it was he, rather than Hind, who stood in the public mind as the classic example of the gentleman highwayman. And when it came to romance and sheer sexual magnetism, no English outlaw before or since enjoyed a comparable reputation.

We have already seen that Duval was credited with creating something of a sea-change in his own day. According to Samuel Butler and the contemporary account entitled *Bloody News from York-shire* he was a "famous artist" who taught highwaymen that bold exploits might be accompanied by a genteel mode of business. An early villain who might have been inspired by Duval was a thief named Thomas Sadler. One of a trio, he pulled off the surprising feat of stealing the Lord Chancellor's mace and purse from a property in Great Queen Street, London. He gaily marched across Lincoln's

Inn Fields preceded by an accomplice who bore the ceremonial booty in mock and brazen imitation of the luckless office-holder they had just impoverished. Tried with others at the Old Bailey on 7 March 1677, Sadler was described as "a fellow who may engage the pity of as many ladies as his famous predecessor, Duval, if he had but a smack of the monsieur." The remark indicates that Sadler was cultivating a like reputation, something also hinted in a contemporary broadside about him. *Groans From Newgate*, published soon after his execution on 16 March, recalled the days

> "When brisk Duval, that French Latroon,
> Received reward of Picaroon,
> And put poor Ladies in a swoon."

Duval's unique standing intrigued the chattering classes of the day, and even entered more creative literature. In Thomas Duffett's lasvicious burlesque, *Psyche Debauch'd*, produced in 1675 and published three years later, Venus attempted to manipulate Psyche, an attractive woman known as None-So-Fair, by using a seductive character disguised as Bruine, "the white bear of Norwich." Unfortunately, the hireling Bruine fell in love with None-So-Fair and revealed to her that he was, in fact, "Du Val, that French prince of padders, that was thought to be hanged; I have lived ever since in this disguise because I would not quite break the kind ladies' hearts to see me hanged twice." But she was to keep his secret, for

> "If Newgate-keeper once should smoke us,
> Thy bear must vanish with a hocus."

In *Psyche Debauch'd* Duval was but one of several leading figures. The first novel to be inspired by the highwayman was *The French Rogue*, a work of some two hundred pages anonymously published in 1672. It related the adventures of a "pretty" French thief in the style of a successful earlier work, *The English Rogue*, and was perhaps written by the same author. The hero's activities in the story bore no resemblance to those of Duval, but there could be no doubt that it was he who had suggested the marketability of such a work, for the preface itself, addressed to the prospective reader, insinuated the highwayman's recent history. "But I have the *English Rogue*, say you," it cajoled, "and what need [have I] of a *French* one? In truth I can give no better answer to this objection [to my book] than the common one; it is the Fashion, and He's the better company for Ladies."

THE
F R E N C H
ROGUE.
Being a Pleasant
HISTORY
OF
His LIFE and FORTUNE,
adorned with variety of other
ADVENTURES
of no less Rarity.
WITH
EPIGRAMS
Suitable to each Stratagem.

LONDON:
Printed by *T. N.* for *Samuel Lowndes,*
and are to be sold at his Shop, over-against
Exeter House in the *Strand.* 1672.

12. Title-page of *The French Rogue*, a novel of 1672. A sequel to *The English Rogue*, although not necessarily by the same author, it was prompted by the popularity of Claude Duval.

Almost twenty years after his death the Duval affair was still being remembered, and entered a work that ran to a third edition in 1696. The author, Titus Oates, the notorious anti-Papist whose allegations of the existence of a 'Popish plot' to murder the king and burn London stirred lethal resentment against Catholics, was predictably willing to share Walter Pope's hostility to all things Gallic. Oates fulminated against the "French whores, French fashions and customs, and French officers and French servants" that England "nourished and cherished with all the caresses imaginable." Inevitably, he illustrated his point by turning his fire upon Duval. "Nay," he declared, "so amorous too had your fine but debauched [English] ladies been of a French Kickshaw that they have even hugged them in their very bosoms, and have lamented the loss, tho' but of the meanest French skips; witness the tears that fell from divers great personages of the feminine sex that on their knees made supplication for that insipid highwayman Du Vall, who, at last, though with great difficulty, was hanged at Tyburn for robberies committed on the highway. It is true he was a man of excellent parts and singular learning, only he could neither write nor read." The passage has occasionally been misconstrued as condemning Duval as an illiterate. But he was, after all, a Frenchman, and it is not surprising that he never grasped written English. His education, of course, had been in his own language.

In the eighteenth century, the new century, the great gangs of highwaymen had all but gone, but Duval's legendary chivalry still inspired. The gentleman highwayman he had popularised made his most notable appearance in fiction in January 1728, when John Gay's *The Beggar's Opera* was first staged in Lincoln's Inn Fields. This ballad opera, which originated in Jonathan Swift's idea for a Newgate pastoral in 1716, turned the conventional Italian opera upon its head, substituting popular street songs and airs for the elevated outpourings of prima donnas, and the lower orders of London for the classical heroes and heroines. It was an instant success, notching up an almost record-breaking run of sixty-two performances in its opening season, and was arguably the greatest English play of that century.

Gay knew enough of his craft to use material which rung bells with his audiences, and suggested parallels between what happened on the stage and in their world outside. We know that he borrowed from established street ditties for his musical interludes, and that some of his characters parodied real-life counterparts, even if they were far from close reproductions of them. Peachum the thief-taker smacked powerfully of Jonathan Wild, who had been executed in 1725, and some have speculated that the central figure of Macheath the highwayman may have been inspired by the recent history of Jack Sheppard. It is true that Macheath's escape from Newgate intentionally recalled Sheppard's escapes from that same penitentiary nearly four years before, but no one informed about the subject could possibly read the famous burglar's life and character into Gay's portrait of Macheath.

Macheath was something that Sheppard never was, a daring highwayman. Moreover, he acted the part of a gentleman, and was therefore able to mix in that level of society. "Sure, there is not a finer gentleman upon the road than the captain," declared Mrs. Peachum. Unfortunately, we were told, he "keeps too good company ever to grow rich." In short, Gay enshrined the gentleman highwayman, popularised by Duval, in literature and art. But it was in the erotic dimension of Macheath that Gay's creation most resembled Claude Duval. He was unashamedly enamoured with the fair sex, upon whom he frittered his money, and received his troop of female admirers with a studied and gallant banter. Pursued by both Polly Peachum, the thief-taker's daughter, and Lucy Lockit, the offspring of the Keeper of Newgate, Macheath owned that he had "two or three wives already" and that he adored women. "I love the sex," he boasted, "and a man who loves money might as well be contented with one guinea as I with one woman. The town perhaps have been as obliged to me for recruiting it with free-hearted ladies."

In the London in which Gay had grown up and worked, Duval was the only well known template for such a figure, and the sensation he had caused, especially among women, was still a powerful folk memory. One telling scene in Act II, in which Macheath receives a bevy of his women with a profusion of compliments, particularly evoked that recollection. "But hark!" he cries. "I hear music. The Harper is at the door. *If music be the food of love, play on.* 'Ere you seat yourselves, Ladies, what think you of a dance? Come in [enter Harper]. Play the *French* tune that Mrs. *Slammerkin* was so fond of." The picture of the handsome outlaw, dressed in his finery, performing *"a dance* a la ronde *in the* French *manner"* could not but summon to mind the famous story of Claude Duval and the lady on the heath, and the emphasis placed upon its Gallic character sturdily reinforced the connection.

13. Gilbert Stuart Newton's 1826 painting of a scene in *The Beggar's Opera*, showing Macheath the highwayman in Newgate with the rivals for his attentions, as reproduced as a lithograph of 1892. John Gay's portrait of Macheath almost certainly reflected memories of Claude Duval, and sealed the public image of the gentleman highwayman.

The Beggar's Opera was a milestone in theatrical history, and no less in the development of the myth of the gentleman highwayman. The principal female rivals for Macheath's attentions, Peachum and Lockit, successfully intercede for the highwayman's life after his final arrest and give the production the happy ending that had eluded the historical Duval, but which, apparently, was demanded by the public. Notwithstanding, the power of the play was undiminished. Thomas Walker, the actor who almost made the part of Macheath his own, was lifted to stardom, and lines inscribed upon his mezzotint portrait boast,

"If wit can please, or gallantry engage,
Macheath may boast he justly charms the age."

In 1729 Sir Archibald Grant commissioned William Hogarth to paint an ambitious picture of *The Beggar's Opera*. Finished about 1732, this early work of the great artist preserves for us the Macheath that appeared on stage, attired in his striking scarlet coat. Even in modern times Gay's depiction of this rakish gentleman highwayman carries conviction. Claud Lovat Fraser, who successfully restored the opera to the London stage in 1921, explained that "Macheath and certain ladies of the town alone 'keep company with lords and gentlemen,' and even then there must have been apparent a distinction. Macheath is unaltered [in the new production]. Here it was essential to keep to tradition. Macheath in a [common] blue coat is unthinkable. The rest of the characters are frankly in the neighbourhood of Newgate." Recalling a Royal Shakespeare Company production of the opera that she had seen as a child, Laura Barnett informed readers of *The Guardian* on 28 April 2014, that "I fell in love with Macheath, with his deep, molasses voice and tumble of dark hair." If Duval had introduced romance into the myth of the highwayman, it was cemented in the public mind by Gay's phenomenal stage success.

Despite Duval and *The Beggar's Opera*, however, there is little doubt that the common highwayman encountered on the rutted roads feeding the capital had little that was romantic or genteel in his character. But imitators did surface often enough for the German historian, Wilhelm von Archenholz, to stereotype the eighteenth-century English road agent in that mould. "They assure you they are very sorry that poverty has driven them to that shameful recourse, and end by demanding your purse in the most courteous manner," he wrote. Readers may remember that this was the very style attributed to Duval, both in the newsletter of 1666 and the story of the highwayman's robbery of two gentlemen, recorded in the contemporary *Life of Deval*. The best identifiable imitator was James Maclaine, who was executed at Tyburn in 1750. A failed grocer, as well as the son of a Scottish Presbyterian minister, Maclaine could credibly claim to have emerged from the lower middle ranks of society. He affected to be a gentleman as well as a highwayman, and some of his robberies were pure Duval, "conducted with the greatest good breeding" and incorporating apologies to the victim and explanations for the unfortunate necessity of his discomfiture.

Scholar Robert Shoemaker, in an interesting essay on the subject of the gentleman highwayman, believed that the tradition declined from about the mid-eighteenth century, and that Maclaine was its last significant exponent. If true, it had persisted for the best part of a century after Duval's death, and was not an inconsiderable legacy. Similar figures also emerged overseas, reputedly including James Freney, an eighteenth-century Irish highwayman who remarkably escaped the noose in 1749, and 'Gentleman' Matthew Brady, a bushranger in Tasmania, who did not, and was executed amidst some sorrow in 1826. Their behaviour may have been matters of class and personal habit, rather than a memory of the Duval tradition, but for all these competitors it was the French original who remained the benchmark. To the poet Leigh Hunt he was the "eternal feather in the cap of highway gentility." Francis Marryat, a son of the noted naval officer and novelist, referred in his *Mountains and Molehills*, published in 1855, to a Californian road agent who accosted a traveller "with the politeness of a Claude Duval."

When the writers of rambling Victorian novels, penny bloods, plays and poems later conferred heroic status on highwaymen, and turned their adventures into a money-spinning industry that bewitched generations, they did not do so by adhering to historical accuracy. Their highwayman was not the fearsome lout, pragmatic thief or rough demobilized soldier. He was the gentleman highwayman artfully fashioned and manipulated by Claude Duval and others, willing to spice their rebellious derring-do with traits of nobility. The highwayman as super-hero was by and large a wayward knight errant, defending women rather than abusing them, and ever ready to assist the unfortunate. He was a gross embellishment of history in almost every way, but drew his only thread of credibility from the tradition popularised by Duval.

Some of the historical characters used by the Victorians had to be considerably rehabilitated to fit this new mould. The best example is that of Richard Turpin, a notorious highwayman of the early eighteenth century who was eventually hanged in York in 1739 for horse stealing. The historical Turpin, we may allow, had measures of courage and ability, but there was little in his character that smacked of romance, gallantry or gentility, as his indefatigable biographer, Derek Barlow, has established. Unprepossessing in appearance, he won his initial notoriety as a member of the Gregory gang, a brutal band of housebreakers, happy to further their aims by terrifying and torturing elderly residents and raping housemaids. Turpin then developed an extremely busy career in highway robbery, but there is nothing to suggest an intrinsic change of character. By writing the novel *Rookwood*, published in 1834, William Harrison Ainsworth ultimately succeeded in turning him into the most famous of all English highwaymen, but only by recasting his character in the nobler frame and pilfering the alleged exploits of predecessors.

In some respects, therefore, it was Duval and his band, almost lost to history, who established the iconic image of the English highwayman. In them the myth of the gentleman thief found its most memorable expression, and in them originated the two most mythological stories of the road. One, of course, was Duval's dance on the heath, with all its attendant romantic connotations; the other the equally storied ride from London to York, which enshrined the thrilling picture of fast riding and noble steeds that was also at the core of the heroic image. In Ainsworth's *Rookwood* the ride was attributed to Turpin, whose fictional relationship with Black Bess became a classic statement of the bond between man and horse. It became the cornerstone of the rise of Turpin the hero. Yet other writers linked the ride with the late seventeenth-century robber John Nevison, but the story, like that of the dance, actually originated with the Duval band.

The two original accounts of it, supplied by Alexander Smith's *History* (1713) and Daniel Defoe's *Tour Thro' the Whole Island of Great Britain* (1724), unequivocally attributed the ride to Swiftnicks, who, as we have already noticed, briefly remained at large after the execution of Claude Duval. In both versions the highwayman rode from the London area to York in a single day in order to establish an alibi for a robbery. Swiftnicks is one of the most interesting of Duval's associates. Duval's death left him the most wanted highwayman in the realm, but he secured a pardon and undertook a new career in the army. He did not forget all his old friends, however. A pamphlet entitled *Jackson's Recantation*, published in 1674, gives us the full name of Swiftnicks. The tract was a confessional narrative by Francis Jackson, a highwayman, entrusted to his "friend" Samuel Swiftnicks "a little before [Jackson's] execution." The title-page and a postscript to the work lead to the conclusion that Swiftnicks visited his old comrade in prison and assumed the responsibility of feeding his narrative to a printer.

Alexander Smith, who gave a brief account of Swiftnicks, was an unreliable chronicler whose supposedly historical accounts were frequently the products of unfettered imagination. Sometimes, however, he gleaned snippets of genuine information. The little he has to say of Swiftnicks contains the famous ride from London to York. According to Smith,

Swiftnicks committed "several most notorious robberies on the road" in partnership with a "Richard Dudley" – although the details he gives of *this* Richard Dudley's trial at the Old Bailey and his execution at Tyburn on 22 February 1681 finds no corroboration whatsoever in the Old Bailey sessions records. More particularly, Smith told how Swiftnicks made the famous ride to establish an alibi. On some unstated date the highwayman left Bosom's Inn in London and robbed a "gentleman" near Barnet "about five in the morning," taking about 560 guineas. By six in the evening he appeared on a bowling-green in York. According to this story, Swiftnicks eventually quitted his rascally career and "was made a captain in Lord Moncastle's regiment in Ireland, where he married a [lady of] great fortune." Smith seemed confused about the highwayman's name. At one point he described him as "Mr. Nicks, otherwise called Swiftnicks," and at another ventured the erroneous theory that "Swift" was appended to "Nicks" as a sobriquet commemorating his famous ride, conferred by no less a person than King Charles II himself!

Smith's account is a cocktail of balderdash and history. He had some facts right. It is evident, for example, that Swiftnicks did square himself with the authorities and receive a pardon, although it was almost certainly in return for supplying information. And he did subsequently serve as an army captain in Ireland. In a letter of July 1687 a correspondent informed Sir Ralph Verney that it was "said that Capt. Swiftnix, who in Ireland would not deliver his commission to the Lord-General," had been "cut to pieces" and killed by a gang of fifteen or sixteen men. "He was formerly a highwayman in England," the writer added.

But the ride itself, through which Swiftnicks achieved his lasting fame, must have been at least a fierce exaggeration if not an absolute fable. In 1724 Daniel Defoe also related the story of the ride of Swiftnicks in his *Tour Thro' the Whole Island of Great Britain*, and as his account is the most detailed we have I will give it verbatim:

"From Gravesend we see nothing remarkable on the road but Gad's Hill, a noted place for robbing of seamen after they have received their pay at Chatham. Here it was that the famous robbery was committed in the year 1676 or thereabouts. It was about four a clock in the morning when a gentleman was robbed by one Nicks on a bay mare, just on the declining part of the hill, on the west side, for he swore to the spot and to the man.

Mr. Nicks, who robbed him, came away to Gravesend, immediately ferried over, and, as he said, was stopped by the difficulty of the boat and of the passage near an hour, which was a great discouragement to him, but was a kind of bait [relief] to his horse. From thence he rode cross the county of Essex, through Tilbury, Hornden [Horndon] and Bilerecay [Billericay] to Chelmsford. Here he stopped about half an hour to refresh his horse, and give him some balls; from thence to Braintre [Braintree], Bocking, Wethersfield; then over the downs to Cambridge, and from thence keeping still the cross roads, he went by Fenny Stanton [Fenstanton] to Godmanchester and Huntington [Huntingdon], where he baited himself and his mare about an hour; and, as he said himself, slept about half an hour, then holding on the north road, and keeping a full larger gallop most of the way, he came to York the same afternoon, put off his boots and riding clothes, and went dressed as if he had been an inhabitant of the place, not a traveller, to the bowling-green, where, among other gentlemen, was the Lord Mayor of the city. He, singling out his Lordship, studied to do something particular that the Mayor might remember him by, and accordingly lay some odd bet with him concerning the bowls then running, which should cause the Mayor to remember it the more particularly, and then takes occasion to ask his Lordship what a clock it was; who, pulling out his watch, told him the hour, which was a quarter before or a quarter after eight at night. Some other circumstances, it seems, he carefully brought into their discourse, which should make the Lord Mayor remember the day of the month exactly, as well as the hour of the day.

"Upon a prosecution which happened afterwards for this robbery, the whole merit of the case turned upon this single point: the person robbed swore as above to the man, to the place, and to the time in which the fact was committed, namely that he was robbed on Gad's Hill in Kent on such a day and at such a time of the day, and on such a part of the hill, and that the prisoner at the bar was the man that robbed him. Nicks, the prisoner, denied the fact, called several persons to [vouch for] his [good] reputation, alleged that he was as far off as Yorkshire at that time, and that particularly, the day whereon the prosecution swore he was robbed, he was at bowls on the public green in the city of York, and to support this, he produced the Lord Mayor of York to testify that he was so and that the Mayor acted so and so with him there as above. This was so positive, and so well attested, that the jury acquitted him on a bare supposition that it was impossible the man could be at two places so remote on one and the same day."

Of Smith's tale that "Nicks" was pardoned by the king and dubbed by him "Swift Nicks" on account of the ride, Defoe was aware, but pointedly remarked that these particulars "I do not take upon me to affirm." In other words, he rightly doubted their veracity. Nevertheless, he allowed the ride itself to pass unscathed. That Swiftnicks was capable of serious horsemanship is not to be doubted, but as a recent commentator has remarked the feat as described is impossible. In recent times the state of California has regularly staged an endurance one-hundred mile horse race known as the Tevis Cup, and to date none of the contestants has completed the course in less than ten and a half hours. And yet Defoe asked us to believe that Swiftnicks traversed twice that distance in some thirteen hours.

We might accept that the story could have had *some* historical foundations. It is possible to believe that Swiftnicks covered exceptional distances by changing mounts along the way, or in substantially more time than reported; far more likely he invented or embellished the story himself, in an effort to explain the pardon he eventually received from the king in 1670, a pardon that was almost certainly won less gloriously by betraying associates. But, as given, the famous ride from London to York has to be taken with the proverbial grain of salt.

Nevertheless, that contemporaries of Swiftnicks believed him capable of such a ride is an indication of the metal they ascribed to his character. Whatever really happened, the great ride passed into the lore of the road, along with Duval's dance, and fiction writers later creamed both for their dramatic potential, creating from the two core dramas the legend of the English highwayman. That they originated with the same "knot" of seventeenth-century robbers is a further illustration of its role in the mythology of outlawry.

This was by no means a one-way process, however. Just as Duval and his accomplices furnished meat for the legends of subsequent highwaymen, so their myths had accrued some of the doings of men before them. As we shall see, the apocryphal story of Duval himself would gather the royalist credentials of the earlier highwayman James Hind. For the history of the French "kickshaw" did not end in the churchyard of St. Giles-in-the-Fields in 1670, nor indeed with the passing of all his contemporaries. He returned to transfix generations of readers and viewers then unborn.

8

The Eternal Feather

The new reading public of Victorian Britain loved stories of highwaymen. By then the breed was effectively extinct. Although the tradition had transferred to Australia, where it was turning such 'wild colonial boys' as Frank Gardiner, Ben Hall and Johnny Gilbert into local legends, it had largely been suppressed in the mother country, where faster communications and improved law enforcement were taking hold. However, as the home-grown highwayman slid into the past, the pain and trouble he had caused tended to be forgotten, allowing the opportunities his story afforded for thrilling, simple and sprawling tales of adventure to be the better exploited. Yet to become literary heroes the highwaymen also had to be sanitized, and it was the daring and chivalry of a Claude Duval that marked their new character in fiction.

These developments must be seen against the growth in population, urbanization and the market for literature during that period. Between 1801 and 1911 the human population of England, Scotland and Wales almost quadrupled, from 10½ million to almost 41 million. There was a concomitant shift from rural to urban living. At the beginning of the nineteenth century the majority of people lived rural lives, but in 1851 a little more than half resided in towns, and by 1901 that proportion had increased to more than three-quarters. Scholars are divided on the vicissitudes of literacy at this time. In the earlier nineteenth century it seems that a rise of literacy in rural areas may have been offset by a fall in the developing industrial regions, but throughout the Victorian and Edwardian periods there was a steady growth, with the 1870 education act, facilitating state funded and eventually compulsory education, driving towards an almost universal literacy. The growing population and levels of literacy were a double-fillip to the popular press, and an unprecedented demand for literature, including cheap publications for working class and younger people, was generated. The growth of towns also expanded the theatre, which proliferated throughout the provinces by means of touring companies, and in 1900 there were architects exclusively specializing in theatre design. It was these changing circumstances, with a flowering culture of their own, that embraced Claude Duval and the image of the highwayman that he represented.

There had, of course, been an early picaresque tradition that dealt in entertaining stories of roguery, but it was probably *The Newgate Calendar*, first published in 1773, that initially prompted the extraordinary appetite that developed for tales, even fictitious ones, of real-life malefactors. Andrew Knapp and William Baldwin edited a popular new edition between 1824 and 1826. In a growing market better writers turned those skeletal accounts into more elaborate works of fast-moving fiction, and two phenomenally popular novels in particular set the trend, Edward Bulwer-Lytton's *Paul Clifford* (1830) and William Harrison Ainsworth's *Rookwood* (1834).

Bulwer-Lytton's purposes included a tilt at the savage penal code, which in his view combined with cruel social environments to create, rather than to reduce, crime. His novel was in part a call for legal reform. But to win the sympathy of his readers, his outlaw hero had not only to be driven haplessly into a world of crime, but also to embody admirable traits. Not surprisingly, Paul Clifford is a gentleman highwayman who wins the heart and hand of a lady, Lucy Brandon.

The hero of Ainsworth's debut novel, *Rookwood*, was the eighteenth-century highwayman, Dick Turpin. Historically, Turpin had won deserved notoriety. Acting alone or with one or two companions, he was dangerous, daring and elusive, and in a remarkably short time became the most infamous road agent of his time. But there was little chivalry in this ruthless desperado, and Ainsworth had first to polish him into the hue of a Hind or Duval in order to render him an acceptable hero. Thus duly rehabilitated, his fictional Turpin was a gentleman; indeed, said he, the "real highwayman would consider himself disgraced if he did not conduct himself in every way like a gentleman."

That this freely borrowed the outfit of a more attractive seventeenth-century predecessor was baldly admitted by the novelist. Ainsworth supplied the desirable pedigree. His Turpin, he said, was the last in a line of gentleman highwaymen created by Claude Duval. "With him [Turpin] expired the chivalrous spirit which animated successively the bosoms of so many knights of the road; with him died away that passionate love of enterprise [and] that high spirit of devotion to the fair sex, which was first breathed upon the highway by the gay, gallant Claude Du-Val, the Bayard of the road – *le filou sans puer et sans reproche.*" As was mentioned earlier, the word 'gay' was here used in its historic sense as a synonym of 'blythe' or 'cheerful' and thus linked the Frenchman with the 'merry men' tradition associated with Robin Hood or the hearty roars of Alexandre Dumas's three musketeers. The characterization of Duval as a carefree adventurer full of merriment and laughter would endure until the 1950s.

In one sense Ainsworth's cleansing of Dick Turpin went beyond Duval, who for all his aversion to violence remained nevertheless a compulsive thief ready to threaten victims with injury or death. In fashioning a new beau ideal of highway robbery for a growing reading public, Ainsworth trivialized Turpin's misdeeds, which were characterized as merry pranks, and legitimized his violence by directing it against such villains of his tale as the eponymous Rookwood family, depicted as a "monster race." But the novelist had unearthed more than a new personality from Turpin's seventeenth-century mentors. For extra measure, the novelist purloined the fictitious ride from London to York – the original property of Samuel Swiftnicks – to inject the necessary derring-do.

Thus rearmed with the legendary persona and feats of seventeenth-century forebears and more, Ainsworth's Dick Turpin rode furiously and fearlessly into the future. *Rookwood* was a great success, and effectively launched the Victorian fad for stories of heroic highwaymen. The novelist's historical acrobatics, fusing the panache and manners of Claude Duval with the benevolent gallantry of St. George and the Lone Ranger, defenders of the weak and abused, had created a figure no real highwayman by definition could ever have been. He became a shining knight of the road, shorn of his more disreputable traits. Turpin was set firmly upon a fictional career that placed him among the most legendary rogues of British history.

Indeed, in the swath of stories that followed *Rookwood*, Turpin, Jack Sheppard and Claude Duval became the first modern British boys' mass-media 'super-heroes,' the veritable ancestors of the comic-book fantasy figures so beloved today. In yarns replete with unbelievable deeds they righted wrongs and punished the wrong-doers with breathtaking speed. They confronted villains of every description, from old-fashioned tyrants, crooked landlords and wicked uncles to spectres and secret societies of malignant masked miscreants. If today boys and boys-at-heart hungrily devour comics and pack cinemas to follow the entirely fabulous adventures of Spiderman, Cat Woman and Superman, so young Victorians and Edwardians were enthralled by penny novels about Turpin, Sheppard and Duval, and even their elders filled theatres to see the latest visual presentations. In one sense it recalled the 'rhymes of Robin Hood' circulated orally in the Middle Ages by troubadours in baronial halls and market places, but this new phenomena was empowered by the growing numbers of the literate and the means to disseminate information. Nothing quite like this avalanche of tall heroes in tall tales had occurred before.

But if the shadow of Duval, or at least Duval as he had tried to present himself, lurked behind this new wave of outlaw literature, influencing the colours in which its highway heroes were painted, more direct employment was needed to extricate that particular individual from the fog of seventeenth-century history and relocate him beside Turpin in the new literary pantheon. As the subject of romance Claude Duval did not lack promise; in some respects his story almost begged fictional embellishment. It harked backwards to the fascination with perilous liaisons between outlaws and fashionable ladies that had given the rolling legend of Robin Hood his Maid Marian, and forwards to the salacious flirtations that would fuel twentieth-century bodice-ripping novels and movie screenplays. Its seventeenth-century context, an age of the masquerade, when men and women used masked balls to deceive, hide and assume multiple personalities, added to the opportunities it afforded romantic novelists.

Yet as the Victorian fad for stories of the road developed, Duval made a slow start. In the wake of the great success of *Rookwood*, Ainsworth proposed writing similar romances about two other celebrated old-time criminals, Jack Sheppard and Claude Duval. *Jack Sheppard* duly appeared in 1839, elevating the novelist's reputation to even loftier heights, but at this time his *Claude Du Val* stumbled. Ainsworth's interest in Duval's story had already been broadcast. Readers of *Rookwood* were left in no doubt that Duval was a unique gallant, "smartly rigged out, all velvet and lace," who "took a purse with the air and grace of a receiver-general," and reduced women to tears of desire. In one of his various prefaces to the different editions of the novel, Ainsworth pronounced the "chivalrous" French highwaymen "the gayest minion of the moon." In *Jack Sheppard* the hero, like the Turpin of *Rookwood*, viewed Duval as a mentor. In idle moments young Jack carved verses about the Frenchman on the beams of the house in which he was serving a frustrating apprenticeship. In both novels, therefore, Claude Duval was represented as the great precursor.

Yet for some reason Ainsworth put his full romance about *Claude Du Val* on the back-burner for thirty or so years, and it was not until 1870 that it was finally published under the title, *Talbot Harland: A Tale of the Days of Charles the Second*. In truth, there was little to distinguish it from the hack literature that had been appearing on Duval since Ainsworth's heyday at the dawn of the Victorian period. The central figure in a romance not overmuch concerned with history, Duval emerges as the usual audacious thief redeemed by charm and nobility of nature. In this story his dancing partner is Dorinda Neville, a niece of Lady Muskerry, from whom the highwayman begs permission for a moonlit "gaillarde," an episode, of course, that provided the volume with its frontispiece. Continuing, we learn that the most famous figures in the realm, including the Duchess of Cleveland, the Duke of Buckingham and the king himself, are held up by the daring outlaw, but in the closing pages of the book the hero receives a mortal wound. With a final bravado, he determines to die with his boots on, and spurs his horse into a deep morass that encloses man and beast in a death grasp. And a thief of hearts to the last, he is followed by a smitten female, who plunges into the quagmire after him. "Leave you! Never!" she cries, "I am yours in life, as in death!" With a belated nod towards history, Ainsworth would have us believe that "a miserable pretender" was hanged in Duval's place at Tyburn to save the blushes of the cheated establishment.

Ainsworth has been variously assessed. For some he was a literary talent never fully developed, and for others nothing more than a lucky hack. *Talbot Harland* was an indifferent piece of work, but it might have had greater impact had it been published in the days when the novelist was at his professional peak. As it was it merely marked another step down in a career that was already slumping towards oblivion. However, in that intervening period, between *Jack Sheppard* and *Talbot Harland*, Duval had paid dividends of a kind to other writers who happily stepped into the void left by the hesitating Ainsworth.

Despite the slow progress of Ainsworth's *Du Val*, interest in the highwayman seems to have been regathering as early as the 1830s. *The New York Mirror* devoted an extensive biographical sketch to him in February 1839, and since the paper was devoted to literature and the arts it may have reflected a new mood. One of the first concrete indications of the revival of interest was to be seen on the stage that year. J. B. Buckstone, who turned Ainsworth's *Jack Sheppard* into an immensely popular play in 1839, tweaked the public's memory of the earlier rogue in song:

"When Claude du Val was in Newgate thrown,
He carved his name on the dungeon stone."

But the first significant piece that treated Duval in his own right appears to have been a one-act thirty-minute play, *Claude Duval, the Ladies' Highwayman, A Farce*, written by Thomas P. Taylor. It premiered at the City of London Theatre on 8 May 1842, with Miss Ellen Daly in the title role, garishly attired in a "green velvet riding doublet, handsomely trimmed with silver, hanging shirt over trunks, high yellow boots with spurs, ringlets, white lace neck-cloth, ruffles, sword, [and a] hat trimmed with gold lace and feathers." In those days it was still common for a woman to portray the leading man in a production. The eponymous hero's misdeeds were largely overlooked, but of course there was a lady to court and defend, in this case one Julia. Taylor's was, allegedly, an "immensely popular drama." Certainly it was revived at the Queen's Theatre in London on 13 December 1845, with another lady, a Miss Rogers, in the main role, and the addition of divers songs. And as late as 1885 Taylor's play was being reprinted as a nine-page pamphlet in John Dick's series of "standard plays" Whatever its merits, it fed upon a rising appetite for Duval.

Further evidence of this last was an original work created by Sir Theodore Martin ('Bon Gaultier') and W. Edmondstoune Aytoun, two eminent balladeers, sometime between 1842 and 1844. Ostensibly satirizing the growing popularity of highwaymen heroes, "The Death of Duval" made a fair fist of imagining the emotions that had run that day the French outlaw perished at Tyburn. The poets used excusable license when they had scores of eager spectators perishing in the crush of the tens of thousands who crowded the streets to see the death cart pass or fought for a place at the gallows themselves:

> "A living sea of eager human faces,
>   A thousand bosoms throbbing all as one,
> Walls, windows, balconies, all sorts of places,
>   Holding their crowds of gazers to the sun.
>   Through the hushed groups low buzzing murmers run;
> And on the air, with slow reluctant swell,
> Comes the dull funeral boom of old Sepulchre's bell.
>
> With step majestic to the cart advances
>   The dauntless Claude, and springs into his seat.
> He feels that on him now are fixed the glances
>   Of many a Briton bold and maiden sweet,
>   Whose hearts responsive to his glories beat.

In him the honour of 'the Road' is centred,
And all the hero's fire into his bosom entered.

His laced cravat, his kids of purest yellow,
    The many-tinted nosegay in his hand,
His large black eyes, so fiery, yet so mellow,
      Like the old vintages of Spanish land,
      Locks clustering o'er a brow of high command,
Subdue all hearts and, as up Holborn's steep
Toils the slow car of death, e'en butchers weep."

Another socially acceptable Duval appeared as the principal hero of Emma Robinson's three-volumed novel, *Whitefriars, Or, The Days of Charles II* (1844), which introduced such historical villains as Judge George Jeffreys and Colonel Thomas Blood as the highwayman's opponents. Both Jeffreys and Blood would become regular characters in the literature of Claude Duval, although neither had anything to do with him in life. That it was an authoress, rather than a male writer, in this case the daughter of an Oxford Street bookseller, who launched Duval's new literary career was singularly appropriate. But hard on the heels of *Whitefriars* thundered Henry Downes Miles, a journalist who published *Claude Du Val, a Romance of the Days of Charles II* (1850) in 28 penny numbers, spurred by the "hope of fame and profit." A bulky novel with footnotes, the new work displayed a considerable knowledge of French history, and about half of its action took place in that country. Miles, like Robinson, retained Duval's reputation for courage and courtesy, but unlike the earlier writer, he socially ennobled the hero by making him the abandoned progeny of a member of the aristocracy. Indeed, here he commences his career as a page boy in the court of Louis XIV. Again Colonel Blood dutifully appears, this time as a one-time associate of the highwayman who turns into his foil.

Robinson and Miles may have failed to repeat the extraordinary success of Bulwer-Lytton and Ainsworth, but they were not without their fans. In fact, a three-act opera, *Claude Duval, the Highwayman of Holloway*, based upon the Miles book, opened at Sadler's Wells on 27 April 1865. The production was sufficiently popular to go on tour. It opened at Yarmouth on 12 May 1866, when the part of Duval, acted by a Mr. Collins in London, now fell to J. S. Beckitt, and that of his paramour, Lady Howard, to Helen Paget.

Emma Robinson had to wait rather longer for *Whitefriars* to transfer to the stage, but it was apparently the inspiration of W. Thompson Townsend's "new historical drama," *Whitefriars, or, Claude Duval, the Dashing Highwayman*, which opened at the Royal Pavilion Theatre in London in July 1862 with a J. H. Richards assuming the guise of the French rogue. This play was also successful abroad. In October 1864 it was introduced to the Royal Victoria Theatre in Sydney, Australia, as an "entirely new historical drama in three acts, full of powerful situations and effects, entitled *Claude Duval, Notorious Highwayman of the 16th* [sic] *Century*," with one J. Rayner in the title role. Six years later it was running to "crowded houses nightly" at the Theatre Royal, Rockhampton, in Queensland, Australia, now under the title of *Whitefriars, or the Days of Claude Duval.* If we recall the title of Robinson's book – *Whitefriars, Or, the Days of Charles II* – it will be concluded that Duval's name had become a bigger box office draw than that of the Merry Monarch himself. When the "great historical drama" ended its run in Rockhampton on 5 April 1870 it was pointed out in the local press that "notwithstanding the genuine success of this drama, it will positively be withdrawn after tonight in order to allow for the production of other novelties now in preparation."

Yet it was none of these authors or dramatists who was responsible for the huge public appetite for a revitalised Duval that marked the middle of the nineteenth century, when hundreds of English penny bloods and American 'dime-novels' turned him into a household name on both sides of the Atlantic. The perpetrator has, unfortunately, never been satisfactorily identified. Suspicion originally fell upon Elizabeth Caroline Grey (1798-1867), whose roles as the proprietor of a girls' school and authoress of several 'silver fork' novels about fashionable life seem an ill fit for such hack work. Today informed opinion prefers to credit all three of the crucial titles to James Malcolm Rymer (1814-1884), a noted writer of cheap blood-and-thunder literature for boys.

What cannot be disputed is the success of the three works on Claude Duval that are now being attributed to Rymer. These books were distinguished not only by their huge size but also for their astonishing popularity in Britain and America. Although they were primarily targeted on working-class adventure-seeking boys, they quickly showed that they could command a more universal appeal, and that men and young and old female readers were not immune to their appeal. They enjoyed a great advantage over the more orthodox novels, which were widely published in relatively expensive parts. Ainsworth's *Jack Sheppard*, for example, ran to fifteen one-shilling parts even in the cheapest edition. By comparison the new *Duval* numbers, printed upon cheap paper, imposed little strain upon modest pockets.

First off the press was *Gentleman Jack, or, Life on the Road*, published by Edward Lloyd of London in 205 parts between 1848 and 1852. An omnibus edition of 1852 extended to 744 crowded pages. A fictional life of Duval, it entirely dispensed with the history, excepting only that the hero was a daring highwayman with an interest in women, and that he once danced a minuet with a lady traveller, an incident here located on Ealing Common. This despite the claim that "many of the surprising adventures of Claude Duval herein mentioned are perfectly authentic." The novel opens in 1780, in the reign of George III, more than a century after the real highwayman's death. Claude and his sister May appear as children, threatening revenge upon one Sir Lionel Faversham, "who [had] persecuted our poor father to death, and yet knew his innocence." Apparently Faversham had framed the senior Duval, whose body hung from a gibbet under which his orphaned children make their fearsome pledge. Without delay Claude disposes of Faversham with a pistol shot, and takes to the road, where he learns the tricks of the highwayman's trade from Sixteen-String Jack Rann (a real character, but one hanged in 1774). After many adventures, in chapter 137 Duval acquires Dick Turpin as his sidekick, although historically that outlaw had perished on a York gallows in 1739.

For the most part Duval lives up to his reputation in *Gentleman Jack*. He quickly fledges as the premier highwayman of his time, renowned for remarkable deeds and a chivalrous nature. When Cicely Brereton, whom he later marries, is stopped on the highway and protests that she has no more money than the small amount that she has already reluctantly revealed, the hero accepts her word and retorts, "That is sufficient. I have the honour, ladies, to wish you good night." Duval raises Cicely's hand and kisses it. But his image is not entirely true-blue, for in other pages we find the highwayman deserting Lucy, "the young girl who had for a time held the unenviable post of Duval's mistress." So stricken was she with the loss of her dashing paramour that she commits suicide.

Gentleman Jack was a top seller, and the publishers were soon claiming that it had "attained an amount of popular favour never before experienced in the annals of periodical literature," and were issuing an omnibus edition. It seems to have prompted a theatrical production that played at the Marylebone Theatre to "overflowing houses" in 1868, and there were reprints of the novel as late as the twentieth century. Not surprisingly, given the book's success, there was an immediate follow-up, another monstrous farrago of derring-do, furious rides and rescues from the house of Edward Lloyd entitled *Claude Duval, the Dashing Highwayman, A Tale of the Road* (circa. 1850), which ran through 202 parts and totalled 1614 pages.

True to form, in this new opus Duval debuts in the first chapter valiantly rescuing a sixteen-year-old girl from a forced marriage. The defences of womanhood, however, are mixed with several sexual liaisons and the same infidelity that had appeared in *Gentleman Jack*. But Duval looks and usually acts in the heroic mould. "Tall and slim of figure, with remarkably small feet, and the most feminine looking hands that could at all look manly," he stood "so fine, so airy and so graceful...His eyes were of the dark and sparkling hazel...and his long silken lashes might have been a proud appendage for a court beauty. His coal black hair...flowed down his back in massive folds rather than curls. His dress was a rich one...At his side hung a sword with a jewelled hilt, but the sparkle of its gems was nothing to be compared to the brilliancy of the rings that adorned his fingers, and the diamond that held together the folds of a long laced cravat..." An "apparition" of "manly grace" he "did not appear to be above twenty-two." No doubt many of the charmed readers were relieved to find that at the end of the book their hero finally escaped with his girl friend and a trusty follower named Luke and settled in Holland.

If anything, *Claude Duval* even outsold *Gentleman Jack*, according to the testimony Abel Heywood, a Manchester dealer, gave to a House of Commons Select Committee in 1851. Heywood kept meticulous records of his sales, and was able to list the sixteen most popular penny bloods of the day. Most had sold between 50 or 350 copies each in his shop. The two exceptions were *Gentleman Jack*, which had notched up 400 sales, and *Claude Duval*, which was running at 550. "A great many boys read that," Heywood said of the latter, "and grown-up people as well as boys buy it." The eagerness with which each episode of these printed dramas was swooped upon by hungry fans was not unlike the excitement that some modern television viewers feel at the approach of weekly diets of dramatised serials or 'soap' sagas.

If Rymer had authored these two sprawling adventure tales, he switched publishers for his final contribution, which was issued by the rival London firm of John Dick about 1865. *Nightshade, or, Claude Duval, the Dashing Highwayman* ran to 60 parts, and consisted of 203 chapters, 488 double-columned pages and 60 engravings by F. Gilbert. This story, which for most of its course ran to expectations, was brought to an abrupt end when Rymer sank his heroes in a boat in the Thames, a termination which suggests that he had more pressing engagements and needed to abort the project. However, readers relished the rescues of more maidens, of which the first is a Lucy Everton, an innocent scooped from the scaffold at the eleventh hour. In this story the flashily dressed knight of the road with the gold-hilted sword is accompanied by a "glossy black" steed of prodigious strength and stamina, the 'Nightshade' of the title. Nightshade, of course, was a literary descendant of Black Bess, the horse that Ainsworth had furnished Dick Turpin in *Rookwood*.

All three of these works extended Duval's fame to the United States, where they were reprinted as a series of cheap novels by Robert M. De Witt of New York in the fifties and sixties. His 'Claude Duval' and 'Nightshade' series, based upon the *Gentleman Jack*, *Claude Duval* and *Nightshade* books, ran to thirty-eight titles, almost all amounting to 100 pages apiece and retailing at twenty-five cents. They included *Claude and the Abbess, or, A Night in the Nunnery*; *Black Bess, or, Claude to the Rescue*; *The Highwayman's Bride; Claude in a Convent*; *Duval Denounced, or, the Haunted Mansion*; *The Struggle for Life, or, Claude and the Skeleton Horseman*; and *Claude in the Cave, or, The Chamber of Death*. In these, as in the English originals, the hero was the defender rather than the pursuer of women; in *Rosa Bell, the Prince's Victim, or Duval in a Boarding School*, for instance, the highwayman foils a "heartless libertine" and rescues an "innocent girl."

These American novels were extremely successful. Some were still being reprinted in the 1870s, and De Witt was by no means the only publisher who dealt in them. About 1860 William B. Dick and Lawrence R. Fitzgerald of New York published a rehash of *Claude Duval, the Dashing Highwayman* called *The Life and Adventures of Claude Duval, the Dashing Highwayman, by the author of 'Dick Clinton,' 'Ned Scarlet,' 'Jack Shepherd,' &c.* In this version of the tale Claude was seized drunk and went to the gallows, as history demanded, but his female companion May, struck down by shock or suicide, was buried beside him. Not satisfied with this concoction (one of a series of the 'Lives of Celebrated Highwaymen') the company added "a companion to *Claude Duval*" entitled *Fearless Fred, or the Highwayman's Bride*. Still hungry, Dick and Fitgerald followed with "a thrilling new series" under the umbrella of 'Celebrated Highwaymen and Housebreakers' which included a further title, *Claude Duval and His Companions, or, The Race on the Road*.

In that same American city of New York one of the great dime-novel kings, Norman L. Munro, also ran a series of at least two dozen ten-cent Claude Duval novels about 1873, with such titles as *Claude in Jail, Claude and the Mohocks, Claude and Adele, Claude and the Beauty, Claude and the Ghost* and *Claude and the Prince*. It would seem that both Dick and Fitzgerald and Norman L. Munro found it profitable to rehash the material De Witt had launched upon a rapacious public.

14. Dime Novel Hero: N. L. Munro & Company of New York advertise their
popular series of Claude Duval novels in the 1870s.

By then Duval's name perhaps carried more currency in the United States than that of any other British highwayman. His stellar reputation enabled De Witt to market 'lives' or stories of other outlaws under the name of Claude Duval. Thus the press issued *Roger O'Donnell; or, The Irish Claude Duval*, and William Llewellyn's fanciful tale of Joaquin Murietta, a legendary American bandit, under the more commanding title of *The Claude Duval of California*. Both were published in the 1860s. Other authors and publishers followed suit. Edward L. Wheeler, the creator of the famous dime-novel western hero Deadwood Dick, penned *Wild Ivan, the Boy Claude Duval, or the Brotherhood of Death* (1878), issued as a 'half-dime' novel by Beadle and Adams of New York, perhaps the best known of all publishers of cheap American literature. It was sufficiently popular to run through several editions.

15. Alexander Franklin (Frank) James (1843-1915), the elder of the legendary James brothers, who terrorised the American Midwest in the years that followed the Civil War. Unlike his brother, Jesse, Frank lived into sedate old age. A devotee of the Claude Duval novels, he was said to have regarded the French highwayman as a mentor.

The robber also made cameo appearances as a gallant bravado in other cheap novels of the day, such as *Tom Ripon; or, The Highwayman and Housebreaker*, published by Dick and Fitzgerald of New York in 1863.

In the Middle Ages Robin Hood had been synonymous with daring outlawry, and successors had sometimes been described in documents as "Robinhoods" merely because they were outlaws. Even in modern times we use Robin's name as a shorthand for extraordinary bandits who exhibit some of his mythical facets, and speak of them as "the Robin Hood of" this place or that. Anyone so designated immediately grows in stature by the comparison. The use of Claude Duval's name in exactly the same way in late nineteenth century America, as evidenced in *The Claude Duval of California*, tells us two things: that it had pulling power and sold books, and that Duval had also become an international benchmark of the ultimate outlaw.

No less a writer than Mark Twain (Samuel Langhorne Clemens) recalled for us the effect of this type of literature on the ragged youths who scrambled around his home town of Hannibal, Missouri. One of the heroes of his greatest novel, *The Adventures of Huckleberry Finn* (1884), the rascally Tom Sawyer, gathers his friends to imagine themselves a gang of highwaymen, similar to those found in the "robber books" that were the required reading of the age. One boy innocently asked whether they would be expected to kill women as well as men in their daring new career. "If I was as ignorant as you I wouldn't let on," scoffs know-all Tom. "Kill the women? No. Nobody ever saw anything in the books like that. You fetch them to the cave, and you're always as polite as pie to them, and, by and by, they fall in love with you, and never want to go home any more." However flickering, in this reference to the obligatory courtesy to women, we can see that even here, on the banks of the broad and muddy Mississippi, the myth of Claude Duval worked upon the minds of barefoot boys.

Other American devotees allegedly included the most notorious outlaws in American history, Frank and Jesse James, who, coincidentally, like Mark Twain, hailed from the 'Show Me' state of Missouri. After their gang robbed the gate at the Kansas City Fair one of their apologists published a justificatory note from the outlaws in the *Kansas City Times* of 15 October 1872. The gang-leaders (presumably the James brothers and Cole Younger) signed themselves "Jack Shepherd, Dick Turpin [and] Claude Duval." The older of the James boys, Frank, was considered to be the more bookish and less violent of the two, and in 1881, when both were still at large, John W. Buel, a Missouri newspaper man, characterized him as a particular disciple of the French highwayman. Frank James, wrote Buel, was "a student, being a lover of books and family...He has murdered many men, and yet he is not destitute of mercy, and finds no gratification in deeds of blood. He has tried to imitate the traditions of Claude Duval, whose fictitious adventures Frank has read until he can repeat them like the written narrative."

Frank James may have dreamed himself a Claude Duval, spicing his outlaw daring with chivalric panache, but again the realities of his business were constantly in conflict with the ideal. The string of gratuitous murders that accompanied the robberies of the James Brothers included, for instance, the deliberate slaughter of an unarmed and injured book-keeper, shot during the famous raid on the Northfield bank in Minnesota in 1876. Needless to say, however, even the catalogue of such outrages as this also prompted comparisons with the doings of Duval and other notorious outlaws. After Jesse's death *The New York Illustrated Times* of 22 April 1882, as if proud of its home-grown talent, declared that "Claude Duval, Robin Hood and Brennan-on-Moor" were "effeminate sun-flowered aesthetes" compared to him.

Back in Victorian Britain Claude Duval rode stirrup to stirrup with the refashioned Dick Turpin as the archetypal English highwaymen. Literature was still a major forum for both. No great writer fashioned a work on Duval, although William Makepeace Thackeray's last and unfinished novel, *Denis Duval*, which opened in *The Cornhill Magazine* in 1863 and was published as a posthumous fragment with a glowing introduction by Charles Dickens in 1864, nodded at the legend. "To plague my wife, who does not understand pleasantries in the matter of pedigree," the novel began, "I once drew a fine family tree of my ancestors, with Claude Duval, captain and highwayman, *sus. per. coll.* in the reign of Charles II, dangling from a top branch. But this is only my joke...None of us Duvals have been *suspercollated* to my knowledge." If the eighteenth-century hero of Thackeray's unfinished book took nothing but his name from the seventeenth-century outlaw, the author did show some knowledge of the history of highwaymen by introducing into his narrative the Weston brothers, who had committed a famous mail robbery in 1780.

However, Duval still belonged not to the serious novelists but to the writers of cheap but often colossal bloods. In the 1860s it was Edward Viles, a new hack, who launched some of the fresh serials. A character named 'Claude Duval' was a subsidiary figure in his *Black Bess, or the Knight of the Road*, although here it was expressly stated that this Duval was merely a namesake of the famous highwayman. He had presumably been introduced to avoid disappointing avid fans of the original. Dick Turpin was the principal hero of *Black Bess*, which ran to 254 penny numbers between 1863 and 1868. Viles may have also been the author of the anonymously published *Gentleman Clifford and his White Mare, Brilliant, or, the Ladies' Highwayman* (1866). Although this work resurrected Bulwer-Lytton's hero as its main protagonist, its title alone betrays origins in the literature and legend of Claude Duval.

That said, by then the myth's successful transition to the stage was rapidly becoming its major conduit, as well as the most obvious manifestation of the century's fascination with Duval's story. Unlike the bloods, the theatre principally attracted adult audiences, who proved themselves equally as vulnerable to the old Gallic charmer. But whether patronised by old or young, the plays also had the advantage of being delivered visually and orally. That meant that the illiterate as well as the literate could enjoy them, and that they could reach a much wider audience than the bloods. One theatre production after another tumbled onto the boards, so many and so frequently, indeed, as to suggest a national obsession.

16. A London Playbill of 1868: At the peak of Duval's popularity as a folk hero theatres scrambled to fulfil demand. Here the 'Pavilion' of Whitechapel simultaneously ran two different Duval vehicles. Reproduced by permission of the East London Theatre Archive.

To take one example, we may examine the productions staged in the Royal Pavilion Theatre on Whitechapel Road in East London. In December 1844 the theatre was running *Adventures of Claude Du Val*, featuring such characters as Gregory Green, Gypsy Ralph, Moonlight Mark and Spanking Jack, in its "Illuminated Garden." June 1852 saw the same theatre staging a different vehicle, *Claude Duval, the Dashing Highwayman*, a three-act "romantic drama" that fairly regularly returned to the venue at least until 1868, sometimes (and perhaps always) running as a serial over different nights. The public demand was so great that in October 1868 the Pavilion ran two different Duval productions within days of each other. At that time *Claude Duval, the Dashing Highwayman* had to share the bill with the "first night of Mr. [James] Harwood's original equestrian drama," *Claude Duval*, an entirely separate three-act entertainment. "N.B.," emphasized the playbill, "This is not the drama generally known as the same title." It seemed that the only thing better than one Claude Duval show was an offering of two.

In fact the proliferation of Duval plays makes it difficult to distinguish between the various productions. The popular dramatist William Thomas Moncrieff, whose career revealed a particular interest in horses, highwaymen and bushrangers, created a *Claude Duval* drama that was posthumously staged at the Marylebone Theatre in 1863. Two or so years later Newton Treen Hicks, known as 'Bravo Hicks', was portraying Duval in the Victoria Theatre in London. Back at the Marylebone, another Claude Duval vehicle by W. Travers, perhaps derived from *Gentleman Jack*, was running to "overflowing houses" in 1868. The noted Francis Cowley Burnand's burlesque, *Claude Duval,*

17. Newton Treen Hicks ('Bravo Hicks') as Claude Duval, one of many portrayals of the highwayman on the Victorian stage.

or, the Highwayman for the Ladies, had perky Patty Oliver in the lead role at the Royalty Theatre in January 1869, while November 1870 saw the East London Theatre on Whitechapel Road premiering a new "great drama" entitled *Knights of the Road*, recounting the early days of Duval, Turpin,

Tom King and Jack Rann. Under such a barrage, it was impossible to live in Britain without becoming familiar with such characters as Claude Duval, Dick Turpin and Jack Sheppard. At the turn of the century, however, many children made their first acquaintance with Duval neither on the stage nor in cheap literature, but in the circus. Gillett's Circus, which successfully toured the country with fairs for many years, regularly featured a Claude Duval equestrian act. Since the owners of this renowned entertainment were of French ancestry and specialized in horses and trick riding, the popularity of Claude Duval gave them an obvious additional attraction.

Like a few of the novels, these plays were by no means all unpolluted juvenilia. They would not have won such universal popularity if they had been. True, they all dealt in derring-do, intrigue and old-fashioned romance, but some were capable of reaching the everyday concerns of adult audiences. No one captured the experience of an evening with a Claude Duval play better than the Scottish author George John Whyte-Melville, who devoted a whole chapter to the subject in his satirical novel, *M. or N.* (1869). It is difficult to read his lengthy description of one such production without believing that he was recording something that he had actually seen. His principal *dramatis personae* are a couple named Dorothea and Jim, who visit the theatre to be spellbound by the "strutting and striding about on the part of an overpowering actor in the inevitable belt and boots of the melodramatic highwayman," Claude Duval. But it was the distaff side of the story that added the real bite to this particular drama. Despite a pedestrian wife at home, ignorant of his true profession, Duval develops a relationship with an aristocratic and beautiful lady with whom he dances on a moonlit heath. The triangular playing-away-from home plot struck primarily at adult viewers.

In the novel both spectators are enchanted by the episode on the heath: "'It's beautiful!' whispers Dorothea, refreshing herself with an orange. 'It reminds me of the first time you and me ever met at Highbury Barn.' Jim grunts, but his grunt is not that of a contented sleeper, rather of one who is woken from a dream." For, whilst Dorothea fancies a romantic parallel with her own past, Jim lusts for the aristocratic beauty on the stage, utterly beyond his physical reach. The theme is then developed by the plight of Mrs. Duval, left in her stifling domesticity whilst her husband, unknown to her, pursues his adventurous career. One scene was set in the Duval household. The faithful wife, "leaving a cradle in the background, and advancing to the footlights, proceeds to hover round her husband, after the manner of stage wives, with neck protruded and arms spread out like a woman who is a little afraid of a wasp or earwig, but wants to catch the creature all the same. He sits with his back to her, as nobody ever does sit but a stage husband at home, and punches the floor with his spur. It is strictly natural that she should sing a faint song with a slow movement on the spot."

The gulf between highwayman and wife ultimately steals into the minds of the spectators, for "Dorothea's sympathies, womanlike, are with the wife," whilst Jim finds the homely "part of the performance rather wearisome" and savours more of "the young lady" of the heath. In this play all ends happily enough, for it is the wife who secures the highwayman a pardon and his escape from the gallows, and who, thereby, regains his attentions. However, a difference of opinion still afflicts the spectators:

"Walking home through the wet streets, under the flashing gas-lights, Dorothea and her companion preserve an ominous silence. Both identify themselves with the fiction they have lately witnessed. The woman, pondering on Mrs. Duval's sufferings and the eventual reward of that good lady's constancy and truth, her companion reflecting, not on the charms of the actress he has lately been applauding, but on another face which haunts him now…thinking how a man might well risk imprisonment, transportation, hanging, for one kind glance of those bright eyes, one smile of those haughty, scornful lips, and comparing in bitter impatience that exotic beauty with the humble, homely creation at his side [Dorothea]."

Such evidence as we have indicates that this was not an unmeasured estimate of the impact of the Duval plays upon many audiences. They furnished room for both romance and adventure, and the best could tap into the lives and dreams of their audiences.

Culturally more impressive than any of these avenues of exploitation, was Duval's debut into serious art in 1859. William Powell Frith, then riding a high wave on account of his sprawling narrative paintings, spent most of that year producing his ambitious *Claude Duval*, which was exhibited at the Royal Academy and sold to an art dealer for £1700. Many illustrators and engravers have attempted to interpret the French highwayman's supposed gallantry. In June 1890 *Harper's New Monthly Magazine*, the famous New York periodical, ran a feature on "Chapbook Heroes" illustrated by the eminent artist Howard Pyle. Perhaps the most reproduced of these fresh creations of Pyle showed Duval and three associates halting a coach at a bleak moorland crossroads. Whilst his men subdue the coachman and a footman with drawn pistols, the elegantly dressed leader of the gang raises his feathered hat to exchange a salute with a gentleman passenger inside, presumably before relieving him of his money. The lesser known British illustrator, Charles Crombie, supplied a lively version of Duval's celebrated dance as a frontispiece to Arthur L. Hayward's *Boys Book of Highwaymen* in 1931. But no one treated the subject as definitively as Frith. The creator of such huge canvases as *Ramsgate Sands*, *Derby Day* and *The Railway Station*, Frith is remembered for his accurate depictions of Victorian life. *Claude Duval* is sometimes seen as a diversion into history, and yet from the perspective we have explored, the obsessive reinvention of Claude Duval and other highwaymen in the nineteenth century, we can see that it was as quintessentially Victorian as any of his other paintings, and portrayed what was then a living part of the Victorian imagination.

Inspired by a passage on Duval in Macaulay's *History of England*, Frith went to considerable lengths to authenticate his picture of the dance on the heath, consulting experts about seventeenth-century costumes as well as the coranto, a dance that had long been extinct by the Victorian period. He located an ancient carriage in Cobham Park, from which he modelled the coach of his heroine, whom he named Lady Aurora Sydney. He based his horses on a heavy duty Flanders variety, and reconstructed the heath from suitable locations in Dorset. Working sometimes by gaslight, Frith brought a marked sense of purpose to the composition, convincing himself, as he wrote in his diary, that "I am doing the most successful picture of its class that I have ever done – better in art than the *Derby Day* – but it will not be so popular by a long way." Both Pyle and Frith captured the blend of terror and charm that characterized Duval. At once, coaches were menaced by masked riders brandishing pistols, and treated to the entertainment and compliments of their leader. Frith owned that he had been attracted to "the dramatic character of the subject" and that he "thought if I could succeed in retaining the beauty of the lady combined with the terror that she would feel, I should perform a feat well worthy of achievement."

Frith prophesied correctly when he supposed that *Claude Duval* would not win the popularity of the best of his other paintings. It is not clear whether any copies were made by the artist, but what seems to have been the original was acquired from one James Gresham in 1917 and now hangs in the Manchester City Gallery. An oil painting on canvas, it measures roughly 3 feet 7 inches by five feet. Despite its relatively modest success, compared to Frith's more famous works, it remains (if we set aside Hogarth's representation of *The Beggar's Opera*) the only serious painting ever devoted to the subject of English highway robbery, and was not without an impact. It was one of only three of Frith's paintings that was turned into a living tableau on the stage, in the manner of the "realizations" of art works that were becoming possible and fashionable in a world where audiences were growing and the technical means of creating theatrical effects improving. The tableau of *Claude Duval* appears to have been part of Burnand's *Claude Duval, or the Highwayman for the Ladies* (1869). Reproductions of the painting have also abounded, as engravings, photographic prints, posters and even biscuit-tin lids, and are still commonly encountered today. All were testimony to a creditable attempt to bridge popular and high culture.

Frith's focus on the famous dance was understandable. This story remained the fulcrum of the popular stories about Duval. As far as history, or pseudo-history, was concerned the dancing partners never met again, but in legend the incident commonly signalled the beginning of ongoing relationships that remained at the core of the plot. Sometimes Duval subsequently championed the lady, rescuing her from unwanted predicaments, such as rascally suitors, but oft it was the highwayman himself who courted her in sagas of clandestine and perilous trysts that married the worlds of the road, the great house and the English court. The scene Frith had painted was the prequel to numerous versions on the theme of forbidden friendships and loves between gallant outlaws and aristocratic beauties.

During the last three decades of the nineteenth century, despite increasing public concern about the popularity of historical criminals, there was no discernible decline in the demand for material about Claude Duval. He had become a ubiquitous cultural artefact, appropriate to hack literature, drama, art, equestrian and circus performances and music alike. Among original musical pieces celebrating the famed highwayman were songs by Prince Jozef Poniatowski (1871) and James Lynam Molloy and F. E. Weatherly (1886), a gavotte by Louis Diehl (1876), and a minuet by Annie Emma Armstrong (1883). Both of the last were written for the pianoforte. More ambitiously, a "new" burlesque musical entitled *Claude Du Val*, written for the company of Arthur Roberts, a music hall entertainer, opened with some success in Bristol and London in 1894. A reviewer hinted that the production "consists of Mr. Arthur Roberts and nothing else besides," but admitted that that performer had the "gift of comic realism." As far as the dominance of Roberts was concerned, others seem to have concurred. "Went in carriage with Maud and Roy (driving cob) to the Prince of Wales's Theatre [London] and saw Arthur Roberts in *Claude Duval*," the illustrator, Edward Linley Sambourne, wrote in his diary in 1895. "Burnand, Mrs. B. and Frank in box opposite. A[rthur] R[oberts] very good in barmaid scene."

18. William T. Carleton, a famous American actor, played Duval in the successful 1882 New York run of Solomon and Stephens's *Claude Duval, or Love and Larceny*, a romatic comic opera from D'Oyley Carte.

But unquestionably the most outstanding contribution in this line, and yet another attempt to raise the subject to a more sophisticated level, was Edward Solomon and Henry Pottinger Stephens's three-act romantic comic opera, *Claude Duval, or, Love and Larceny* (1881). The subject was an "excellent" one, opined a newspaper reviewer, although the music was "more in the direction of grand opera than romantic or comic" and the mixture uncertain. Notwithstanding which, the work won considerable if not outstanding popularity in both Britain and the United States. Opening at the Olympia Theatre in London on 24 August 1881, with the famous F. H. Celli portraying Duval, it clocked up fifty-four performances, no mean run. Richard D'Oyly Carte sent it to Scotland, where it played Glasgow, Edinburgh, Aberdeen and Dundee with G. Byron Browne in the title role, and New York, where it opened in March 1882 featuring the celebrated William T. Carleton as the fearless highwayman. Set in 1670, when the real highwayman was in fact dead, it was predictable fare in terms of plot. Duval enjoyed himself befriending a young man swindled out of his estate, and helped him regain his fortune as well as the hand of his beloved, a young lady threatened with an arranged and distasteful marriage. The piece was still being published as late as 1922.

One interesting feature of the later Victorian period was its tendency to return Duval to his own historical time period and to do away with the bloods of the 1850s and early 1860s, which had transported him to the age of George III. Solomon and Stephens had no doubt that they were portraying the reign of Charles II, and the newer 'literary' works galloped happily in the same direction. Along came *Claude Du Val, the Dashing Knight of the Road*, published about the 1870s by A. Richie and Company of London in their 'Paragon Library' of complete penny bloods; and R. J. Lambe's *By Command of the King; or the Days of the Merrie Monarch*, serialised in the *Boys of England* paper from January to April 1883 and subsequently reissued in 12 parts.

The most ambitious of such late nineteenth century works was billed as the "most interesting and thrilling story ever presented to the Boys of Albion." Anonymously authored, *Dashing Duval, or the Ladies' Highwayman* was published by Palmer of London in 18 parts about 1875. The story was set in the 1660s, and the famous dance was not only described but allowed an illustration by H. M. Brock. Beyond that, and allusions to such time markers as Titus Oates, it contained little history. Not for the first time the villain was Colonel Blood, who, despite the assistance of the no less appropriately styled Vampyre Vaughan, failed to triumph. Two of Duval's loyal friends, Paul Clifford and Gentleman Jack, taken straight from earlier works, were eventually allowed to make new lives for themselves on the North American prairies, while the great highwayman himself retired with "his fondly loved Maude" to a Norman chateau to raise "a numerous progeny."

At the close of the Victorian period, Duval was as much the touchstone of his profession as ever, and in 1895, when Fergus Hume ventured a novel about a modern highwayman, he entitled it *Claude Duval of Ninety-Five, A Romance of the Road*. Today, the nineteenth-century fad for stories of these old-time highwaymen seems strange. It fed, of course, upon the rise of a popular press, and the growth of literacy, even among sections of the poorer classes who patronized little more than the penny bloods or 'dreadfuls', as these serials were increasingly called. One reason for their popularity was their simplicity. Unlike tales of national heroes, such as Nelson, Wellington, Gordon or even Drake, they involved no complicated political situations. No difficult historical circumstances had to be mastered to understand them. On the contrary, they dealt largely in the everyday adventures of hearth-sized heroes, who could ride at will, frustrating bullies and bounders, confronting smugglers and spectres, discovering secret caves and spooky houses, and rescuing innocent damsels or the downtrodden as they cantered along on their noble steeds. It was unchallenging escapist fare. The fact that these heroes had all, in life, been predators, sometimes violent predators, was easily obscured in wandering yarns of mystery and adventure.

Some of the more successful subjects had actually possessed usable attributes. Jack Sheppard (1702-24), whose literary afterlife was richer than that of any other product of this 'Newgate' fiction, had been a persistent and remorseless small-time thief. He had also been party to a brutal attack upon a drunken pedestrian, but was not withal an inherently violent man and exhibited the same cheerful demeanour as Duval whilst lingering in prison. And he possessed astonishing ability as a prison-breaker, making bold escapes from the New Prison and Newgate. Claude Duval had also been, in some respects, a disarming villain, able to slip into the character of the 'knight of the road' *par excellence*. The real Dick Turpin, it is true, wore a more difficult complexion, but he was seriously reconstructed for mass consumption. In the fictions that dealt in these individuals attempts were also made to excuse, if not to justify, the lifestyles they adopted. They were usually wronged in some way, perhaps dispossessed or falsely charged, and driven into criminal existences by necessity or revenge.

But even layers of whitewash could not entirely absolve such heroes of a moral ambiguity that raised considerable vocal dissent at the time. The very popularity of the stories, which maximised their influence upon the young, sharpened the criticism. They diverted people from more serious literature, some complained, and much more importantly, they contaminated and criminalized the immature and foolish. This was a period in which crime was generally believed to be on the increase, and if the numbers of people committed for trial in England and Wales are any guide there was probably much truth in it. There was a widespread fear that juvenile crime, in particular, was becoming a serious problem, a fear that fed the movements for ragged and reform schools. Industrialization, poverty and the booms and slumps in manufacturing and agriculture also created considerable unrest and political disquiet. It is impossible to estimate the extent to which these tales of highwaymen reinforced, condoned or triggered deviant tendencies. No doubt it did happen. When the nineteen-year-old James Dinham was questioned in connection with an attack two footpads had made upon a carriage on Blackheath on 28 May 1877, a copy of *Claude Duval, the Dashing Highwayman* was found in his possession. Dinham, with one Thomas Hyslope, was convicted of highway robbery under arms at the Old Bailey on the following 22 October, and both men received seven year prison sentences. Thus, in a strange and ugly legacy, Duval impinged upon the last case of highway robbery to come before the English courts, and the end of Blackheath's notorious connections with that dead trade.

The possible pernicious influence of criminal heroes, especially on the young and poor, became a hot potato before the end of the nineteenth century. In 1864 Henry Mayhew – he of Mayhew's *London* – interviewed 170 London vagrants between the ages of six and thirty-five, and was somewhat perturbed to find that their favourite books were those dealing with Claude Duval, Dick Turpin and Jack Sheppard. Ten years later one James Greenwood was similarly complaining of the "singular and startling fact" that "thousands of young gentlemen varying in years from ten to eighteen, and born and bred in and about the most enlightened city in the world...find their *beau ideal* of a hero not in Lord Nelson or the Duke of Wellington, but in Blueskin, Claude Duval, or some similar ruffian." A man who claimed to have been an inmate in a London workhouse recalled in 1885 the questionable reading material strewn about this grim institution, "a dozen detached numbers of the cheapest illustrated publications – things relating the deeds of Claude Duval, Dick Turpin and other desperadoes" that passed through the hands of even "the youngest inmates." And as late as the 1930s Thomas Okey could still remember an impoverished childhood which he thought had been lightened a little by the "romantic stories of highwaymen" that "circulated freely from boy to boy until reduced to rags," especially those of "the gallant Claude Duval, gracefully dancing with the ladies he had robbed."

In the new century, the twentieth century, the purveyors of the Duval stories began to grapple with the notion that their business was not entirely wholesome, and posit a solution. In that brief Edwardian summer before the First World War the myth was still a marketable force to be reckoned with. In fact it was then that the legend infiltrated what would become one of the nation's most popular poems. Alfred Noyes's "The Highwayman" became more than anything else the classic expression of the romantic, free and fast-riding English outlaw of the open road. The fame of the poem even outlived the other seminal manifestations of the gentleman highwayman myth created by Bulwer-Lytton, Ainsworth and Frith.

About the time Noyes composed his enduring poem, the compilers of august reference works, normally some decades behind popular taste, also began including the 'Newgate' heroes in encyclopaedias and biographical dictionaries. You will not find Claude Duval, Jack Sheppard or Dick Turpin in the sober pages of the ninth edition of *Encyclopaedia Britannica* published at the turn of the century, but the new century thought them entirely worthy of such commemoration. Rightly acknowledging the strong demand for information about historical figures who were now staples of popular entertainment, later editors of *Britannica* relented and opened their literary doors.

And yet the sun was beginning to set on the highwayman hero, and even the enchanting lens supplied by Noyes could not turn back Time. It was perhaps a reflection of the growing controversy about the effects of this literature upon juvenile minds that the interpretation of Duval tended to change as the nineteenth century merged into the twentieth. A political dimension increasingly appeared. Duval became a royalist rebel, valiantly fighting the cause of the Stuart kings during the years of the Civil War and Cromwell's Protectorate. Just as Dick Turpin had successfully imbibed the qualities of more romantic rogues to recommend him to Victorian audiences, so the twentieth century Duval purloined the character of James Hind, the alleged cavalier highwayman of the Civil War period, to further his appeal. Like Hereward the Saxon resisting the minions of William the Conqueror's Normans, and Robin Hood, transformed over time into the champion of the good but absent King Richard, Claude Duval became a patriot, the stalwart enemy of a usurping and undesirable regime. Now he was not outlawed because he found other people's money irresistible, but because he had loyally supported the king against Parliament. In other words, he was a political rebel and worthy hero.

The most important manifestation of this nature was the last of the mountainous works of penny-pinching fiction that had long characterized the subject. This one was issued by the Aldine Publishing Company of London between October 1902 and May 1906. The author was Alfred Sherrington Burrage (1850-1906), who used the pseudonym of 'Charlton Lea' to produce forty-eight *Claude Duval* novels. They were published between dramatic and colourful covers illustrated by Robert Prowse junior, in which the hero almost invariably appeared in a fetching slashed scarlet suit, riding boots and a feathered hat. The success of the series, which built into a single shambling odyssey creaking under its own weight, caused it to be launched overseas, where it also flourished. The rights were purchased by A. Eichler, who issued editions in New York in the United States and in Dresden, Germany, the latter published in 1907 and 1908 as *Claude Duval, Historischer Roman Aus Der Puritanerzeit*. However, arguably Eichler's most successful edition was the French translation by Bernard-Henri Gausseron, *Claude Duval, ou Au Temps des Puritains d'angleterre (Claude Duval, or, the Days of the Puritans of England)*, issued in Paris between 1910 and 1912. Gausseron (1845-1913) was one of France's most accomplished translators, with skills honed on editions of Defoe, Dickens, Goldsmith, Swift and Lewis Carroll, among others, but none of these illustrious tomes demanded the massive commitment that must have gone into reproducing Lea's sprawling epic on Duval. Surviving numbers of these French versions of *Claude Duval* are currently more abundant on the collectors' market than any others of an Aldine series, either in English or a foreign language, which points to the international appeal of their subject.

Lea's stories were supposedly "centred on actual episodes in the life of the Cavalier highwayman," but such instalments as *Strike For the King* and *The Sword of Vengeance, or, How Claude Duval and Prince Rupert Became Comrades*, presented the highwayman as a royalist cavalier, a survivor of the English Civil War continuing the struggle against the victorious Parliamentarians and their damnable curs, including such story-book villains as Judge Jeffreys and Colonel Blood. In the first number, for example, Duval makes the acquaintance of Prince Rupert, the famous cavalier general, whom he disarms in a clash of swords before becoming his firm friend. Duval had thus been shot back a couple of decades in time, where he had metamorphosed into the royalist highwayman, James Hind, making that legend part of his own.

Nor was it the only liberty taken with history, for in Lea's fable Duval was actually Raphael Claude Vallerie, the orphaned son of a French countess, who had been cheated out of his considerable inheritance by an unscrupulous English guardian. Thus, again like Robin Hood, Duval was ennobled and disinherited before being turned into a patriot. His activities were therefore doubly vindicated. He was an avenger seeking common justice as well as a servant of his king. And if Robin had had his Maid Marian, Lea's Duval was obligingly furnished with his own female companion, Diane. Despite these adjustments and an extensive run, the series ended abruptly while another four parts were actually in preparation. Burrage died in Newbury, Berkshire, the same year and his death, and perhaps also illness, accounts for the sudden suspension of the Duval works. However, its success had spawned a "companion" series on Dick Turpin. *Turpin* apparently made less headway than *Duval* on the European continent, but at home it prodigiously outran all of its competitors, trebling the size of its predecessor and turning into one of the most gigantic fictional works ever written upon an historical figure.

In these dying decades of the Duval myth the patriotic cavalier surfaced as often as the renowned ladies' highwayman so beloved by earlier generations. But the trauma of the First World War seemed to draw a veil over many of the pleasures of past times, and the vogue for highwaymen in general quickly ran out of steam. In 1881 a rather snooty reviewer had summarised Duval as "the highwayman of Bulwer Lytton, the polite thief of school-girl fancy [and] the king of the road familiar to boys who read the 'penny dreadfuls' of unscrupulous publishers." But those cohorts of boys who had patronized the wondrous adventures of Duval and his fictional imitators were wasted on the battlefields of Belgium, France and Gallipoli. With the whole generations so mercilessly cut down went the folklore, memories and proclivities they had harboured and perhaps treasured. The culture they had embraced and enjoyed, with its real or fictional heroes, a culture that might, had they lived, been passed to their children, was buried in their graves. This, along with the fast turnover in boys' heroes being created by such new media as the cinema and television, probably accounted for the relatively steep decline of interest in the 'Newgate' school of fiction in the years after the war. By the mid twentieth century names once universally known had been forgotten, and highwaymen had been swept aside by fresh and more compelling figures from World War II, the American 'Wild West', the exploration of Space and the ranks of the cloaked fantasy 'super-heroes' purveyed in American comics. And unlike their pirate brethren, who periodically attempted to reassert themselves against these new waves, the highwaymen seemed incapable of recovery.

There was not five yards now between Claude and Diana and the foremost bloodhound. Unflinchingly he spurred his horse forward for the terrible leap. "Now 'tis life or death!" he cried, as they flew over the abyss.

19. Penny Dreadfuls: Duval as his admirers wanted him to be, the saviour of endangered women. This is a Robert Prowse front cover for Charlton Lea's *Claude Duval*, a penny dreadful that ran to 48 issues between 1902 and 1906.

20. Lea's Duval saga was successfully marketed in London, New York, Dresden and Paris. This is a front-cover from the extremely popular Parisian edition.

As most who remember the mid-twentieth century will confirm, this decline did not affect the old literary heroes equally. Dick Turpin survived as a household name rather longer than either Claude Duval or Jack Sheppard, who some might have deemed historically more attractive personages. All three had made a robust beginning of the twentieth century. But Sheppard had largely been forgotten by the Second World War, despite the isolated book or film that attempted to revive his reputation, while Duval only struggled into the fifties as a regular comic-book and television swashbuckler. Turpin, however, could still be recalled by most Britons at the end of the twentieth century.

Claude Duval McKenna (to Welsh victim). "ROBBING YOU! WHY, I'M LETTING YOU KEEP SIX-AND-EIGHTPENCE IN THE POUND."

21. Political Satire: Liberal Chancellor of the Exchequer, Reginald McKenna, was lampooned as "Claude Duval McKenna" by *Punch* for his 'Stand and Deliver' budgets during the First World War.

The items that were produced on Duval were increasingly forlorn. At the end of the First World War the subject was wearying, but still had some legs to stand upon. The last original drama seems to have been the "romantic play" scripted by the Irish nationalist politician, writer and historian, Justin Huntly McCarthy. His *Stand and Deliver* opened in His Majesty's Theatre in the Haymarket in March 1916 with Arthur Bourchier, a noted actor, as the lead. Bourchier "provided an admirable study of Claude Duval," said one reviewer, and since the highwayman was "a likeable fellow" it was mere "poetic justice...that he should escape the gibbet and marry the lady of his choice," played in this instance by Miss Kyrlo Bellew. The play had a measure of success, it seems. At least, when a Liberal Chancellor of the Exchequer, Reginald McKenna, imposed his famous duties upon the importation of luxuries in 1915 and 1916 he was lampooned for "Stand and Deliver" policies, and derided in *Punch* cartoons as 'Claude Duval McKenna.'

At that time Duval also had a little more mileage left in boys' comics, perhaps the final bastion supporting his legend. Between 9 March and 13 April 1918 six numbers of *Chums*, a boys' favourite comic, ran "With Claude Duval on the King's Highway," written by one David Harold Parry under the pseudonym of 'Morton Pike'. Early in 1924 the same author penned a sequel, "The Night Rider, a Tale of Claude Duval," for *The Popular*, which was also published by The Amalgamated Press of London and proclaimed itself "the finest boys' paper on the market." The comic's editor informed his readers that "the wonderful highwayman serial" was being "extolled sky-high" in his post-bag, but expressed no surprise on that account, for Duval was "a born fighter and a real leader of men...in the rough-and-ready days...when swords were always flashing out of their scabbards." In this new story, set in 1667, Pike had Duval again helping "a sturdy lad of fifteen" to regain his rightful fortune from rascally adults, but he managed to insert an explanatory "historical" account of the hero's real background, drawn entirely from Pope. That Duval was still capable of exciting boys was also evident from his simultaneous appearance in another Amalgamated Press vehicle. In announcing that "another thrilling instalment" of Pike's "powerful serial" could be found in the following week's *Popular*, the editor chipped in the news that "an exciting story introducing Claude Duval [also] appears in this week's *Young Britain*," published on 14 February.

Duval even tottered into the new age of film. The first motion picture to use the story was *Beau Brocade* (1916), based upon a novel of the same name by Emma, Baroness Orczy, published in 1907 and shortly afterwards turned into a play. For her hero the creator of the Scarlet Pimpernel took the name Beau Brocade from an 1892 poem by Austin Dobson. But whereas Dobson's highwayman had nothing but that name to suggest the fashionable template inherited from Duval and others, Orczy elaborated with generous helpings from the myths of Duval and Robin Hood. Her gentleman highwayman, one handsome Jack Bathurst, an army captain masquerading under the aforementioned sobriquet, both plundered the rich in the interests of the poor and had a ready eye for the ladies; almost inevitably he filled one chapter of the novel by handing an aristocratic beauty from her carriage to dance with him beneath the moon. On its part, the silent film cast the stalwart leading man Matheson Lang in the role of the Duval neophyte.

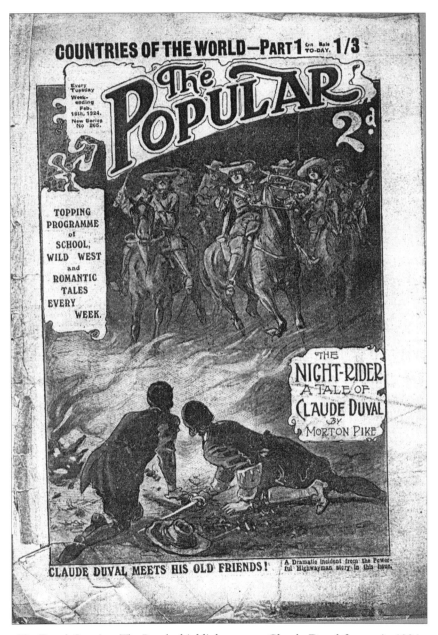

22. Boys' Comics: *The Popular* highlights a new Claude Duval feature in 1924.

A substantial and more direct British silent film of 1924, *Claude Duval*, made by Gaumont, starred Nigel Barrie and Fay Compton in "a romance of a highwayman and a duchess in the Old Days of Merrie England." Written by Mary Bennett and Louis Stevenson, and directed by George A. Cooper, it may have been influenced by the 1881 comic opera; in both, for example, Duval dances with a lady he subsequently rescues from a villainous suitor. *The Kinematograph Weekly* regarded the movie as "one of the best British costume romances yet seen," but thought Barrie rather lack-lustre in the title role.

23. Motion Pictures: Nigel Barrie as the eponymous hero of *Claude Duval*, the successful big-screen movie from Gaumont, released in 1924. The film posters proudly proclaimed it "a romance of a highwayman and a duchess in the Old Days of Merrie England."

The lingering potency of the link between fashionable ladies and highwaymen was also demonstrated in one of the most famous of British pictures, Gainsborough's *The Wicked Lady*, a 'talkie' released in 1945 with Margaret Lockwood as the scheming Lady Barbara Skelton, who turns to highway robbery herself, partly to allay the boredom of her life as the wife of a nobleman. The film was based upon Magdalen King Hall's novel, *The Life and Death of the Wicked Lady Skelton*, published the same year. The story was supposed to have been based upon the career of Katherine Ferrers, an actual historical personage who lived between 1634 and 1660. But there is simply no evidence whatsoever that the historical original either committed highway robberies or was ever alleged to have done so during her lifetime. At best the story may have been a Victorian legend. The novel and film made no use of the story of Claude Duval, although in its seventeenth-century context and association of ladies and highwaymen, the tale possibly originated in the nineteenth-century popularity of the stories about Duval or other gentleman rogues. The idea of turning the lady, the victim or love interest of so many thrilling yarns, into a highway robber herself was certainly successful. The 1945 film was one of the most popular

British motion pictures of the decade, and the yarn was remade in 1983 with Faye Dunaway in the leading part.

Another example of the manner in which the Duval story could transmute itself can be found in Daphne Du Maurier's most famous essay into historical romantic fiction, *Frenchman's Creek*, published in 1941. In this Restoration adventure it is the Lady Dona St. Columb who finds life at the court of Charles II stifling, and takes to more adventurous wiles. But after the briefest flirtation with playing a highwayman, the heroine quits London to retire to Du Maurier's favourite geographical locale, the seas, hidden coves and moors of her native Cornwall, where Lady Dona is enamoured of the chivalrous and gallant French pirate, Captain Jean-Benoit Aubery. *Frenchman's Creek* was not Du Maurier's best novel, and there was nothing original in the theme. It was the old formulae of glamorous lady and romantic French outlaw that had been the staple of the Duval stories for more than a century, stories with which the authoress and all the readers of her generation were respectably familiar. Nevertheless, it still had enough oomph to inspire film versions in 1944 and 1998.

24. "The Duchess and Claude Duval": William H. Barribal's attractive design for a fashionable set of playing cards produced by the John Wadddington company in the 1920s.

A different manifestation of the same Duval legend at this time was its use by the famous John Waddington company of Leeds and London, then more renowned for manufacturing stylish playing cards than the board games that would later become its international trademark. In the 1920s the company hired an accomplished designer and painter, William Henry Barribal, to beautify the backs of its playing cards. His numerous depictions of fashionable and glamorous Edwardian and Art Deco gentlewomen are now highly collectable, but one early double set of cards carried the title, *The Duchess and Claude Duval*. The design portrayed the highwayman in ambush, preparing to descend upon a fairy-tale coach that might have come from a production of *Cinderella*. While pleasant enough, Barribal's work recalled the chronological confusion so common in the previous century, for he gave Duval clothes that were strikingly eighteenth-century.

That particular anachronism, however, did not trouble another full novel written about Duval. Edwin T. Woodhall's *Claude Duval, Gentleman Highwayman and Knight of the Road* (1937) was a rather slender tome of 96 pages compared to many of its elephantine predecessors. Woodhall's Duval was the son of a royal servant, who had assisted the future Charles II to escape to the continent after the monarchy's cause went down in the Civil War. But Claude becomes the Restoration highwayman of history and legend, in this version assisted rather than endangered by Thomas Blood, as well as a fictional Irishman named Paddy O'Rourke. When Duval meets his end on the gallows, the king is shocked and chagrined to learn that he had been the son of a faithful old retainer.

The thirties and forties had, on the whole, little to say about Duval, and there were no new serial productions of any kind, but a minor revival of the subject occurred in the 1950s. The Amalgamated Press, which had published Charlton Lea, attempted to recapture old glories by reintroducing the highwayman as a comic-strip hero, this time in the weekly *Comet*, a popular boys' paper. Abandoning their ancient format, in which columns of small print had been interspersed by occasional illustrations, the new strip was more visual, adopting the increasingly prevailing practice of using a fast-moving sequence of pictures and short captions and speech bubbles to deliver a truncated text. Surprisingly at this time it was a modest success, and "Claude Duval, the Laughing Cavalier," illustrated by Fred T. Holmes, ran from 1953 to 1959, and inspired four independent comic books in the 'Thriller Picture Library', published between 1955 and 1957. Today they would be called "graphic novels." Again, the artist was Holmes, and as their titles (*Claude Duval, The Laughing Cavalier*; *Claude Duval, Swordsman of the King*; *Claude Duval and the Roundhead's Revenge*; and *Claude Duval and the Traitor Cavalier*) indicate they, like the strip that gave them birth, reflected the Aldine tradition popularised by Charlton Lea and set the highwayman's adventures in the Civil War period. He was either a royalist during that conflict, or an agent for the exiled Charles II, executing dangerous missions or otherwise harassing the tyrannical forces of Cromwell's England.

George King, a successful film producer, was sufficiently moved by the Amalgamated Press's hero to transfer the story to the small screen, and through the Associated Rediffusion company made thirteen half-hour swashbucklers for Independent Television. They aired in 1957 as *The Gay Cavalier*, starring the neatly moustached debonair French actor and film director Christian Marquand as 'Captain Duval' and Larry Burns as his Irish henchman, Dinny O'Toole. The fictitious Major Mould of the comic strip, portrayed by Ivan Craig, became the duo's principal foil. With alternating directors Lance Comfort and Terence Fisher, some established actors such as Greta Gynt and Christopher Lee, and a team of scriptwriters (Jack Andrews, Gordon Wellsesley, Charlotte Hastings and Brock Williams), the series continued to flog the Civil War theme, as the signature tune proudly proclaimed:

"It's the Gay Cavalier, has a song for the King;
It's the Gay Cavalier, here's the song that we sing;
Duval is out a riding, and we have no cause to fear,
For the Roundheads will be hiding from the Gay Cavalier."

But the stories did not evade the feminine aspects of the legend, as episodes entitled 'The Masked Lady', 'The Lady's Dilemma', 'Girl of Quality' and 'Springtime for Julia' attested. Indeed, Duval frequently appeared with a female companion, but in a vehicle designed principally for adventure-loving boys, the emphasis was upon horse and rapier work, and the films, like Charlton Lea's *Claude Duval* series and the Amalgamated Press comic strips, occupied exactly the same territory as versions of Alexandre Dumas's classic sword and buckler saga of *The Three Musketeers*. Indeed, one of Dumas's heroes, Charles, Comte d'Artagnan, captain of musketeers, in fact an historical personage, had also featured in Lea's sprawling epic as an ally of Duval. The comic strips had gone further than Lea, and provided Duval with two henchmen, almost as jovial, intrepid and skilled with a blade as himself, whose names just happened to be Hind and Nevison, two other seventeenth-century highwaymen. This trio made the parallel with the *Three Musketeers* inescapable. But, notwithstanding all such embellishments, however, the television series ran for only a single season. It was repeated at least once, in 1960, but surprisingly no print of it is known today, and it has consequently never appeared in a digitalised format.

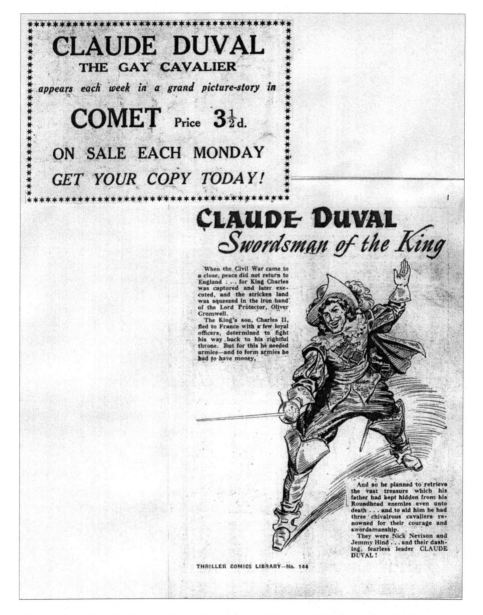

25-26. Comic-Strip Hero: Above, Amalgamated Press of London advertise its regular series in the weekly *Comet* in the mid 1950s; and below the first page of a spin-off, *Claude Duval*, number 144 of the Thriller Picture Library.

It is arguable that these final manifestations of Duval the boys' hero might have overplayed their hand. Politics had been imported into the tale to confer legitimacy upon the dubious hero, but they were politics that were now of a very stale kind. They were predicated upon a conservative loyalism, an unquestioned belief in the worthiness of the monarchy, and a consequent repugnance for the seventeenth-century 'roundheads' who had executed their king. They not only belonged to a forgotten time but sat ill at ease with the less deferential and more assertive, even rebellious, younger generations that emerged after the Second World War. The new youth culture would not be known for its readiness to stand up for the establishment of any kind. And if Duval's appeal as a sword-swishing patriot had tired, his other card, emphasizing sexual shenanigans with ladies, was then generally deemed unsuitable for younger audiences.

That said the latter could still gull some of the consumers of adult historical romances, and underlay the highwayman's return to the big screen. Warner Brothers produced a version of *The Beggar's Opera* in 1953, with Laurence Olivier as the sex-driven highwayman, while two years later a Restoration swashbuckler entitled *The King's Thief* starred Edmund Purdom as a dashing knight of the road. It drew some inspiration from the Duval stories, but rather more from Thomas Blood's historic attempt to steal the crown jewels. More on target was another British movie, *The Lady and the Highwayman*, released as late as 1989. In all but name and nationality the English hero 'Silver Blade' was the Claude Duval of the most recent penny dreadfuls, comic strips and television dramas. In a story set in the periods of the Protectorate and Restoration, Hugh Grant played the patriotic

27. Advertising for a movie of 1989. The title (*The Lady and the Highwayman*) and accompanying description ("the story of a dashing swordsman who, in the 17th century, must rescue a beautiful lady from a jealous rival and former mistress of Charles II") alone suggest its roots in the Duval myth.

royalist, who happened to be a highwayman, chivalrous in disposition and dexterous with a sword, dedicated to frustrating the "brutish" Roundheads, serving the king, and of course rescuing maidens in distress, in this case Lady Panthea Vyne, played by the alluring Lysette Anthony. Oliver Reed acted the part of William Morton, the relentless justice, in all but name. Not surprisingly, this recapitulation of the theme of dashing cavalier outlaw and aristocratic female sweetheart had appealed to the *doyen* of formulaic historical romantic fiction for women, Barbara Cartland, whose novel, *Cupid Rides Pillion* (1952), had provided the inspiration for the motion picture. But the film may have also owed something to its executive producer, Lew Grade, whose independent television company had earlier been responsible for *The Gay Cavalier*. Despite an impressive cast that included Claire Bloom and John Mills, this new Grade venture made little headway with cinema-goers and furnished yet another testimony to changing times.

Indeed, while the fifties had seen some return to the days of old, with serial comics and television stories, the signs of decay were writ large. Even the Amalgamated Press's illustrated comic strips and books were demonstrably shifting their ground. Their most popular series of comic books in the fifties was entitled the 'Cowboy Picture Library' and featured monthly pamphlets of *Buck Jones*, *Kit Carson* and *Davy Crockett*, the historical and cinema heroes associated with America's frontier days. Their companion 'Thriller Picture Library' did publish prolific runs of *Robin Hood*, *Dick Turpin* and the like, including the four issues of *Claude Duval* already mentioned, but their day was over. The 'Thriller Picture Library' ran from 1951 to 1963, but by the sixties it was dispensing with its old-time sword and longbow heroes and devoting itself almost entirely to new breeds of heroes belonging to World War II and the murky fields of modern detection and espionage.

The fifties can, in fact, be considered the dying spasm of the popular Duval myth. Turpin survived a little longer, but within a few decades he, too, had become an anachronism. The technological revolution contributed to their decline, for the minds of boys were abandoning men on horses for faster and as they saw it more exciting tales of motor cars, ironclad warships, fighter aeroplanes and space rockets.

9

And What Remains

Claude Duval deserves to be remembered as a key figure in the development of the myth of the English outlaw, and as one of the great popular criminal 'heroes' of the past. Few generated such a sustained demand for versions of their life histories, however fanciful. In that he ranks with Hereward, Robin Hood, Jack Sheppard, Rob Roy MacGregor and Dick Turpin, and perhaps no other who inhabited these islands. They were all freebooters and thieves of a kind, who challenged the authorities of their times, and yet who, at some time or another, the nation embraced as its own and garlanded in literature and legend. Notwithstanding their dubious historical activities, they generated an appeal that says something about the British psyche.

But what remains of Claude Duval today, at the beginning of the twenty-first century, apart from crumbling pamphlets, novels, comics, playbills and other vestiges of a celebrity that has finally all but disappeared?

Almost nothing that was physically connected to our subject can now be seen. In London the Old Bailey Sessions house, in which the highwayman was tried, was a temporary wooden structure, raised after its predecessor had perished in the Great Fire; it gave way to a new permanent building in 1674.

The old Newgate prison had also been damaged by the Great Fire, and the exact circumstances of Duval's incarceration there are unknown. There is no doubt that he and other prisoners were held in Newgate in the period 1668 to 1670, but extensive repairs were then being made, and after 1672 the place was substantially rebuilt. Thus restored, the prison survived for more than a century until it was destroyed by an insurgent mob during the Gordon riots of 1780. As for Tyburn, it is still possible to stand upon the site of the macabre gallows where Duval and so many others died. It is now commemorated by a plaque, but the area, which in the seventeenth century was a borderland between town and country, has long since been enveloped by urbanization.

The one grim survival from the last days of Claude Duval is the church of St. Sepulchre-without-Newgate, parts of which, including the tower, the porch and a portion of the outer wall, are believed to be much as they were in 1670. Inside the building today visitors may also see the 'execution bell', a hand-bell said to have been the one used to alert prisoners in the condemned cell of Newgate that the day of their reckoning had come. But the two churches associated with the burial of the French highwayman have not survived as they were. That of St. Giles-in-the-Fields, the apparent site of his interment, was rebuilt in the early eighteenth century and consecrated in 1733, while St. Paul's in Covent Garden, erroneously stated to have been his last resting place, was destroyed by fire in 1759. One supposes that Duval's bones still sleep somewhere in the churchyard of St. Giles, which has been transformed into a pleasant garden conducive to reflections upon times past.

Traditions of uncertain age have claimed several houses for Claude Duval. It was once said, for example, that he had owned a cottage in Highwater Lane in Wokingham, Berkshire. Another and more vocal candidate was situated in the capital itself. In August 1841 the watercolour artist John Wykeham Archer made a drawing of a wooden red-roof tiled house on the east side of the Hornsey Road, Holloway, near its junction with the Seven Sisters road. It was moated, as if prepared for defence, and sheltered by trees, and it was rumoured to have been a house of ill fame as early as the beginning of the Jacobean period. For this reputation it was styled 'the Devil's House' in a survey of 1611. But later, and more enduringly, it was believed to have been a refuge of Claude Duval. Archer's drawing was inscribed, "The house of Claude Duval, the highwayman, near Holloway – moated," and it was engraved and published as such.

Yet it must be doubted that it preserved a genuine memory of the outlaw. An adjoining pathway had been variously known as 'Duval's Lane' or 'Devil's Lane', and it is to be feared that the former nomenclature was little more than a corruption of the latter that thrived in times of resurging interest in the highwayman. Archer's annotation is the first we have found that associates Duval with the Holloway district of London, although soon afterwards it featured in some of the mid-Victorian literature about the outlaw. It may be that both were born of oral traditions. Despite our healthy scepticism, we have sometimes met instances when lingering local memories of famous or infamous connections have ultimately been verified, although not many. We must leave "Claude Duval's house" at that. Unfortunately it, as well as any neighbourhood stories that may have informed Archer, have long since disappeared.

CLAUDE DUVAL'S HOUSE, IN 1825. (*See Page* 381.)

28. "Claude Duval's House" on the Hornsey Road in Holloway, London, in 1841, an engraving of a drawing now in the British Museum. While accepted in the early nineteenth century, the connection to the highwayman was almost certainly apocryphal.

The alleged associations between historic inns and highwaymen are, of course, commonplace. Throughout the country old taverns claim to have been the hideouts of famous robbers, but few of these traditions rest upon hard historical evidence. There was commercial capital to be tailored from tales of smugglers and highwaymen once the terror they had inspired had gone. But again, it is possible to doubt too readily, for highwaymen certainly did use inns and wayside stables, and many of them must still stand in one form or another. Unfortunately, we know little of Duval's geographical range, although it could have been considerable. Public houses advertising a connection to him once included the 'The Black Boy' on the Windsor Road in Slough, until its demolition in 1910. A plain brick and timber structure with two storeys and tall chimneys, it served travellers between Bath and London, and on that score alone had as good a claim to Duval as any other contender. We know that he frequented the western roads into London, and that the nearby Maidenhead Thicket was a notorious black spot for travellers. The 'The Bell' in East Molesey in Surrey, an ancient hostelry near Hampton Court, was also said to have been used by Duval, but perhaps a stronger claim might be made for the 'The Claude du Vall' on the High Street of Camberley in the same county. It is close to the site of Bagshot Heath, once noted for its highwaymen and almost certainly one of the Frenchman's hunting grounds.

In the twentieth century there was also a tradition that Duval worked the rural areas of northern Oxfordshire. The 'Hopcroft Holt Hotel' near Steeple Aston commemorates the association with a striking highwayman inn sign and the in-house 'Claude Duval Restaurant'. In the sixties publicity for the 'Hopcroft Holt' featured an imaginative legend that the Frenchman's ghost had murdered one of the hotel's landlords and his lady. The Oxfordshire tradition has also been recently recognized by the British Horse Society, which collaborated with local government councils and the Southern Tourist Board to establish the fifty mile 'Claude Duval Bridle Path' for riders, walkers and cyclists, running between Quainton in Buckinghamshire and Great Barrington in the Oxfordshire Cotswolds. A twenty-three mile 'Claude Duval 2' was later added across western Oxfordshire, connecting the bridleway to the famous Ridgeway near Ashbury.

In London itself the 'Swan' at 66 Bayswater Road, a mile beyond the route felons once took from Newgate to Tyburn, once claimed the questionable honour of being the very tavern at which Duval stopped to take his final drink before proceeding to the triple tree. It is not entirely clear that the tavern, perhaps the one formerly known as 'The Saracen's Head', even existed in 1670 but the building still bears a plaque commemorating its association with the highwayman. But perhaps the strongest case for any public house or inn can be made for another London hostelry. At 51 and 52 Chandos Place, near Covent Garden in London, the interested tourist will find 'The Marquis' public house, formerly 'The Marquis of Granby'. Previous to the 1930s Chandos Place was known as Chandos Street, and 'The Marquis' was either built upon the site of the 'The Hole-in-the-Wall' tavern, where Duval was captured, or is a modernisation of the ancient taproom itself. Today it is the only habitation in which Duval's spirit may be said to have a genuine home. A plaque outside of the establishment proudly boasts of the tavern's lineage as one of the oldest in London, and delights in its twin claims to fame: in a mistress of the Duke of Buckingham, who is said to have once owned the house, and in its "romantic highwayman."

The bridle paths are the most notable modern commemorations of the French highwayman, but others can be found in appropriate places. Very recently a row of residential dwellings in Hounslow, once thick with the knights of the road, was officially designated 'Claude Duval House'. But if original buildings connected with the highwayman are few, those searching for the remains of Duval's world may wonder whether somewhere there may be survivors of a very different kind; a progeny maybe?

If Duval was even half the man contemporaries described, it would be surprising if he had not sired illegitimate offspring by the "girls" said to have been his regular companions. Sadly, while it is theoretically possible that descendants of the highwayman are still with us today, we are unable to trace a line. We do not even know what happened to Elizabeth Morris, the highwayman's last mistress.

She was probably one of several paramours of Duval, and since he was a handsome young man who by all accounts had his choice of women, she was likely to have also been young and reasonably attractive in 1670. Still, we have too little information to track her down in available records. London church registers record that several children were baptised Elizabeth Morris at that time. Such infants were christened, for example, in Whitechapel in August 1641, in Southwark in June 1643, in the parish of Westminster in October 1643, and in St. Botolph-Without in Aldgate in 1647. There are others too, but any or none of them might have been our girl. Women are notoriously difficult to trace because most changed their names, either in formal marriages or loose associations. Unmarried women often adopted the surnames of men with whom they were temporarily living.

Apart from the references concerning Duval in 1670, already noted, nothing is to be had about an Elizabeth Morris in the Middlesex Sessions books up to 1672, but one or more offenders of that name had business with the Old Bailey in years thereafter. On 18 November 1687 a woman of that name burgled the house of Thomas Phillips with two confederates. The men escaped, but she was found in possession of the goods and on 22 February 1688 received a death sentence. She successfully "pleaded her belly," which is to say her unborn child, in mitigation. By the practices of the time, she would have been eligible for execution at a later date, when her baby had been delivered, but it was not uncommon for women in her situation to have their sentences commuted, perhaps to transportation to the Americas, or even waived entirely. Although this particular woman was described as "an old offender" there are grounds for disbelieving that she was the former mistress of Duval. No one mentioned the celebrated highwayman in referring to her bad record; they only adverted to her husband, Oliver Morris, a desperate character executed the previous year for a burglary in St. Giles-in-the-Fields parish. Moreover, the profile of this individual suggests that she was also known as Elizabeth Clancy. The most likely inference is that Clancy was her former name, and that she had more recently acquired the surname Morris from her marriage to the unwholesome Oliver. Our Elizabeth Morris, alias Duval, was using the name Morris in 1669, almost twenty years before.

Another trial of an Elizabeth Morris occurred three years later. Whether she was the former defendant or another is uncertain. On 23 April 1691 she stole a number of items from Nathaniel Haughton: a gold and jewelled ring worth £60, three pearls valued at £12, two gold earrings, half a yard of lace worth £1, two pairs of sheets worth £6 and sundry other items of "good value." Some of the booty was found in her possession, and her explanation, that she had had them from her mother in Worcestershire, could not be confirmed. Tried on 27 May this Elizabeth was convicted of grand larceny and sentenced to hang. She, too, was pregnant, but significantly failed to broach the subject at her trial, something that suggests that she was a different woman than the aforementioned offender, who at least had learned the efficacy of pleading her belly. Nevertheless, her condition was discovered, and by "the Queen's clemency and grace" she escaped the trip to Tyburn, taken on 3 June by all but one of the other felons with whom she shared a place on "the Dead Warrant." On 9 September Morris moved to have her pardon allowed, by which one assumes she applied for a permanent release, but her appeal failed "for want of a Writ of Allowance." Again, the sequel is unknown. We can only hope that, given a reluctance to execute mothers, she eventually secured her reprieve or at least that she secured a reduction of sentence and made something better of her life.

A final Elizabeth Morris was tried on 21 February 1694. She and Grace Denby had stolen four pewter pots, six draper napkins and other goods to the value of thirteen shillings from Nathaniel Rosewell in the parish of St. Clement Dane. Unfortunately, Elizabeth persuaded her accomplice to help her sell them "at the ditch side, where they were stopped." Technically, the prisoners had committed grand larceny, which in those days was defined as the theft of a good or goods over the value of a shilling. But in this case the jurors did not believe that the crime merited severe punishment, and found the defendants guilty of stealing goods worth only ten pence, two pence short of the shilling threshold. Nevertheless, the punishment for petty larceny itself was humiliating and painful. These women were publicly whipped for their transgressions.

Now, Duval's mistress might well have escaped retribution in 1670 only to turn into a middle–aged recidivist. But we cannot make that assumption. She may have been one or all of the defendants between 1688 and 1694, and she may have been none of them. We simply do not know, and the whole illustrates the almost impenetrable fog that so eagerly descends upon the affairs of 'the common people' of the seventeenth century.

Consequently there is little likelihood of anyone today tracing a lineage to the notorious outlaw. The only place that can be regarded as an occasional residential haunt of Claude Duval is the Covent Garden area, where he was eventually tracked down. And while the parish church of St. Paul's carries no record of the alleged burial of the man himself, it can testify to the existence of other Duvals in the period after his death. A 'Peter' was baptised there in 1695, the son of 'Peter Deval' and his wife Priscilla. If the elder Peter was thirtyish at the time of the birth of this, seemingly his first, child, he could easily have been a son of the highwayman. Peter, we know, was a name often adopted by Claude Duval; indeed, it may even have been his real name, rendered Pierre in French. This Peter and Priscilla had at least four other children in Covent Garden, Edward in 1699, Ann in 1701, John in 1706 and Mary in 1708. The elder Peter was buried in St. Paul's church on 22 August 1731 and his widow on 25 April 1736. The family appear in the records as 'Deval' or 'Davall'.

It is tempting to suggest that this might have been one of the lines left by the most picturesque of the knights of the road, but really we are tilting at windmills. Bearing in mind the verified mathematical existence of coincidences, we may be maligning a family that had no such formidable ancestry.

Moreover, there is an alternative affiliation for our 'Peter Deval' senior of Covent Garden, for another 'Peter Duval' met a sticky end in Restoration London. The session records of the Old Bailey reveal that on 27 August 1679 one Peter 'Duval' or 'du Val', formerly the keeper of a tobacco and dram shop near St. Giles-in-the-Fields, and an associate, Thomas Thompson, were sentenced to hang for the murder of an "honest" man named Jenkins outside an alehouse in Soho fields. Duval's business had foundered, and he and Thompson, another ne'er-do-well, had taken up with "two baggages of the other sex...of ill fame" and in their company come across a company of labourers "innocently sitting" at the alehouse door late one evening. Duval, who seems to have been inebriated, argued with the men, drew his sword and threatened "to fight with any of them." During an ensuing scuffle Thompson thrust his sword into the abdomen of Jenkins and killed him outright. Although the prostitutes appeared in court to "excuse" their paramours, the offenders were jointly convicted of murder and sentenced to hang. Now this unsavoury Peter Duval of 1679 was too old to have been sired by the famous highwayman, but he is a credible alternative to him if we are seeking a father to the Peter Deval of Covent Garden.

There, indeed, is our problem. There may not have been many Duvals in the London area, but enough existed to create confusion about who belonged to whom. There was, for example, the Chelsea baker, Peter Duval, who died in 1711, and his wife, Elizabeth, who died in Stepney in Spitalfields, and whose will, proven on 7 October 1724, mentioned a son John and her losses in the South Sea Bubble speculation. A John Duval was indicted for felonious theft but acquitted at the Old Bailey on 4 April 1722, and an Abraham Deval or Daval, convicted of forgeries involving lottery tickets, died on the gallows protesting ill usage on 11 November 1724, aged "near thirty." Whether any of these were connected to the infamous Claude in any respect is a moot point, although in most cases the link seems unlikely. Nevertheless, despite the difficulties of jumping to obvious or desired conclusions, there are still people today who fancy that they are descendants of the most stylish of highwaymen.

It is clear that Claude Duval fascinated our ancestors in the nineteenth and early twentieth centuries, in Britain, North America and Australasia. It was for that reason that his name was included in the encyclopaedias and biographical dictionaries that I saw in my youth. Their editors were members of an older generation that had grown up with the legend of the French outlaw. But Time has gradually dimmed those memories of the Victorian stage, circus and penny dreadful, and the name of Duval no longer sparks instant recognition, nor does anyone salivate at his physical charms or fictitious deeds. His standing as a popular cultural artefact died with our forefathers.

That said, a small rear-guard action is still occasionally heard, even in this twenty-first century. Every now and again someone is moved to brush the cobwebs from this hoary old tale. In 2005 Donald Heller's traditional folk group, the Hurdy Gurdy Band, based in the state of Connecticut in the United States, created an "outrageous tragic-comical shadow figure ballad opera," *The Adventures of Claude Duval*, in which shadow puppetry interacted with such period instruments as hurdy-gurdies, violins and harpsichords. A year later another American folk music act, the Band of Brothers, included "The Highwayman Waltz" on their original album, *Railroads, Hobos and Cowboys*. It was a fresh recounting of Duval's famous dance, written by Michael Scott Smith.

Britain also saw spasmodic interest. In 1997 there was an almost inevitable skirmish with homosexuality when Chris Hunt's *Duval's Gold* became one of the more successful examples of 'gay literature.' So pronounced a ladies' man as Claude Duval was in no danger of losing his heterosexual character, even in the most imaginative fiction, but his association with dandyism perhaps appealed to a different niche audience. In this three-hundred paged novel set in the early eighteenth century, it is, in fact, an admirer and imitator of Duval, raised on stories about "the greatest of highwaymen," who takes to the road and is eventually drawn into the colourful world of London homosexuality. Nine years later, in 2006, the no less glamorous original himself was more conventionally stirring female hearts in Mary Hooper's *The Remarkable Life and Times of Eliza Rose*, an historical novel written for young adults. In 2009 Nicholas Duval, a publican, created something of a local controversy in Kidlington by renaming his inn on the Banbury Road 'The Highwayman' in the belief that he was a descendant of the notorious outlaw. The following year Carl Reid, a sculptor, created a 200 mm. resin bust of a masked Duval for Stormtroopers Ltd., one of the foremost British companies in military modelling.

If the interest in highwaymen has been eclipsed, in some respects Duval is weathering the hiatus rather better than most. His name still stands high in rosters of robbers. In 2003 one chronicler of "eight centuries of crime, cruelty and corruption" opined that Duval, above all others, "brought class and dignity to the profession of highwayman." Seven years later, riding on a news story about a modern criminal, the American *Time Magazine* selected ten historic international bandits who had "given the police a run for their money." In terms of time period, "Claude Du Val" was the oldest chosen, as well as one of only three who avoided serious vilification. Rather Du Val was "known for defying the norm of armed road thievery by not resorting to violence when ripping people off. He used charm. Legend has it that Du Val was a bit of a fashionista who presented himself differently than your average dirty uncouth robber. He is described as 'dashing, witty and handsome'...Women flocked to his wake, fighting for a chance to touch his body." A current website is even more enthusiastic. "We take Duval... at his mythological acme," it explained. "He is the patron saint of the early modern bandit, the superman of English outlawry, succouring with the fantasy of freedom upon the road the thousands of porters and scullery maids and apprentices chained to their oars below-decks upon Britannia's ship of state." Even now, three and a half centuries after his death, Claude Duval can apparently still weave his Gallic spell.

It worked upon two enterprising new American writers, Jessica Cale and Michelle Lowe, respectively based in North Carolina and California, who published E-book novels in 2014. Cale's story of the seamier side of seventeenth-century life, *Tyburn*, opens with the execution of Claude Duval. The heroine of the novel is a prostitute who had known the Frenchman in better times, and who remained haunted by the last kiss he gave her or anyone else, on his final journey to the Triple Tree. The Duval of *Tyburn* was tragic and sexually enchanting as well as "the very picture of a swaggering hero." As for Lowe, she bravely set herself the task of writing a "non-fiction" study of Duval, but found the accessible material too threadbare, and opted to flesh out the picture in a biographical novel. Nevertheless, *Cherished Thief* ran to some four hundred pages. It sticks fairly closely to the popular seventeenth-century story, and can claim to be the most earnest of all the fictionalized attempts to reconstruct the career of the French highwayman.

Robin Hood acquired a timeless formula, in which good successfully confronts evil and liberty triumphs over tyranny within the setting of adventure and romance, but the English highwayman is now, for the most part, an unfashionable figure. Nevertheless, Claude Duval, probably more than any other, had defined the mythical persona that had sustained the interest in these bandits of the road for so long. He may not have been the first highwayman to display or affect a gentlemanly bearing, but he was better at it than any of the others, and turned it into something of an industry. In doing so he set the pattern for the romantic notion of the road that tantalised Gay, Ainsworth, Bulwer-Lytton, Stevenson, Frith and Noyes, as well as generations of hack writers, and in turn many of them embroidered his reputation in tales of breathless adventure, intrigue, sex and old-time patriotism. The defining visual image of the romantic highwayman remains Frith's painting of the dance. Even today it breathes narrative power. Looking at it, one can almost see the sweeping bows and hear the seductive French accent of a remarkable outlaw.

Claude Duval was a scoundrel, and the most famous leader of a destructive robber-band. Schooled in a dangerous world, he is said to have held his life cheaply, and to have boasted that he would rather die with sword and pistol in hand than risk a lingering death by disease. In the end, he died more ignominiously, but his impact upon the popular imagination of these islands would be more than anyone could have foreseen that day he swung beneath Tyburn Tree.

Appendices

Appendix 1

Devol's Last Farewell, Containing an Account of Many Frolicksome Intrigues and Notorious Robberies which he committed, Concluding with his Mournful Lamentation on the Day of his Death (1670), a ballad to the tune of *Upon the Charge*.

You bold, undaunted souls attend
To me, who did the laws offend;
For now I come to let you know
What prov'd my fatal overthrow,
And brought my glory to decay;
  It was my gang for whom I hang,
Well a day, well a day.

Unto a duke I was a page,
And succour'd in my tender age,
Until the devil did me intice,
To leave of[f] Virtue and follow Vice;
No sooner was I led astray
  But Wickedness did me possess,
Well a day, well a day.

If I my crimes to mind shou'd call,
And lay them down before you all,
They would amount to such a sum,
That there is few in Christendom,
So many wanton pranks did play;
  But now, too late, I mourn my fate,
Well a day, well a day.

Upon the road, I do declare,
I caused some lords and ladies fair,
To quit their coach and dance with us:
This being done, the case was thus,
They for their musick needs must pay:
      But now, at last, those joaks [sic] are past,
Well a day, well a day.

Another time I and my gang,
We fell upon a noble man;
In spite of all that he could do,
We took his gold and silver too,
And with the same we rid away;
      But, being took, for Death I look.
Well a day, well a day.

When I was mounted on my steed,
I thought myself a man indeed;
With pistol cock'd and glittering sword,
Stand and deliver, was the word
Which makes me now lament and say,
      Pity the fall of great Devol.
Well a day, well a day.

I did belong unto a crew
Of swaggering blades as ever drew;
Stout Witherington and Dowglas both,
We were all three engag'd by oath
Upon the road to take our way;
      But, now, Devol must pay for all.
Well a day, well a day.

Because I was a Frenchman born,
Some persons treated me with scorn;
But, being of a daring soule,
Although my deeds was something foul,
My gaudy plumes I did display;
      But, now, my pride is laid aside.
Well a day, well a day.

I reign'd with an undaunted mind,
Some years, but now, at last, I find
The Pitcher that so often goes
Unto the well, as proverb shows,
Comes broken home, at last, we say;
      For, now, I see my destiny.
Well a day, well a day.

Then being brought to Justice Hall,
Try'd and condemn'd before them all;
Where many noble lords did come,
And ladies, for to hear my doom,
Then sentence pass'd, without delay,
      The halter first, and Tybourn last.
Well a day, well a day.

Appendix 2

Walter Pope, *The Memoirs of Monsieur Du Vall, ContainingThe History of his Life and Death. Whereunto are annexed his Last Speech and Epitaph. Intended as a Severe Reflection on the too great Fondness of English Ladies towards French Footmen, which, at that Time of Day, was a too Common Complaint* (1670)

-----------------------Si quis
Opprobriis dignos latraverit, integer ipse,
Solventur risu tabulae--------------------- Horat.

Claude du Vall was born, anno 1643, at Domfront in Normandy, a place very famous for the excellency and healthfulness of the air, and for the production of mercurial wits. At the time of his birth, (as we have since found, by rectification of his nativity, by accidents) there was a conjunction of Venus and Mercury, certain presages of very good fortune, but of a short continuance. His father was Pierre du Vall, a miller; his mother Marguerite De la Roche, a taylor's daughter. I hear no hurt of his parents, they lived in as much reputation and honesty, as their conditions and occupations would permit.

There are some that confidently aver he was born in Smock-alley without Bishopsgate; that his father was a cook, and sold boiled beef and porridge. But this report is as false as it is defamatory and malicious, and it is easy to disprove it several ways. I will only urge one demonstrative argument against it: if he had been born there, he had been no Frenchman, but if he had been no Frenchman, it is absolutely impossible he should have been so much beloved in his life, and lamented at his death by the English ladies.

His father and mother had not been long married, when Marguerite longed for pudding and mince pie, which the good man was fain to beg for her at an English merchant's house in Rouen, which was a certain sign of his inclination to England. They were very merry at his christening, and his father, without any grumbling, paid also then the fees for his burial, which is an extraordinary custom at Domfront, not exercised anywhere else in all France, and of which I account myself obliged to give the reader a particular account.

In the days of Charles the Ninth of that name the curate of Domfront (for so the French name him whom we call parson and vicar), out of his own head began a strange innovation and oppression in that parish; that is, he absolutely denied to baptise any of their children if they would not at the same time pay him also the funeral fees; and what was worse, he would give them no reason for this alteration, but only promised to enter bond for himself and his successors, that hereafter all persons, paying so at their christening, should be buried gratis. What think ye the poor people did in this case? They did not pull his surplice over his ears, nor tear his mass-book, nor throw crickets at his head? No, they humbly desired him to alter his resolution, and amicably reasoned it with him, but he, being a capricious fellow, gave them no other answer but, 'What I have done, I have done. Take your remedy where you can find it; 'tis not for men of my coat to give an account of my actions to the laity.' Which was a surly and quarrelsome answer, and unbefitting a priest. Yet this did not provoke his parishioners to speak one ill word against his person or function, or to do any illegal act. They only took the regular way of complaining of him to his ordinary, the Archbishop of Rouen. Upon summons, he appears. The Archbishop takes him up roundly, tells him. He deserves deprivation, if that can be proved which is objected against him, and asked him what he had to say for himself. After his due reverence, he answers that he acknowledges the fact to save the time of examining witnesses, but desires his Grace to hear his reasons, and then do unto him as he shall see cause. 'I have been,' says he, 'curate of this parish these seven years. In that time I have, one year with another, baptised a hundred children, and buried not one. At first I rejoiced at my good fortune to be placed in so good an air, but, looking into the register-book, I found, for a hundred years back, near the same number yearly baptised, and not one above five years old buried. And, which did more amaze me, I find the number of the communicants to be no greater now than they were then. This seemed to me a great mystery but, upon further enquiry I found out the true cause of it, for all that are born at Domfront were hanged at Rouen. I did this to keep my parishioners from hanging, encouraging them to die at home, the burial duties being already paid.'

The Archbishop demanded of the parishioners whether this was true or not. They answered that too many of them came to that unlucky end at Rouen. 'Well then,' said he, 'I approve of what the curate has done, and will cause my secretary, *in perpetuam rei memoriam*, to make an act of it,' which act the curate carried home with him, and the parish cheerfully submitted to it, and have found much good by it, for within less than twenty years there died fifteen of natural deaths, and now there die three or four yearly.

But to return to Du Vall it will not, I hope, be expected that I should, in a true history, play the romancer and describe all his actions from his cradle to his saddle, telling what childish sports he was best at, and who were his play-fellows. That were enough to make the truth of the whole narration suspected. Only one important accident I ought not to omit.

An old friar, accounted very expert in physiognomy and judicial astrology, came on a time to see the old Du Vall and his wife (for so we call him to distinguish him from his son). They had then, by extraordinary good fortune, some Norman wine, that is, cider, in their house, of which they were very liberal to this old friar, whom they made heartily welcome, thinking nothing too good for him.

For those silly people who know no better, account it a great honour and favour, when any religious person, as a priest or friar, are pleased to give them a visit and to eat and drink with them. As these three were sitting by the fire, and chirping over their cups, in comes Claude, and broke the friar's draught, who fixed his eyes attentively upon him without speaking one word for the space of half an hour, to the amazement of Claude's parents, who, seeing the friar neither speak nor drink, imagined he was sick and courteously asked him, 'Brother, what ails you? Are you not well? Why do you look so upon our son?' The friar, having roused himself out of his ecstasy, 'Is that stripling,' says he, 'your son?' To which, after they had replied, yes. 'Come hither, boy,' quoth he, and looking upon his head, he perceived he had two crowns, a certain sign that he should be a traveller. 'This child,' says he, 'will be a traveller, and he shall never, during his life, be long without money; and, wherever he goes, he will be in extraordinary favour with women of the highest condition.' Now, from this story, the certainty of physiognomy and judicial astrology is evidently proved; so that from henceforward whoever shall presume to deny it ought not to be esteemed a person in his right wits.

Pierre and Marguerite looked upon the friar as an oracle, and mightily rejoiced at their son's good fortune; but it could not enter into their imagination how this should come to pass, having nothing to leave him as a foundation to build so great a structure upon.

The boy grew up, and spoke the language of the country fluently, which is lawyer's French, and which (if I should not offend the ladies, in comparing our language with theirs) is as much inferior to that at Paris, as Devonshire or Somersetshire English to that spoken at White-hall.

I speak not this to disgrace him for, could he have spoke never so good French, it is not in such high esteem there as it is here, and it very rarely happens that upon that account alone any great man's daughter runs away with a lackey.

When he was about thirteen or fourteen years old his friends mustered their forces together to set him up in the world. They bought him shoes and stockings, for (according to the laudable custom of that country, of inuring their youth to hardship) till then he had never worn any. They also bought him a suit of[f] the brokers, gave him their blessing and twenty sous in his pocket, and threw an old shoe after him, and bid him go seek his fortune. This throwing of an old shoe after him was looked upon as a great piece of prodigality in Normandy, where they are so considerable a merchandise; the citizens' wives of the best quality wearing old shoes chalked, whence, I suppose, our custom of wearing white shoes derives its original.

His friends advised him to go to Paris, assuring him he would not fail of a condition [position] there, if any could be had in the world, for so the French call Paris. He goes to Rouen, and fortunately meets with post-horses, which were to be returned, one of which he was proffered to ride *gratis*, only upon promise to help to dress them at night. And, which was yet more fortunate, he meets several young English gentlemen with their governors going to Paris to learn their exercises to fit them to go a-wooing at their return home; [and] who were infinitely ambitious of his company, not doubting but, in those two days' travel, they should pump many considerable things out of him, both as to the language and customs of France, and, upon that account, they did very willingly defray his charges.

They arrive at Paris, and light in the Fauxbourg St. Germain, the quarter wherein generally the English lodge, near whom also, our Du Vall did earnestly desire to plant himself. Not long after, by the intercession of some of the English gentlemen (for in this time he had endeared himself to them) he was admitted to run on errands and do the meanest offices at the St. Esprit, in the Rue de Boucherie, a house in those days betwixt a tavern, an ale-house, a cook's shop, and a bawdy-house, and, upon some of these accounts, much frequented by the English his patrons. In this condition he lived unblameable during some time, unless you esteem it a fault to be scabby and a little given to itching qualities, very frequent in persons of his nation and condition.

The restoration of His Majesty [Charles II], which was in 1660, brought multitudes of all nations into England to be spectators of our jubilee; but, more particularly, it drained Paris of all the English there, as being most concerned in so great a happiness. One of them, a person of quality, entertained Du Vall as his servant, and brought him over with him.

What fortunes he ran through afterwards is known to every one, and how good a proficient he was in the laudable qualities of gaming and making love. But one vice he had which I cannot pardon him, because it is not of the French growth, but northern and ungenteel, I mean that of drinking; for, that very night he was surprised, he was overtaken.

By these courses (for I dare not call them vices) he soon fell into want of money to maintain his sport. That, and his stars, but chiefly his own valour, inclined him to take the generous way of padding [highway robbery], in which he quickly became so famous that in a proclamation for the taking several notorious highway-men he had the honour to be named first.

This is the place where I should set down several of his exploits, but I omit them, both as being well known, and because I cannot find in them more ingenuity than was practised before by Hind and Hannum, and several other mere English thieves.

Yet, to do him right, one story there is that savours of gallantry, and I should not be an honest historian, if I should conceal it.

He, with his squadron, overtakes a coach, which they had set over night, having intelligence of a booty of four-hundred pounds in it. In the coach was a knight, his lady, and only one serving-maid, who, perceiving five horse-men making up to them, presently imagined that they were beset; and they were confirmed in this apprehension by seeing them whisper to one another and ride backwards and forewards. The lady, to show she was not afraid, takes a flageolet out of her pocket and plays. Du Vall takes the hint, plays also and excellently well upon a flageolet of his own, and in this posture he rides up to the coach side. 'Sir,' says he to the person in the coach, 'your lady plays excellently, and I doubt not but that she dances as well. Will you please to walk out of the coach and let me have the honour to dance one currant [coranto] with her upon the heath.' 'Sir,' said the person in the coach, 'I dare not deny any thing to one of your quality and good mind;

you seem a gentleman, and your request is very reasonable,' which said the lackey opens the boot, out comes the knight, Du Vall leaps lightly off his horse and hands the lady out of the coach. They danced, and here it was that Du Vall performed marvels the best master in London, except those that are French, not being able to show such footing as he did in his great riding French boots. The dancing being over he waits on the lady to her coach. As the knight was going in, says Du Vall to him, 'Sir, you have forgot to pay the music.' 'No, I have not,' replies the knight, and, putting his hand under the seat of the coach, pulls out a hundred pounds in a bag and delivers it to him, which Du Vall took with a very good grace, and courteously answered, 'Sir, you are liberal, and shall have no cause to repent your being so. This liberality of yours shall excuse you the other three-hundred pounds,' and, giving him the [pass] word that, if he met with any more of the crew, he might pass undisturbed, he civilly takes his leave of him.

This story, I confess, justifies the great kindness the ladies had for Du Vall, for in this, as in an epitome, are contained all things that set a man off advantageously, and make him appear, as the phrase is, *much a gentleman*. First, here was valour, that he and but four more durst assault a knight, a lady, a waiting gentlewoman, a lackey, a groom that rid by to open the gates, and the coachman, they being six to five, odds at football; and beside, Du Vall had much the worse cause, and reason to believe that whoever should arrive would range themselves on the enemy's party. Then he showed his invention and sagacity that he could *sur le champ*, and, without studying, make the advantage of the lady's playing on the flageolet. He evinced his skill in instrumental music by playing on his flageolet; in vocal by his singing, for (as I should have told you before) there being no violin, Du Vall sung the currant himself. He manifested his agility of body by lightly dismounting off his horse, and with ease and freedom getting up again when he took his leave; his excellent deportment by his incomparable dancing, and his graceful manner of taking the hundred pounds; his generosity in taking no more; his wit and eloquence and readiness at repartees in the whole discourse with the knight and lady, the greatest part of which I have been forced to omit.

And here (could I dispense with truth and impartiality, necessary ingredients of a good history) I could come off with flying colours, leave Du Vall in the ladies' bosoms and not put myself out of a possibility of ever being in favour with any of them.

But I must tell the story of the *sucking bottle*, which, if it seem to his disadvantage, set that other against it which I am come from relating. The adventure of the sucking-bottle was as follows:

It happened another time, as Du Vall was upon his vocation of robbing on Black-heath, he meets with a coach richly fraught with ladies of quality, and with one child who had a silver sucking-bottle. He robs them rudely, takes away their money, watches, rings and even the little child's sucking-bottle. Nor would he, upon the child's tears, nor the lady's earnest intercession, be wrought upon to restore it, till at last one of his companions (whose name I wish I could put down here, that he may find friends when he shall stand in need of them), a good natured person (for the French are strangers both to the name and thing) forced him to deliver it. I shall make no reflexions upon this story, both because I do not design to render him odious, or make this pamphlet more prolix.

The noise of the proclamation and the rewards promised to those who should take any therein named made Du Vall retire to France. At Paris he lives highly, makes great boastings of the success of his arms and amours in England, proudly bragging he could never encounter with any of either sex that could resist him. He had not been long in France but he had a fit of his old disease, want of money, which he found to be much augmented by the thin air of France; and therefore, by the advice of his physicians, lest the disease should seize upon his vitals and make him lie by it, he resolves to transport himself into England, which accordingly he did, for in truth the air of France is not good for persons of his constitution, it being the custom there to travel in great companies well armed, and with little money. The danger of being resisted and the danger of being taken is much greater there, and the *quarry* much lesser than in England. For, if by chance a dapper fellow with fine black eyes and a white peruke be taken there and found guilty of robbing, all the women in the town do not presently take the alarm and run to the king to beg his life.

To England he comes, but alas! His reign proves but short, for within a few months after his return, before he had done anything of great glory or advantage to himself, he fell into the hands of justice, being taken drunk at the Hole-in-the-Wall in Chandos Street, and well it was for the bailiff and his men that he was drunk. Otherwise they had tasted of his prowess, for he had in his pocket three pistols, one whereof would shoot twice, and by his side an excellent sword, which, managed by such a hand and heart must without doubt have done wonders. Nay, I have heard it attested by those that knew how good a marksman he was, and his excellent way of fencing, that had he been sober it was impossible he could have killed less than ten. They farther add, upon their own knowledge, he would have been cut as small as herbs for the pot before he would have yielded to the bailiff of Westminster; that is to say, he would have died in the place, had not some great person been sent to him, to whom he might with honour have delivered his sword and himself. But taken he was, and that too *a bon marche*, without the expence of blood or treasure committed to Newgate, arraigned, convicted, condemned and on Friday, January the 21st, executed at Tyburn in the twenty-seventh year of his age (which number is made up of three times nine) and left behind him a sad instance of the irresistible influence of the stars and the fatality of climacterical years.

There were a great company of ladies, and those not of the meanest degree, that visited him in prison, interceded for his pardon, and accompanied him to the gallows, a catalogue of whose names I have by me, nay, even of those who, when they visited him, durst not pull of[f] their vizards [veils] for fear of showing their eyes swollen and their cheeks blubbered with tears.

When I first put pen to paper I was in great indignation and fully resolved, nay, and I think I swore, that I would print this muster-roll. But upon second thoughts and calmer considerations I have altered my fierce resolution, partly because I would not do my nation so great a disgrace, and especially that part of it to whom I am so entirely devoted. But principally because I hoped milder physic might cure them of this French disease, of this inordinate appetite to mushrooms, of this degenerous doting upon strangers.

After he had hanged a convenient time he was cut down and by persons well-dressed carried into a mourning coach, and so conveyed to the Tangier Tavern in St. Giles's, where he lay in state all that night, the room hung with black cloth, the hearse covered with escutcheons, eight wax tapers burning, and as many tall gentlemen with long black clokes attending. *Mum* was the word, great silence expected from all that visited, for fear of disturbing this sleeping lion. And this ceremony had lasted much longer had not one of the judges (whose name I must not mention here, lest he should incur the displeasure of the ladies) sent to disturb this pageantry. But I dare set down a mark whereby you may guess at him. It is one betwixt whom and the highwaymen there is little love lost, and who thought the fellow had honour enough done him, that he was not buried under the gallows.

This story of lying in state seemed to me so improbable and such an audacious mockery of the laws that till I had it again and again from several gentlemen, who had the curiosity to see him, I durst not put it down here for fear of being accounted a notorious liar.

The night was stormy and rainy, as if the heavens had sympathised with the ladies and echoed again their sighs, and wept over again their tears.

As they were undressing him in order to his lying in state, one of his friends put his hands in his pocket and found therein the speech, which he intended to have made, written with a very fair hand; a copy whereof I have, with much cost and industry, procured, and yet do freely make it public, because I would not have any thing wanting in this narrative.

Du Vall's Speech

'I should be very ungrateful (which amongst persons of honour, is a greater crime than that for which I die) should I not acknowledge my obligation to you, fair English ladies. I could not have hoped that a person of my nation, birth, education and condition could have had so many and powerful charms to captivate you all, and to tie you so firmly to my interest that you have not abandoned me in distress or in prison, that you have accompanied me to this place of death, of ignominious death.

From the experience of your true loves I speak it; nay, I know I speak your hearts. You could be content to be with me now, and even here, could you be assured of enjoying your beloved Du Vall in the other world.

How mightily and how generously have you rewarded my little services. Shall I ever forget that universal consternation amongst you when I was taken; your frequent, your chargeable [expensive] visits to me at Newgate; your shrieks, your swoonings when I was condemned; your zealous intercession and importunity for my pardon?

You could not have erected fairer pillars of honour and respect to me had I been a Hercules, and could have got fifty sons in a night.

It has been the misfortune of several English gentlemen, in the times of the late usurpation, to die at this place upon the honourablest occasion that ever presented itself, the endeavouring to restore their exiled sovereign [Charles II], gentlemen, indeed, who had ventured their lives and lost their estates in the service of their prince. But they all died unlamented and uninterceded for, because they were English. How much greater, therefore, is my obligation, whom you love better than your own countrymen, better than your own dear husbands? Nevertheless, ladies, it does not grieve me that your intercession for my life proved ineffectual, for now I shall die with little pain, an healthful body, and I hope a prepared mind. For my confessor has showed me the evil of my way, and wrought in me a true repentance. Witness these tears, these unfeigned tears. Had you prevailed for my life, I must in gratitude have devoted it wholly to you, which yet would have been but short, for, had you been sound, I should soon have died of a consumption; if otherwise, of the pox.'

He was buried with many flambeaux, and a numerous train of mourners, most whereof were of the beautiful sex. He lies in the middle isle in Covent-Garden church, under a plain white marble stone, whereon are curiously engraved the Du Vall's arms, and, under them, written in black, this epitaph.

Du Vall's Epitaph

Here lies Du Vall: Reader, if male thou art,
Look to thy purse; if female, to thy heart.
Much havock has he made of both; for all
Men he made stand, and women he made fall.
The second conqu'ror of the Norman race;
Knights to his arms did yield, and Ladies to his face;
Old Tyburn's Glory, England's illustrious thief;
Du Vall, the ladies' joy, Du Vall the ladies' grief.

The Author's Apology, Why he Conceals His Name

Some there are, without doubt, that will look upon this harmless pamphlet as a libel and invective satire because the author has not put his name to it, but the bookseller's printing his true name and place of abode [Henry Brome at 'The Gun' tavern] wipes off that objection.

But if any person be yet so curious as to inquire after me I can assure him I have conjured the stationer not to declare my name so much as to his own wife. Not that I am ashamed of the design; no, I glory in it, nor much of the manner of writing, for I have seen books with the authors' names to them not much better written. Neither do I fear I should be proud if the book takes, and crestfallen if it should not; I am not a person of such a tender constitution:

---------------------- Valeat res ludicra, si me
Palma negate macrum, donata reducat opimum.

But upon other pressing and important reasons, though I am resolved not to be known, yet I intend to give you some account of myself, enough to exempt me from being so pitiful and inconsiderable a fellow as possibly some incensed females may endeavour to represent me.

I was bred a scholar, but let none reproach me with it, for I have no more learning left than what may become a well-bred gentleman. I have had the opportunity if not the advantage of seeing all France and Italy very particularly, Germany and the Spanish Netherlands *en passant*. I have walked a currant in the hands of Monsieur Provosts, the French king's dancing-master, and several times pushed at the *plastron* of Monsieur Filboy le Vieux. Now I hope these qualities, joined with a white peruke, are sufficient to place any person *hors de la portee*, out of the reach of contempt.

At my return from France I was advised by my friends to settle myself in the world, that is to marry. When I went first amongst the ladies upon that account I found them very obliging, and as I thought *coming*. I wondered mightily what might be the reason could make me so acceptable, but afterwards found it was the scent of France, which was then strong upon me, for, according as that perfume decayed, my mistresses grew colder and colder.

But that which precipitated me into ruin was this following accident. Being once in the company of some ladies, amongst other discourses, we fell upon the comparison betwixt the French and English nations. And here it was that I, very imprudently maintained, even against my mistress, that a French lackey was not so good as an English gentleman. The scene was immediately changed. They all looked upon me with anger and disdain. They said I was unworthy of that little breeding I had acquired, of that small parcel of wit (for they would not have me esteemed a mere fool because I had been so often in their company) which nature had bestowed upon me, since I made so ill use of it as to maintain such paradoxes. My mistress forever forbids me the house, and the next day sends me my letters and demands her own, bidding me pick up a wife at the plough-tail, for it was impossible any woman well bred would ever cast her eyes upon me.

I thought this disgrace would have brought me to my grave. It impaired my health, robbed me of my good humour. I retired from all company, as well of men as of women, and have lived a solitary melancholy life and continued a bachelor to this day.

I repented heartily that at my return from my travels, I did not put myself into a livery, and in that habit go and seek entertainment in some great man's house, for it was impossible but good must have arrived to me from so doing. It was *a la mode* to have French servants, and no person of quality but esteemed it a disgrace if he had not two or three of that nation in his retinue, so that I had no reason to fear, but that I should soon find a condition [position].

After I had insinuated myself into one of those houses I had just reason to expect, if I could have concealed myself from being an Englishman, that some young lady with a great portion [fortune] should run away with me and then I had been made for ever. But if I had followed bad courses and robbed upon the highway, as the subject of this history did, I might have expected the same civilities in prison, the same intercessions for my life, and, if those had not prevailed, the same glorious death, lying in state in Tangier Tavern, and being embalmed in the ladies' tears. And who is there worthy of the name of a man that would not prefer such a death before a mean, solitary and inglorious life?

I design but two things in the writing this book. One is that the next Frenchman that is hanged may not cause an uproar in this imperial city, which I doubt not but I have effected.

The other is a much harder task: to set my countrymen on even terms with the French, as to the English ladies' affections. If I should bring this about, I should esteem myself to have contributed much to the good of this kingdom.

One remedy there is which, possibly, may conduce something towards it.

I have heard that there is a new invention of transfusing the blood of one animal into another, and that it has been experimented by putting the blood of a sheep into an Englishman. I am against that way of experiments, for should we make all Englishmen sheep, we should soon be a prey to the *loure*.

I think I can propose the making that experiment a more advantageous way. I would have all gentlemen who have been a full year or more out of France be let blood weekly, or oftener if they can bear it. Mark how much they bleed, transfuse so much French lackey's blood into them, replenish these last out of the English footmen, for it is no matter what becomes of them. Repeat this operation *toties quoties*, and, in process of time, you will find this event: either the English gentlemen will be as much beloved as the French lackeys, or the French lackeys as little esteemed as the English gentlemen.

But to conclude my apology, I have certainly great reason to conceal my name, for if I suffered so severely for only speaking one word in a private company, what punishment will be great enough for a relapsed heretic publishing a book to the same purpose? I most certainly do as that Irish gentleman that let a scape in the presence of his mistress, run my country, shave my head and bury myself in a monastery, if there be any charitable enough to harbour a person guilty of such heinous crimes.

Appendix 3

*The Life of Deval. Shewing How he came to be a Highway-Man;
and how he committed Several Robberies afterwards. Together with his
Arraignment and Condemnation. As also his Speech and Confession at
the place of Execution* (1670)

Lewis Deval, alias *John Brown*, was born of *French* parents, by whose care he
was so educated that he was made capable of any employment that might
offer itself, that was either gentle or profitable. Neither was Fortune more
backward in assisting of him than his friends had been indulgent towards
him, for no sooner is he come to be capable of any thing, but he is entered
into the service of a person of quality, where (if he had had as much grace
as Nature had bestowed on him parts) he might in time have acquired a
considerable preferment, but being wild and very extravagant, he could not
confine himself in his expenses and attendance within the narrow bounds
and limits of a servant. He is acquainted with a parcel of lewd people, and he
must have some new way to get money if he means to be welcome, neither
shall he need to go far for advice what course he should take, those people
being as excellent to persuade and encourage any unlawful ways of getting,
as they are prodigal in spending.

He is not long unresolved what course to take, for being brought
acquainted with a knot of highwaymen (having before observed their way
of living) a little persuasion now serves his turn. He resolves to make one
with them, and in he falls with his resolution, Never to be taken alive.

Now he goes on successfully, taking many rich prizes, having found out
a way how to be welcome to his girls and be as heartily embraced as the
best of their associates. Now money comes in so fast he hardly knows how
to spend it. His girls shall not have all. He hath something to spare for the
game-houses, whither, with others of his crew, he oft resorts.

This way he concludes to be the best that ever he could have fallen into; yea, better than an estate in land, for he could not have his rent till it were due, and many times should have a bad tenant that would leave him in the lurch. Neither is any place he could have attained to be equalled with this, for now if he wants money 'tis but taking his horse and riding out, and he's a poor landlord and tenant too of whom *Deval* gets nothing if he meets with them. As soon as one parcel of money is gone, 'tis but out and fetch in another; 'tis no matter who suffers for it, he resolves never to want so long as there is any money in *England*, but when all is gone here then he resolves for *France* (if nothing happen that may hinder his journey).

Another thing also that might move him to like this course the better was he not caring to die a natural death if a long disease should afflict him, or the gout should get him and make him cry out, '*O his legs, O his toes.*' This does not like him. He had rather be hanged out of the way, but that he does not much like neither. He therefore resolves to die in the field and will think himself injured if he be suffered to die in his bed.

Now *Deval* and his consorts harass the country to purpose, taking rent from many tenants before it is due, and giving them no receipts for it; and as little kindness had they for landlords, when they fell into their hands, taking all they could light on, though the money were intended for some purchase, or for a son or a daughter's portion, all's one to them, though the poor girl lose a good husband by it, which makes the poor maids pray backwards for them, yet will they be thus kind to them, rather than they shall lead Apes in Hell. *They will truck with them for their maidenhoods if they have a convenient opportunity*, for which kindness the maids resolve to gratify them with their prayers when they go to be hanged, and cry them up for the *handsomest* men they ever saw.

But those which complain most are the poor market folks who are forced to lie in London all night or else go home without their money, which makes the graziers come off by weeping-cross, the money they should have had of the butchers for their sheep, oxen and hogs being seized by *Deval* and his consorts to spend on their ladies. Now before we leave the market folks we will tell you how they served a parcel of them. About a dozen or fourteen market men and women having been at *London* at market and made an end betimes rode merrily homewards with their money, being very joyful they had done so soon that they might escape robbing, but those that reckon without their host must reckon again. For coming up a narrow lane they were made to stand, their hampers turned off their horses, and every one set by their hampers, so that it seemed to some passengers that they came by afterwards as if they had been set down on purpose to make an end of their market.

More kindness had two gentlemen that were coming towards *London*, and were set upon by *Deval* and one other, coming up with their pistols and presenting them to their servants' breasts, took such money from them as they had in their pockets, came up to one of the gentlemen and took away his sword and belt, but meddled not with their money. Afterwards they restored the sword and belt, declared their names, called the gentlemen by theirs, told them they would not have meddled with them, but that they had but four shillings among twelve of them, that they would pay it them again on any place of the road they would appoint, *Deval* telling one of the gentlemen how he was armed, what number of pistols he had ready charged, and that he was resolved never to be taken alive, *for he knew he should be hanged if he were.*

But thus they must not go on always, *sweet meat will have sour sauce*, also it will spoil the proverb. They have used the trade so long (and there are so many outcries after them) that many of their haunts are found out, and they begin to be taken notice of: some of them are seized about *London*, tried, condemned and executed, which, though it at present broke their haunts and made them more careful, yet did it not put an end to that way of living, they have tasted the sweet of it, and resolve that nothing but death shall part them. And it is not long ere another parcel of them are taken, and very kindly parted at the gallows.

But though so many are taken about *London* and other places about the country, yet *Deval* escapes still, but it will not be long ere we hear of him. He goes on in the old trade still, no warning will serve his turn, he can but into *France* at last, which he means shortly to be (as he told a gentleman he met upon the road) who told him again he would take his leave of the gallows first, and he will now escape very well if he miss it. Little does he think where he must keep his Christmas; his game is now almost at an end. He will still venture to come and spend his money with his old acquaintance, but it will cost him dear; his haunts are found out, and in one of them he is apprehended and carried before a magistrate, by whom he is sent to Newgate. And because he shall not keep his Christmas alone, he shall have his wife to keep him company and other his comforts.

In Newgate he carries it out very cheerfully, seeming to be very little daunted at what had befallen him, lamenting nothing more than that he was not in a condition to die upon the place when he was taken.

On Friday *Jan.* 14 he was carried down to the Sessions House in the Old Bailey, where he had several indictments read against him, to which he pleads *Not Guilty*, and then was conveyed back again to Newgate.

On Saturday *Jan.* 15 he was again carried down to his trial, where, after the examining of witnesses and proving the indictments, he was found guilty by the jury and thence conveyed to Newgate again. The concourse of people both these days being such as the like hath seldom been seen on such an occasion.

On Monday *Jan.* 17 he was again carried down to the Session House, where he received his sentence to be carried back to the place from whence he came, and thence to be carried to the place of execution, there to be hanged till he was dead, according to Law.

Jan. 21 Monsieur Deval was carried from Newgate to the place of execution, where being come, he spake to this purpose: *That he had taken many men's money, and had been a very lewd liver, and that he had justly deserved this end he was come to; and that as he hoped for forgiveness from God, so he desired forgiveness from all whom he had any ways injured.* After which he was turned off, and soon dead.

Licensed Jan. 22 1669 [1670],

Roger L'Estrange [Licensor].

Appendix 4

A True and Impartial Relation of the Birth and Education of Claudius du Val, Together with the Manner of his Apprehending, Commitment to New-gate; as also his Tryall at the Sessions-house in the Old-Baily the 14 and 15, and his Condemnation on the 17 Day of this Present Month. And Likewise his Deportment in the said Gaol, How he had been Preferred, and by what Means at first He became Debauched, by his Own Confession. And Lastly the Manner of his Execution at Tyborn on Friday the 21 of this Present January 1669 [1670]. (1670)

Claudius du Val, who is the present subject of all persons' discourse, and now of the author's writing, [who] out of a desire to satisfy all people, and that they might not be abused by false pamphlets or erroneous suggestions, took upon him this work (as presuming himself not ignorant of the condition of *du Val*), having it as an Eye-Witness to matter of trial, and for his actions from his own mouth during his confinement, as may be testified by credible witnesses, if any one scruple the truth hereof.

Various hath been the reports concerning his birth, being strongly averred to be in *London* and *Westminster*, and that in several places, as *Chancery-Lane, Drury-Lane, Covent-Garden, White-Chappell* and many other places, but he himself owned none of all these, but declared to have drawn his first breath in *Paris* in *France*. His parents he did not boast of; his education was there, till a gentleman of quality, liking his person, in which Nature was bountiful, brought him over to England in the nature of a page; with whom he lived till a noble and eminent peer desired of his master to have him, with whom he continued some years, who was pleased to prefer him from his [post as a] page to a more honourable service, where he continued till his lady died. After which he was transmitted to the service as gentleman to a person of honour, related to the said noble family, and there continued till about two years and a half ago, and then a difference arising, his master was willing to part with him, and advised him to retire home to his own country lest bad company might debauch him, and that he might have no excuse to derogate [deviate] from this wholesome advice (after his noble master had caused to be paid him what was his due) he gave him a gelding worth twenty pieces, and twenty pieces in broad gold to defray his charges; and so they parted, and *du Val* came to London, intending his passage for France; but in the interim fell into the acquaintance of some of the Old Gang of highwaymen, who by debauchery corrupted his nature, for that (by his own confession) it was since he left his last service that he fell into those lewd and wicked ways.

I shall waive particulars which I might insist on, but, in short, for his short time he was a great offender, being put into two several proclamations, and being often sought after [he] at last was taken (by the vigilancy of Mr. *Bennett* the bailiff of the City and Liberty of Westminster) at the sign of the *Hole in the Wall* in *Shando's-Street*, being an alehouse. At his taking he was well armed, having three pistols in his pocket when he was seized on, but being surprised by a stratagem, he made no resistance, and so was committed unto His Majesty's gaol of *New-Gate* on *Christmas* day last, before whom he stood accused of several robberies and other crimes.

The Manner of His Trial Followeth

On the 14 day of *January* the Court being set at the Sessions-house in the *Old-Bayly*, he was arraigned and pleaded to seven several indictments, and then the court rose. Saturday being the 15, he came again upon his trial for robbing of *John Cox*, servant to a noble lord, which he confessed.

The next was for robbing *Thomas Lawrence*, servant to the said lord, to which he had pleaded not guilty, but it was sufficiently proved. Amongst others, *Thomas Lawrence* behaved himself very stoutly, fighting a long time with *Humble Ashenherst* (another member of the gang), from whom he received and gave several wounds, and had he had fair play undoubtedly *Ashenherst* had been secure in gaol or a grave.

The third indictment was for robbing Master *Thomas Hastings* and his wife in a coach about two years ago, and taking away to the value of 17 pounds 10 shillings. The robbery was proved by Mr. *Hastings*, but [he] could not accuse the prisoner at the bar, which was only *du Val*; but that was proved by *George Withrington*, who was best able to give an account of that, having been one of the party, and by whose evidence some of the offenders were formerly convicted and suffered.

The fourth was an indictment for felony and burglary for entering the house of *Lancelot Johnson*, Esquire, stealing several goods to a great value. The fact was proved by Mr. *Johnson*'s man and others, who were deluded [tricked] under pretence to take the said house and desired to be admitted in to leave a note in writing, seized upon the servants, secured the gate and doors, and ransacked the house. There was a great many more concerned in this robbery, for which, and others, they justly suffered the Law. This was proved by the said *George Withrington*, an actor in the same.

The fifth indictment was for robbing *Thomas Browning* and *Mary Trotman* to the value of thirty pounds, which was likewise proved.

The sixth indictment was for robbing one *Thomas Harris*, a poor man, of fourteen pounds ten shillings, all that he had, which did so trouble him that he desired them even to kill him. Upon which they sportingly asked him, 'What death would you willingly die?' '*Any*,' said he. 'What, would you be run through?' '*What you please*,' said he. Says another, 'Would you be pistoled?' '*What you please*,' said he. 'Would you have your throat cut?' said another. '*What you please*,' said he. But God restrained them that they did him no other hurt, leaving him to lament his loss. This was proved also.

The seventh indictment was for robbing one *William Hopkins*, taking away his bridle, valued at twelve pence, and eleven shillings in money, which was proved.

Of all which robberies the jury brought him in guilty, and for the felony and burglary committed in the house of *Lancelot Johnson*, only guilty of felony and not burglary; the reason was because it was not done in the night-time.

There was another indictment against him for murder, for killing one *James Tyrrell* near the *Golden Lyon* in the Strand, about four or five years ago. But there was no proof, for the coroner's jury of enquiry that then sat found that a Dutchman committed the fact, although *Withrington*, upon this trial, said that upon discourse with *du Val* and others of his wicked society, and boasting of their manhood, otherwise villainies, *du Val* should say he did kill a man near *Durham-yard* in the *Strand*, but it was believed it was but a boast, the better to fit himself for so wicked a company, of which he was then to be a member. So that the jury acquitted him of that, and brought him not guilty of that indictment.

There were several more indictments, which for want of evidence, or at leastwise [the court] thinking there was enough [already], the sessions ended.

Concerning His Deportment Before and After Trial

I cannot but write something as to his deportment both before and after his trial, during his confinement. Never had [a] prisoner such a concourse of people come to see him, and most out of novelty, and whatever their opinions were before they went up, they pitied his condition when they came from him, which I impute to his youth. He was very temperate as to drink, and his actions very modest, and discourse civil.

A long time he was in hopes of obtaining a reprieve, which, when he found to the contrary, he was much dejected, and said, '*Never man had more or better friends, and worse success.*' From that time, as I am informed, he was very penitent, and on the morning of his execution, hearing the bell toll, said, '*I hear my summons for another world.*'

As to the gallows, he prayed very earnestly that God would forgive him his world of sins, and that the world would forgive him; that he died in charity with all men, and craved the prayers of them all, and that they would take example by him to amend their lives lest they fall into the like ways, for then God's judgement would overtake them, as it had done him. And so committing his soul to God almighty, and often calling upon Christ for mercy, the executioner discharged his office.

Appendix 5

Samuel Butler, *To the Happy Memory of the Most Renowned Du Val. A Pindarick Ode* (1671).

1

'Tis true, to compliment the dead
Is as impertinent and vain
As 'twas of old to call them back again,
Or, like the Tartars, give them wives,
With settlements for after lives;
For all that can be done or said,
Though e'er so noble, great, and good,
By them is neither heard nor understood.
All our fine sleights and tricks of art,
First to create, and then adore desert,
And those romances which we frame
To raise ourselves, not them, a name,
In vain are stuff'd with ranting flatteries,
And such as, if they knew, they would despise.
For as those times the Golden Age we call
In which there was no gold in use at all,
So we plant glory and renown
Where it was ne'er deserv'd nor known,
But to worse purpose, many times,
To flourish o'er nefarious crimes,
And cheat the world, that never seems to mind
How good or bad men die, but what they leave behind.

2

And yet the brave Du Val, whose name
Can never be worn out by Fame,
That liv'd and died to leave behind
A great example to mankind;
That fell a public sacrifice,
From ruin to preserve those few
Who, though born false, may be made true,
And teach the world to be more just and wise;
Ought not, like vulgar ashes, rest
Unmention'd in his silent chest,
Not for his own, but public interest.
He, like a pious man, some years before
The arrival of his fatal hour,
Made ev'ry day he had to live
To his last minute a preparative;
Taught the wild Arabs on the road
To act in a more gentle mode;
Take prizes more obligingly than those
Who never had been bred *filous* [thieves];
And how to hang in a more graceful fashion
Then e'er was known before to the dull English nation.

3

In France, the staple of new modes,
Where garbs and miens are current goods,
That serves the ruder northern nations
With methods of address and treat;
Prescribes new garnitures and fashions,
And how to drink and how to eat
No out-of-fashion wine or meat;
To understand cravats and plumes,
And the most modish from the old perfumes;
To know the age and pedigrees
Of points [laces] of Flanders or Venice;
Cast their nativities, and, to a day,
Foretell how long they'll hold, and when decay;

T' affect the purest negligences
In gestures, gaits, and miens,
And speak by repartee-routines
One of the most authentic of romances,
And to demonstrate, with substantial reason,
What ribands, all the year, are in or out of season.

4

In this great academy of mankind
He had his birth and education,
Where all men are s' ingeniously inclin'd
They understand by imitation,
Improve untaught, before they are aware,
As if they suck'd their breeding from the air,
That naturally does dispense
To all a deep and solid confidence;
A virtue of that precious use,
That he, whom bounteous Heav'n endues
But with a mod'rate share of it,
Can want no worth, abilities, or wit,
In all the deep Hermetic arts,
(For so of late the learned call
All tricks, if strange and mystical).
He had improv'd his nat'ral parts,
And with his magic rod could sound
Where hidden treasure might be found:
He, like a lord o' the manor, seiz'd upon
Whatever happen'd in his way
As lawful weft and stray,
And after, by the custom, kept it as his own.

5

From these first rudiments he grew
To nobler feats, and try'd his force
Upon whole troops of foot and horse,
Whom he as bravely did subdue;
Declar'd all caravans, that go

Upon the king's highway, the foe;
Made many desperate attacks
Upon itinerant brigades
Of all professions, ranks, and trades,
On carriers' loads, and pedlars' packs;
Made them lay down their arms, and yield,
And, to the smallest piece, restore
All that by cheating they had gain'd before,
And after plunder'd all the baggage of the field,
In every bold affair of war
He had the chief command, and led them on;
For no man is judg'd fit to have the care
Of others' lives, until h' has made known
How much he does despise and scorn his own.

6

Whole provinces, 'twixt sun and sun,
Have by his conqu'ring sword been won;
And mighty sums of money laid,
For ransom, upon every man,
And hostages deliver'd till 'twas paid.
Th'e excise and chimney-publican [collectors of the chimney tax],
The Jew forestaller and enhancer [profiteers],
To him for all their crimes did answer.
He vanquish'd the most fierce and fell
Of all his foes, the Constable;
And oft had beat his quarters up,
And routed him and all his troop.
He took the dreadful lawyer's fees,
That in his own allow'd highway
Does feats of arms as great as his,
And, when they encounter in it, wins the day:
Safe in his garrison, the Court,
Where meaner criminals are sentenc'd for't,
To this stern foe he oft gave quarter,
But as the Scotchman did t' a Tartar,
That he, in time to come,
Might in return from him receive his fatal doom.

He would have starv'd this mighty town,
And brought its haughty spirit down;
Have cut it off from all relief,
And, like a wise and valiant chief,
Made many a fierce assault
Upon all ammunition carts,
And those that bring up cheese, or malt,
Or bacon, from remoter parts:
No convoy e'er so strong with food
Durst venture on the desp'rate road;
He made th' undaunted waggoner obey,
And the fierce haggler [itinerant dealer] contribution pay;
The savage butcher and stout drover
Durst not to him their feeble troops discover;
And, if he had but kept the field,
In time had made the city yield;
For great towns, like to crocodiles, are found
I' th' belly aptest to receive a mortal wound.

8

But when the fatal hour arriv'd
In which his stars began to frown,
And had in close cabals contriv'd
To pull him from his height of glory down,
And he, by num'rous foes opprest,
Was in th' enchanted dungeon cast,
Secur'd with mighty guards,
Lest he by force or stratagem
Might prove too cunning for their chains and them,
And break through all their locks, and bolts, and wards;
Had both his legs by charms committed
To one another's charge,
That neither might be set at large,
And all their fury and revenge outwitted.

As jewels of high value are
Kept under locks with greater care
Than those of meaner rates,
So he was in stone walls, and chains, and iron grates.

9

Thither came ladies from all parts,
To offer up close prisoners their hearts,
Which he receiv'd as tribute due,
And made them yield up love and honour too,
But in more brave heroic ways
Than e'er were practis'd yet in plays:
For those two spiteful foes, who never meet
But full of hot contests and piques
About punctilios and mere tricks,
Did all their quarrels to his doom submit,
And, far more generous and free,
In contemplation only of him did agree:
Both fully satisfy'd; the one
With those fresh laurels he had won,
And all the brave renowned feats
He had perform'd in arms;
The other with his person and his charms:
For, just as larks are catch'd in nets
By gazing on a piece of glass,
So while the ladies view'd his brighter eyes,
And smoother polish'd face,
Their gentle hearts, alas! were taken by surprise.

10

Never did bold knight, to relieve
Distressed dames, such dreadful feats achieve
As feeble damsels, for his sake,
Would have been proud to undertake;
And, bravely ambitious to redeem
The world's loss and their own,
Strove who should have the honour to lay down

And change a life with him;
But, finding all their hopes in vain
To move his fixt determin'd fate,
Their life itself began to hate,
As if it were an infamy
To live, when he was doom'd to die;
Made loud appeals and moans,
To less hard-hearted grates and stones;
Came, swell'd with sighs, and drown'd in tears,
To yield themselves his fellow-sufferers,
And follow'd him, like prisoners of war,
Chain'd to the lofty wheels of his triumphant [execution] car.

Appendix 6

Alexander Smith, "DuVall, a Notorious Highwayman," in *The Complete History of the Lives and Robberies of the Most Notorious Highwaymen* (1713)

[Much of this account was copied almost verbatim from Pope's pamphlet, and is not repeated here. However, excerpts of additional material were interspersed throughout the narrative. They are now unique to Smith, who either invented them or copied them from another, now unknown, source, and it is these that are reproduced below.]

> Of all the highwaymen which have ever been executed within the limits of Great Britain, none have been more noted than Claude Du Vall, who (as some say) was born in Smock Alley, without Bishopsgate, though, indeed, he received his birth at a place called Domfront in Normandy in France. His father was a miller, and his mother a tailor's daughter. They bestowed as much education originally upon him as qualified him for a footman, and bred him up very strictly in the Romish religion, which made him generally talk more of good cheer than the church, of great feasts than his faith, of good wine than good works, and of courtesans than Christianity. But though he died a Roman Catholic, yet we may reasonably suppose his religion was to choose, for being once so very sick that there was great hopes of his dying then a natural death, a ghostly father comes to him with his *Corpus Domini* and tells him that hearing of the extremity wherein he was, he had brought him his saviour to comfort him before his departure. Whereupon Du Vall, drawing his curtain and seeing a good fat friar with the Host in his hand, said, 'I know it is our Saviour because He comes to me as He went to Jerusalem, C'est un asne qui le porte, he is carried by an ass.'

[There followed an account of Duval's youth, passage to England, fall into crime and increasing notoriety, all drawn exclusively from Pope. After describing the dance with the lady and relating the story of the sucking-bottle in a like manner, Smith continues...]

One time Du Vall being in company with some strolling players at Oxford, the chiefest of them inviting him to supper, as looking upon him for some foreign gentleman, he accepted of his civility. And being entertained in the player's chamber, but the victuals not yet brought up, he (to divert Du Vall the while) proceeded to act in gestures and expressions, some fragments of a tragedy, made upon a Scythian King, who, flying through a forest with his queen, was himself after a stout resistance seized on and got under the feet of a bear. He acted this part till just as the wench was coming up with a dish of custards which the player had ordered with the rest of the supper, the poetic rapture took him in the noddle, and fancying himself in the bear's clutches, he thus in a passionate, magniloquent, and very earnest tone besouth his queen to save herself by flight:

'O! Fly my queen from this devouring bear;
Let it suffice he me alone does tear.
O! Save thyself, the bloody bear's jaws fly;
Why shouldst thou, whilst thou may'st escape him, die?
O! Haste, be gone, or thy death, too, is nigh.'

The maid being by this time at the stairhead in a great fright, concluded that some bear broken loose was got into the chamber a-worrying him, and that it was to her that he spoke so eagerly to save herself, lest the beast having made but half a supper of him, she should come in for the second course to make up his meal. Thereupon she made but one leap downstairs, yet tumbling head over heels at the bottom, beat all the custards in pieces, and lying with her coats over her head, her bare buttocks and heels up the stairs, she fancied the bear would now have her by the breech, which made her roar out lamentably for help. Being taken up, all embued in, and almost blinded with custard, and demanded of how this disaster came to pass, 'Oh!' said she, 'for the love of God don't stand asking of questions, but arm, arm and run up quickly to the poor gentleman's rescue, whom a monstrous bear, come from I know not whence, is now tearing to pieces and eating.' Upon this, though somewhat startled, they catched up what weapons came first to hand, and upstairs they ran, rushing in upon the player and Du Vall in a very furious manner, so that they knew not what to think should be the meaning of it, 'till they all cried out in a breath, 'Where's this bear? Where's this bear that the maid says was worrying a man?' The player as soon as he could be heard assured them it was only a mistake of the maid's, who had heard him perhaps repeating such a passage of a play, and by her fear suggested it a reality. This occasioned much laughter in the house, but the player had the least cause to be merry, for whilst the hurly-burly was in his chamber, by half a score country fellows with clubs and staves to kill poor Bruin if he had been there, Du Vall had the opportunity of taking £30, which lay in a bag on the player's trunk, and slipping downstairs, mounted his horse and rode away.

A little after this accident Du Vall lighted into another as profitable, for coming into Beaconsfield, where at the Crown Inn he heard a great singing and dancing to an hautboy and violin, enquiring the reason thereof he found there was a country wake kept, at which was present most of the young men and maids for several miles about. Here, setting up his horse, whilst he was drinking a pint of sack in the kitchen, an old rich farmer with £100 tied up in a bag under his arms, and which he had just received, must step into the inn to see this mirth and pastime before he went home with his money, which was not above a quarter of a mile out of the town. Du Vall seeing him admitted into the room where the wake was kept, he asked the landlord whether he might be permitted to see this country diversion without any offence to the company. He told him he might and welcome, so entering the room likewise, his eyes were more fixed upon the old farmer's bag of money than the young folks dancing, and perceiving that the room had a chimney with a large funnel he came out and communicated his design to the ostler. He, for the reward of two guineas, dressed up a great mastiff dog in a cowhide he had in the stable, and placing the horns just on this forehead, by the help of a ladder and a rope he let him hastily down the chimney into the chamber, where they were assembled, and whither Du Vall was returned again before the acting of this scene.

The dog howling as he descended, and rushing among them in that frightful figure, turned all into hurry and confusion, the music silenced, the table overthrown, the drink spilled, the people screaming and crowding downstairs as fast as they could, everyone striving to be foremost lest the Devil, as they supposed this to be, should take the hindmost. Their heels flew up, the women's coats over their heads, and the men's noses some of them in their breeches, lying higgledy piggledy, heads and tails, whilst their backstrings loosing, gave full flushes and put them into a very unsavoury condition. The pipe and the fiddle were trod in pieces, and the supposed demon making his way over all, he got into the stable, where the ostler hasting after him uncased him. So that when they came a little to themselves, and saw no more of him, they concluded he had vanished into the air. But in the time of this hurly-burly the old farmer being in as great a fright as any of 'em, and his breeches as well befouled, he dropped his hundred pound bag and fled for safety into the house of office. Du Vall securing the money under his cloak at once took horse, and spared not whipping and spurring 'till he got safe into London. But as soon as all things were in order again, there was a sad outcry for the £100, which being not to be found, high nor low, the whole company supposed the late devil had took it away, and imputed the loss as a judgment inflicted on the old farmer, who was a very covetous fellow, whose chief studies were how to cozen this tenant, beggar that widow or undo some orphan.

One time Du Vall meeting with Squire Roper, Master of the Buckhounds to King Charles the Second, hunting in Windsor Forest, having the opportunity of enjoying his company in a private thicket, he commanded him to deliver his money, or else he would shoot him. The squire, to save his life, gave a purse of fifty guineas to Du Vall, who then tying him neck and heels, with his horse fastened by him, he rode away. All the pastime of hunting was over before the squire was found out by the forester, who, accidentally going by there, unloosed the bound person, who then making what haste he could into Windsor was met in the town by Sir Stephen Fox [one of the king's political followers], who asking him whether he had met with any sport, he replied in a great passion, 'Yes, Sir, I have had sport enough shown me by the son of a whore, but he made me pay damned dear for it; for tying me neck and heels, he then took fifty guineas to pay him for the trouble of taking such pains about me.'

But the noise of the proclamation and the rewards promised to those who should take any therein named made Du Vall retire to France. At

Paris he lived highly, made great boastings of the success of his arms and amours in England, proudly bragging he could never encounter with any of either sex that could resist him. He had not been long in France, but he had a fit of his old disease, want of money. This obliged him to use his wits again, for having heard of a learned Jesuit who was confessor to the French king, and that his politics had rendered him very eminent, but that he was withal very covetous and still craving, though exceeding rich, it came into Du Vall's noddle to venture a bold stroke that he might unhoard some of the gold he so much doted on. In order to do this, he put himself into a scholar's garb, and waited a fit opportunity to address himself to this miser. It was not long ere he found a fit one, for seeing him alone in the Piazzas of the Faubourg, he thus addressed him, 'May it please your reverence, I am a poor scholar, that has been travelling many strange lands to gain experience in sciences that may turn to the good of all France, if I might be under your patronage for protection.' 'And what may that be?' replied he, very much pleased. 'If it be advantageous to my country, I assure you no fitting encouragement shall be wanting.' Then, assuming more boldness, Du Vall said, 'I have spent most of my study in alchemy, or the transmutation of metals, and at Rome and Venice have profited so much from great men learned in that science that I can transmute several metals into gold with a philosophical powder I can speedily make.'

The father confessor appeared to brighten with joy at this, and told him such a thing would be very grateful indeed to his country, and particularly to the king, who, as his affairs went, stood much in need of so rare an invention. But he must see experiments made before he could credit it, or recommend him where he should not fail of advancement. And so he conducted Du Vall to his house, and furnished him with money to build and purchase such materials as he told him were requisitie in this precious operation, charging him to keep it as a secret from everybody but themselves 'till he thought fit to communicate it. Du Vall promised to be obedient, and when he had fixed his utensils, and melted some base minerals which the Jesuit viewed as he put them into the crucible, he stirred them with a hollow stick into which he had conveyed some sprig of pure gold (just as black lead is concealed in a pencil) which burning, as he stirred the flaming metal, the gold unperceived of him, sank in and melted likewise.

When the excessive fire had consumed or evaporated the lead, tin and brass, with the powder he threw in for a show, the gold remained pure to the quantity of an ounce and a half. This he caused to be assayed, and finding it (what it really was) all pure gold, it made the Jesuit so blinded with covetousness that after several other experiments producing the like effect, he totally gave himself over to believe whatever Du Vall said or did. And in the hopes that he had of the promises he made him to instruct him how to do it himself, that the fame of such a project might redound to him, as the inventor of it, he supplied him with what money he asked for, and he became so dear to him that he shewed him his treasure and many rich jewels that had been presented him for court favours. In this Du Vall resolved to be his partner, for when he had often produced the gold in the manner above mentioned, the Jesuit began to press him to discover the secret, after delaying him for a few days he concluded that if he stayed much longer his trick must be discovered, so he took his opportunity to steal into his chamber, where he usually slept after dinner, and finding him sleeping with his mouth open, he gagged and bound him, took his keys and unhoarding as much of his treasure as he could carry out unsuspected, he bid him adieu for ever.

[Smith's account concludes with Pope's material about Duval's return to England, capture, trial, execution and funeral.]

Appendix 7

De Witt's Claude Duval Novels & I.T.V.'s Small Screen Films

A: DE WITT'S CLAUDE DUVAL NOVELS

This list depends heavily upon the work of Allen J. Hubin. The 'Claude Duval' series was published by De Witt and Davenport from 1852 to 1857, and by De Witt thereafter into the 1860s. The 'Nightshade' series ran from 1864 to 1867. The works are listed in alphabetical order.

Black Bess; or, Claude to the Rescue

The Cask of Gold; or, Claude in the Tower, Containing the Interesting Details of Claude Duval's Marvellous Adventures in the Gloomy Tower Vaults at Midnight

Claude and the Abbess; or, a Night in a Nunnery

Claude and the Countess; or, Nightshade Near Newgate

Claude Captured; or, A Night in Newgate, Containing Vivid Descriptions of..the Daring Claude Duval and the Fair Dora

Claude Duval and his Companions; or, The Race on the Road

Claude in a Convent; or, The Nuns and the Highwayman

Claude in his Dungeon; or, Maggs the Traitor

Claude in the Cathedral; or, A Night in the Vaults

Claude in the Cave; or, The Chamber of Death; Strange, Wild and Terrible Deeds of Daring and Startling Adventures Give Interest to Every Page

Claude's Last Bullet; or, The Price of Three Lives

Claude to the Rescue; or, The Escape of Duval and the Maniac Heiress

Dare-Devil Dick; or, The Road and its Riders

Death to the Traitor; or, Claude Duval and the Poachers, Containing the Remarkable Adventures in the Secret Cave

Duval and the Duchess; or, A Midnight Row at St. James's

Duval at Bay; or, Claude's Career Closed

Duval Denounced; or, The Haunted Mansion

Duval in a Duel; or, The Abduction of Lucy

Duval in Newgate; or the Traitor Jew

The Fatal Tree; or, The Gibbet Bears Fruit

Gentleman Jack; or, Life on the Road

The Girl in the Gibbet; or, Claude Saves the Captive

Grace Manning; or, The Vengeance of Claude Duval

The Highwayman's Bride; or, The Capture of Claude Duval, in which are Related the Remarkable Adventures in Hornsey Church-Yard and the Fight of the Mohocks

The Highwayman's Doom; or, The Road and the Riders

The Highwayman's Stratagem; or, Claude on the Scaffold

Hounslow Jack; or, Duval and the Dark Lantern

Jack and his Bride; or, The Highwayman's Flight

The Last Leap; or, The Reward of Crime

Lucy Thornton; or, Claude in the Chateau

Luke the Lurker; or, Duval Dares All

Moonlight Jack; or, Claude and His Captors, filled with…the Very Remarkable Exploits and Strange Adventures of the Lovely Dora and The Fearless Claude

Nightshade; or, Claude Duval, the Dashing Highwayman

Nightshade on the Heath; or, Claude and the King

The Renegade Gipsy; or, The Betrayal of Claude Duval

The Ride for Life; or, Claude in Jeopardy

Rosa Bell, the Prince's Victim; or, Duval in a Boarding School, Showing How Claude Foiled the Heartless Libertine and Rescued an Innocent Girl

The Struggle for Life; or, Claude and the Skeleton Horseman

B: I.T.V.'S SMALL SCREEN FILMS

The Gay Cavalier television series premiered in Britain on 6 February 1957; the thirteenth and final episode was shown on 13 September 1957. The half-hour stories, each complete in itself, and opening to the stirring scenes of 'Duval' galloping furiously towards the camera, were, in the order of being screened:

A Throne At Stake
Girl of Quality
Angel Unawares
Springtime for Julia
Dragon's Heart
The Lady's Dilemma
The Masked Lady
Flight of the Nightingale
The Sealed Knot
The Lost is Found
The Little Cavalier
The Return of the Nightingale
Forsaking All Others

Select Bibliography

MANUSCRIPT SOURCES

Archives Departementales de l'Orne, register of baptisms, Domfront, Sept. 1638-Nov. 1647, 3NUMECRP145/AC145_1, pp. 1-76.

Register of baptisms, marriages and burials, Saint-Front, 1638-1647, 3NUMECRP145/AC145_11, pp. 35-151.

London Metropolitan Archives: Gaol delivery certificates, 1670, MJ/SR/1361-81. These certificates are in a poor condition, extremely difficult to use, and ideally should be conserved mounted in books. Some potentially rewarding packets, such as 1367-68 and 1371, are currently deemed unfit for use, and could not be examined. Where they exist or are accessible, however, these certificates frequently supply greater detail about offences than the "session books." A valuable source, but largely unused by historians.

Sessions books, 1667-70, MJ/GB/B/007-008. Rough minutes taken at the Middlesex sessions, listing justices and defendants, with allusions to charges and results.

Gaol delivery registers, vol. 6, 1656-72, MJ/GB/R6. A more polished record, furnished from the above; more considered, but also a step further removed from the actual proceedings.

St. Giles-in-the-Fields burial registers, Microfilm: X 105/022.

National Archives, Kew (formerly the Public Record Office): Domestic State Papers, 1665-72 (SP 29/100-306), Ms. 29/257.

Probate 4/7063 (Ashenhurst estate, 14 November 1671).

Probate 11/599/360 (Elizabeth Duval, widow).

Portland Papers, Longleat House, England: "Duval's Epitaph" by "Mr. Edwards," in a collection of English and Latin verses dated 1694, Volume 17, f. 102.

Shropshire Archives, Shrewsbury: documents of 21 June and 23 September 1668 relating to Humble Ashenhurst, Haslewood Collection, XD 3614/5/2/13-14.

PUBLISHED SOURCES

Adcock, John, *Yesterday's Papers* (yesterdayspapersarchive.blogspot.com).

Ainsworth, William Harrison, *Rookwood* (1834).

Ainsworth, William Harrison, *Talbot Harland* (1870).

Barlow, Derek, *Dick Turpin and the Gregory Gang* (1973).

Beattie, J. M., *Crime and the Courts in England, 1660-1800* (1986).

Blackledge, Catherine, *A Biography of William Lilly, the Man Who Saw the Future* (2015).

Bloody News from York-shire; or, the Great Robbery, Committed by Twenty Highwaymen...Two of Whom Confess Themselves to have been Pupils to the famous Du-Val and of his Gang Heretofore (1674).

Boulenger, Jacques, *The National History of France: The Seventeenth Century* (1920).

Bowyer, Frederick, John Crook, Lionel Monckton and Payne Nunn, *Mr. Arthur Roberts and His Own Company in a New Musical Piece Founded on an Episode in the Life of Claude Duval* (1894).

Burrage, Alfred Sherrington (Charlton Lea), *Claude Duval* (48 parts, 1902-1906).

Butler, Samuel, *To the Happy Memory of the Most Renowned Du Vall, A Pindarick Ode* (London, 1671; reprinted in John Mitford, ed., *The Poetical Works of Samuel Butler* [1835], 2, pp. 252-58.

Cale, Jessica, *Tyburn* (E-book, 2014).

Clark, Andrew, ed., *The Life and Times of Anthony Wood* (1891-95, 5 vols.).

Claude Du Val, the Dashing Knight of the Road (London, c. 1870s).

Claude Duval (Thriller Picture Library, nos. 99, 144, 164, 181, 1955-57).

"Claude Duval, the Laughing Cavalier," *The Comet* (1953-59).

Cockburn, J. S., ed., *Crime in England, 1550-1800* (1977).

Cressy, Edmund, *Captivity Improved to Spiritual Purposes, Or, Spiritual Directions given to Prisoners of all Sorts, Whether Debtors or Malefactors* (1675).

Daniell, F. H. Blackburne, ed., *Calendar of State Papers, Domestic Series, 1671-72* (1897).

Dashing Duval, or, the Ladies' Highwayman (c. 1875, 18 parts).

Defoe, Daniel, *A Tour Thro' the Whole Island of Great Britain* (1724, 2 vols.), volume 1.

Devol's Last Farewell, Containing an Account of many…Robberies…with his Lamentation on the Day of his Death (London, 1670; reprinted in Charles Gordon, *The Old Bailey and Newgate* (1902), pp. 77-79.

Dobson, R. B. and Taylor, J., ed., *Rymes of Robyn Hood* (1976).

Duffett, Thomas, *Psyche Debauch'd* (1678).

East London Theatre Archive, University of East London: Victorian Playbills (www.elta–project.org).

Earle, Peter, *A City Full of People: Men and Women in London 1650-1750* (1995).

Emsley, Tim, et. al., *The Proceedings of the Old Bailey, 1674-1913* (a project of the Universities of Hertfordshire and Sheffield and the Open University, www.oldbaileyonline.org).

'Eye-Witness', *A True and Impartial Relation of the Birth and Education of Claudius du Val, Together with the Manner of his Apprehending, Commitment to New-gate; as also his Tryall at the Sessions-house in the Old-Baily…and likewise his Deportment in the said Gaol…* (London, 1670).

The French Rogue, Being a Pleasant History of His Life and Fortune (1672).

Frith, William Powell, *Autobiography and Reminiscences* (1887–88, 3 vols.).

Gay, John, *The Beggar's Opera* (1728; 1921 edition).

Gladfelder, Hal, *Criminality and Narrative in Eighteenth-Century England* (2001).

Gordon, Charles, *The Old Bailey and Newgate* (1902).

Green, Mary Anne Everett, ed., *Calendar of State Papers, Domestic Series, 1664-65* (1863).

Green, Mary Anne Everett, ed., *Calendar of State Papers, Domestic Series, 1666-67* (1864).

Green, Mary Anne Everett, ed., *Calendar of State Papers, Domestic Series, 1667* (1866).

Green, Mary Anne Everett, ed., *Calendar of State Papers, Domestic Series, 1667-68* (1893).

Green, Mary Anne Everett, ed., *Calendar of State Papers, Domestic Series, 1668-69* (1894).

Green, Mary Anne Everett, ed., *Calendar of State Papers, Domestic Series,1670, With Addenda, 1660-1670* (1895).

Griffiths, Arthur, *The Chronicles of Newgate* (1884, 2 vols.).

Grovier, Kelly, *The Gaol. The Story of Newgate, London's Most Notorious Prison* (2008).

Harper, Charles G., *Half-Hours With Highwaymen* (1908, 2 vols.).

Hayward, Arthur L., *The Boys' Book of Highwaymen* (1931).

Head, Richard and Swiftnicks, Samuel, [Francis] *Jackson's Recantation, or the Life and Death of the Notorious Highwayman now Hanging in Chains at Hampstead* (1674).

Hibbert, Henry George, *A Playgoer's Memories* (1920).

Hobsbawm, Eric J., *Bandits* (1969; revised ed., 2001).

Holt, J. C., *Robin Hood* (1989).

Hunt, Chris, *Duval's Gold* (1997).

Hunt, William H., ed., *The Registers of St. Paul's Church, Covent Garden, London* (1906–1909, 5 vols.).

Hutton, Ronald, *The Restoration: A Social and Religious History of England, 1658-1667* (1985).

Indoor Pauper by 'One of Them': Life Inside a London Workhouse (1885; reprinted in 2013).

James, Elizabeth, and Smith, Helen R., *Penny Dreadfuls and Boys' Adventures* (1998).

Katanka, Margaret, *Women of the Underworld* (1973).

Katanka, Margaret, "Captain Smith's Plagiarism," *Notes & Queries*, 24 (1977): pp. 222-23.

Keen, Maurice H., *The Outlaws of Medieval Legend* (1977).

Lambe, R. J., *By Command of the King* (1883).

Le Fleming, Stanley Hughes, '*The Manuscripts of S. H. Le Fleming, Esquire, of Rydal Hall* (1890).

Lennox, Charles Henry Gordon, Duke of Richmond, *Records of the Old Charlton Hunt* (1910).

Life and Adventures of Claude Duval, the Dashing Highwayman by the author of Dick Clinton and *Ned Scarlet* (1860).

The Life of Deval (London, 1670).

"The Literature of the People," *The London Review*, 13 (October 1859–60): pp. 1-31.

The London Gazette (copies in the Burney Collection, British Library).

Lough, John, *An Introduction to Seventeenth Century France* (1955).

Loveland, Richard L., *Sir John Kelyng's Reports of Crown Cases in the Time Of Charles II* (1873).

Lowe, Michelle, *Cherished Thief: Based on the True Story of Britain's Most Notorious Highwayman, Claude Du Vall* (Kindle, 2014).

Macaulay, Thomas Babington, *History of England from the Accession of James II* (1848-61, 5 vols.).

Mackie, Erin, *Rakes, Highwaymen, and Pirates: The Making of the Modern Gentleman in the Eighteenth Century* (2009).

Maland, David, *Culture and Society in Seventeenth Century France* (1970).

Marks, Alfred, *Tyburn Tree* (1908).

Marshall, John Alan, *Sir Joseph Williamson and the Development of the Government Intelligence System in Restoration England in 1660 to 1680* (Ph.D., University of Lancaster, 1991).

Marshall, J. Alan, "Sir Joseph Williamson and the Conduct of Administration in Restoration England," *Historical Research*, 69 (1996): pp. 18-41.

Martin, Sir Theodore (Bon Gaultier), and Aytoun, W. Edmondstoune, *The Book of Ballads* (1845; 16th edition, 1903).

Mathew, Colin, and Harrison, Brian, ed., *The Oxford Dictionary of National Biography* (2004, 60 vols.).

Maxwell, Gordon S., *Highwayman's Heath* (1935).

Medcraft, John, *Bibliography of the Penny Bloods of Edward Lloyd* (1945).

Miles, Henry Downes, *Claude Du Val, A Romance of the Days of Charles The Second* (1850).

Morgan, William, *London &c. Actually Surveyed and a Prospect of London And Westminster Taken at Several Stations to the Southward...*[1682] (1977).

Morrison, Alfred, *The Bulstrode Papers* (1897).

Murphy, Theresa, *The Old Bailey: Eight Centuries of Crime, Cruelty and Corruption* (2003).

A Narrative of the Life, Apprehension, Imprisonment and Condemnation of Richard Dudly, the Great Robber (London, 1669).

Nevins, Jess, *Fantastic, Mysterious and Adventurous Victorians* (www.oocities.org/jessnevins/vicintro.html).

Oates, Titus, *Eikon Baziaikh, or, The Picture of the Late King James* (1696).

Okey, Thomas, *A Basketful of Memories* (1930).

The Ordinary of Newgate, His Account of the Behaviour, Confession and Last Dying Words of the Three Malefactors Executed at Tyburn on Wednesday the 11th of this Instant November, 1724 (1724).

Parry, David Harold (Morton Pike), "With Claude Duval on the King's Highway," *Chums*, 9 March-13 April 1918.

Parry, David Harold (Morton Pike), 'The Night Rider, A Tale of Claude Duval," *The Popular*, flourished 16 February 1924.

Peter, Rex, *Hereward, the Last Englishman* (2005).

Piep, Karsten H., 'The Merry Life and Mad Exploits of Capt. James Hind,' or, How the Popular Press Created the First Outlaw-hero in the Wake of the English Revolution (www.academia.edu.)

Pope, Walter, *The Memoirs of Monsieur Du Vall, Containing the History of his Life and Death* (London, 1670).

Pringle, Patrick, *Stand and Deliver, the Story of the Highwayman* (1951).

Pugh, Ralph D., "Newgate Between Two Fires," *Guildhall Studies in London History*, 3 (1978): pp. 137-63, 199-222.

Richards, Jeffrey, *Swordsmen of the Screen* (1977).

Roberts, W. "Claude Duval in Literature," *The National Review*, 508 (June 1925): pp. 582-91.

Robinson, Emma, *Whitefriars, or, the Days of Charles the Second* (1844, 3 vols.).

Royal Commission on Public Records, with Minutes of Evidence, Appendices And Indexes (1912-19, 9 vols.).

Rumbelow, Don, *The Triple Tree: Newgate, Tyburn and Old Bailey* (1982).

Rymer, James Malcolm, *Gentleman Jack, or, Life on the Road* (1848-52, 205 parts).

Rymer, James Malcolm, *Claude Duval, the Dashing Highwayman* (c. 1854, 202 parts).

Rymer, James Malcolm, *Nightshade, or, Claude Duval, the Dashing Highwayman* (c. 1865, 60 parts).

Settle, William A., Jr., *Jesse James Was His Name* (1967).

Sharpe, James, *Dick Turpin: The Myth of the English Highwayman* (2004).

Sheehan, Wayne Joseph, *The London Prison System, 1666-1795* (Ph.D., University of Maryland, 1975).

Shoemaker, Robert, "The Street Robber and the Gentleman Highwayman: Changing Representations and Perceptions of Robbery in London, 1690-1800," *Cultural and Social History*, 3 (2006): pp. 381-405.

Smith, Alexander, *A Complete History of the Lives and Robberies of the Most Notorious Highwaymen* (1713; edited by Arthur L. Hayward and reprinted, 1923).

Smith, Helen R., *New Light on Sweeney Todd, Thomas Peckett Prest, James Malcolm Rymer and Elizabeth Caroline Grey* (2002).

Solomon, Edward and Stephens, Henry P., *Claude Duval, or, Love and Larceny* (1922).

Spurr, J., *England in the 1670s* (2000).

Steele, Robert, *Tudor and Stuart Proclamations, 1485-1714* (1910, 2 vols.).

Stephen, Leslie, and Lee, Sidney, ed., *The Dictionary of National Biography* (1885-1900; revised edition, 1908-1908, 22 vols.).

Strype, John, *Survey of the Cities of London and Westminster* (1720, 2 vols.).

Sugden, Philip, "William Page," *The Oxford Dictionary of National Biography*, 42 (2004): pp. 334-35.

Sugden, Philip, "John Rann," *The Oxford Dictionary of National Biography*, 46 (2004): pp. 43-44.

Sugden, Philip, *Forbidden Hero: The Georgian Underworld of Jack Sheppard* (forthcoming).

Taylor, Thomas P., *Claude Duval, the Ladies' Highwayman, A Farce* (1885).

Thornbury, George Walter, and Walford, Edward, *Old and New London* (1897-98, 8 vols.)

The People's Ancient and Just Liberties Asserted in the Tryal of William Penn and William Mead at the Sessions Held at the Old-Baily in London (1670).

Verney, Frances Parthenone, Lady, and Verney, Margaret M., *Memoirs of The Verney Family* (1892-99, 4 vols.), volume 4.

Vian, Alsager, "Claude Duval," *The Dictionary of National Biography*, 7 (1917), pp. 271-72. First published in 1888-89.

Viles, Edward, *Gentleman Clifford and the White Mare, Brilliant, or, the Ladies' Highwayman* (1866).

Wales, Tim, "Thief-takers and their Clients in Later Stuart London," in Paul Griffiths and Mark S. R. Jenner, ed., *Londinopolis. Essays in The Cultural and Social History of Early Modern London* (*2000*), pp. 67-84.

Weinreb, Ben, and Hibbert, Christopher, *The London Encyclopaedia* (1986).

White, Barbara, "Claude Duval," *The Oxford Dictionary of National Biography*, 17 (2004), pp. 445-47.

White, Jerry, *London in the Eighteenth Century* (2013).

Whyte-Melville, George John, *M. and N. 'Similis Similibus Curantur'* (1869, 2 vols.).

INDEX

than Nelson and Wellington, 135, 142-43; transformed into a patriotic cavalier defending the monarchy, 136-38, 146-50; decline in popular interest, 136, 138, 141, 149, 158; in political satire, 141-42; in motion pictures and television, 142-45, 147, 149-50; enduring appeal of association of fashionable ladies and highwaymen, 144-47, 149-50; and surviving sites and buildings, 151-54; Claude Duval's house, 152-53; alleged connections with historic inns, 153-54; commemorated in buildings, bridleways and plaques, 154-55; possibility of descendants, 157-58

Du Val, Claude, of Saint-Front, 18

Duvals of Covent Garden, 157-58

Duvals in records of the Old Bailey, 157-58

Eaton, Francis, 51, 52

Edgware Road, London, 78

Eichler, A., 136, 140

Encyclopaedia Britannica, 136

Enfield Chase, 30

Eustace the Monk, 94

Exeter, 8, 31, 60, 86

Eye-Witness, *True and Impartial Relation*, 19-20, 24-27, 67, 79, 96-97, 182-85

Fielding, Henry, 98

Finchley Common, London, 31

Fire of London, 30, 70, 78, 151

Fitzwarin, Fulk, 94

Flushing, 31

Fox, Sir Stephen, 43-45

France, 6, 8, 14, 16-24, 30, 36, 60-61, 94-96, 102, 137, 140

Fraser, Claud Lovat, 105

The French Rogue, 101-102

Freney, James, 106

Frith, William Powell, 5, 129-31, 136, 160

Gad's Hill, Kent, 108-109

Gausseron, Bernard-Henri, 136

The Gay Cavalier, 9, 147-48, 150, 200-201

Gender issues (seventeenth-century), 14, 22-24, 35, 42, 67, 73, 79-84, 100-101

Gillett's Circus, 128

Godberd, Roger, 94

Grade, Lew, 150

Granger, Thomas, 31, 85-87

Grant, Sir Archibald, 105

Grant, Hugh, 149-50

Great Plague, 30, 81

Great Queen Street, London, 100

Greenbury, Nicholas, 60

Gregory Gang, 106

Grey, Elizabeth Caroline, 118

Groans from Newgate, 101

Hals, Richard, 49

Hanwell, Middlesex, 60

Harris, Thomas, 60, 77

Hastings, Thomas, 58, 61, 76-77

Hastings, William, 49-50

Hawkin, John, 53

Hereward the Wake, 4-5, 94, 100, 136, 151

Hersham, Surrey, 87-88

Heston, Middlesex, 61

Heywood, Abel, 120

Hicks, John, 88

Hicks, Newton Treen, 127

Highwaymen, in fiction, 2-5, 111-50, 158-60; threats from, 2, 6, 28, 32-33; state intervention and royal proclamations against, 4, 46, 53-54, 57, 59-61, 85, 92; large gangs, 5-6,

About the Authors

Twins John and Philip Sugden won international acclaim as historians and writers. They were born in Kingston-upon-Hull in Yorkshire in 1947, educated in local schools, and worked briefly in industry and administration before returning to full-time study.

Philip (pictured on the left in 1960) graduated from Hull University with the departmental prize in History in 1972, and taught in several schools and colleges. He had a lifelong interest in the history of crime in London, and his classic study of the Whitechapel Murders of 1888, *The Complete History of Jack the Ripper* (1994), established itself as the standard work in the field; shortlisted for the Anthony Award in the United States, it has sold more than 130,000 copies. For more than forty years Philip worked on a study of *The Georgian Underworld of Jack Sheppard*, pioneering the use of many neglected or unused collections of manuscripts, but although he published a number of scholarly articles his book remained unfinished at the time of his untimely death in 2014 and is now being prepared for publication by his brother. A brief study of *Amy's Last Flight: The Fate of Amy Johnson in 1941* is also in the press.

Dr. John Sugden (pictured right) graduated from three English universities with a doctorate in Modern History, and pursued a trans-Atlantic career as a lecturer, writer, Senior Research Fellow and academic editor. He has conducted research in more than a hundred archives, specialist libraries and museums world-wide. John was unanimously awarded the A. W. Thompson Memorial Prize in Florida History at Fort Lauderdale in 1982 for his first important article, and went on to author over a hundred articles, research notes and book reviews, some for the Oxford University Press's prestigious *American National Biography* project, of which he was an associate editor. He has appeared in television documentaries in Britain and the United States, and his books have won great critical acclaim. Of *Sir Francis Drake* the author Byron Farwell wrote in the 1991 *Washington Times*, "It is not an easy task to bring to life those so long dead, but surely no author today could have succeeded so brilliantly." For his studies in early American frontier history he travelled extensively to consult relevant books and manuscripts in Europe and America, and connected with present day Native American communities, visiting more than a dozen 'reservations' in the United States and Canada. His three award-winning books on the Indian tribes between 1760 and 1815, and the role they played in French, British and American international rivalry (*Tecumseh's Last Stand*; *Tecumseh, a Life* and *Blue Jacket*) helped to reshape the way historians interpreted the Anglo-American War of 1812 and led the Ohio State University to honour him "with the title 'Founder' for your lifetime commitment to understanding Native Ohio" in 2006. In Britain, John is best known for his books on maritime and naval history, especially his two-volume life of Nelson (*A Dream of Glory* and *The Sword of Albion*) which has been acclaimed the most thoroughly researched and comprehensive biography of the admiral ever written. The volumes were shortlisted for several awards, including the James Tait Black prize, and cited by the *Sunday Times* as one of the two best biographies of the year.

Both brothers were fascinated by natural history, as well as conventional history, since childhood; Philip once wanted to be a zoologist and John a palaeontologist. Both were, consequently, lifelong supporters of environmental causes. Philip spent most of his life in western Hull, a few minutes of walking from the countryside, and John continues to live with his long-term partner, Terri, in 'an area of outstanding beauty' near the Lake District National Park.